How to Be, and Remain, a Compassionate Educator

As educators, the attitude with which we approach our work has considerable impact on the outcome for students. Our assumptions and expectations influence learning both positively and negatively.

This book adopts a compassionate acceptance that all children, no matter what they say, don't say, or do, are doing the best they can in that moment. It is in the adults' power, and their responsibility, to understand children and barriers they experience in their learning. By exploring neuroscience, psychology, and learning theory, we can increase our awareness of brain organisation and function to help us understand why a child isn't doing what we have asked. With understanding comes both our compassion and ability to support. The case studies and examples from the author's practice illustrate how we can learn from effective strategies for neurodivergent children to build insight into all pupils.

When we adopt a non-judgemental and encouraging approach, we form positive collaborative relationships with children and their families that increase engagement with and enjoyment of learning and reduces our own frustration and stress. This book is valuable reading for all educators, equipping them with an understanding that allows them to work flexibly and creatively to meet the learning and emotional needs of all pupils.

Anne Emerson is a former speech and language therapist who now works as an educator, trainer and psychotherapist. She has had a long career working in schools, residential services, universities teaching psychology and education, and families, both in the UK and internationally, all of which has contributed to building her approach to her work. She is a school governor and is on the editorial board of the Journal of Pastoral Care in Education.

Praise for This Title

'This book covers such an important topic. How I wish I'd read this when I was a trainee teacher or early in my teaching career! I honestly do believe it would have made such a difference to my own wellbeing as well as to my classroom practice, my understanding of pupils' needs and to my daily interactions. I really do feel this is a truly valuable resource. It is essential reading for everyone working in all schools.'

Victoria Honeybourne, Specialist Teacher, Neurodiversity Trainer and Author

How to Be, and Remain, a Compassionate Educator

Learning from Neurodivergent Students for the Benefit of All

Anne Emerson

LONDON AND NEW YORK

Designed cover image: Getty Images

First published 2025
by Routledge
4 Park Square, Milton Park, Abingdon, Oxon OX14 4RN

and by Routledge
605 Third Avenue, New York, NY 10158

Routledge is an imprint of the Taylor & Francis Group, an informa business

© 2025 Anne Emerson

The right of Anne Emerson to be identified as author of this work has been asserted in accordance with sections 77 and 78 of the Copyright, Designs and Patents Act 1988.

All rights reserved. No part of this book may be reprinted or reproduced or utilised in any form or by any electronic, mechanical, or other means, now known or hereafter invented, including photocopying and recording, or in any information storage or retrieval system, without permission in writing from the publishers.

Trademark notice: Product or corporate names may be trademarks or registered trademarks, and are used only for identification and explanation without intent to infringe.

British Library Cataloguing-in-Publication Data
A catalogue record for this book is available from the British Library

Library of Congress Cataloging-in-Publication Data
Names: Emerson, Anne, author.
Title: How to be, and remain, a compassionate educator : learning from neurodivergent students for the benefit of all / Anne Emerson.
Description: Abingdon, Oxon ; New York, NY : Routledge, 2025. | Includes bibliographical references and index.
Identifiers: LCCN 2024046426 | ISBN 9781032848549 (hardback) | ISBN 9781032848358 (paperback) | ISBN 9781003515319 (ebook)
Subjects: LCSH: Neurodivergent children—Education. | Educational sociology. | Teacher-student relationships. | Parent-teacher relationships. | Educators—Social conditions.
Classification: LCC LC4717 .E44 2025 | DDC 371.94—dc23/eng/20241226
LC record available at https://lccn.loc.gov/2024046426

ISBN: 9781032848549 (hbk)
ISBN: 9781032848358 (pbk)
ISBN: 9781003515319 (ebk)

DOI: 10.4324/9781003515319

Typeset in Optima
by codeMantra

Contents

Acknowledgements		viii
1.	**Introduction**	**1**
	Why educators join the profession	1
	The relevance of educator attitude	2
	My personal philosophy	3
	My background and experience	5
	Children others find challenging	10
	The focus of this book	12
	Who this book is for	13
	Chapters and contents	14
	A note on language and identity	16
2.	**Theoretical models**	**19**
	Introduction	19
	Understanding of difference	20
	Neurodiversity as a concept	26
	Development and assessment	28
	Growth mindset	30
	Person-centred approach	33
	School well-being, emotions, stress and trauma	35
	Summary	39
	Least dangerous assumption	39
	Conclusion	44
3.	**Attending**	**46**
	Introduction	46
	Paying attention	47
	Eye-contact	50
	Eye gaze	52
	Pointing	53

Contents

Attention and distraction	55
Listening	58
Observable lack of attention	58
How we support attention	60
Kim: Persistent disruptive behaviour	66
Conclusion	72

4. Executive functioning — **75**

Introduction	75
Impulse control	77
Working memory	85
Cognitive flexibility	88
Organisation and planning	89
Self-monitoring and emotional control	91
General approaches to improving EF	92
Carol: Giftedness as a mixed blessing	93
Conclusion	97

5. Helping children to engage — **100**

Introduction	100
Types of engagement	103
A culture of engagement	104
Engagement and neurodivergence	107
Sensory differences	109
Motor impairments	111
Pace and timing	113
Self-perception	114
Mona: Teaching pointing	115
Emotional responses	118
Motivation	119
Building engagement	124
Attitudes and beliefs	124
Child-centred approaches	126
Fisal: The importance of routine	130
Conclusion	135

6. Supporting communication in the classroom — **139**

Introduction	139
Communication as the foundation of learning	142

	Aspects of communication	144
	Speech	144
	Expressive language	146
	Selective mutism	147
	Bilingualism	149
	Understanding	150
	Prosody	151
	Pragmatics	152
	Language and literacy	155
	Typical development	155
	Emergent literacy	156
	Areas of difficulty with communication	160
	Impact of communication difficulties	160
	Ben: Acquired difficulties	161
	How to support communication – the MORE model	165
	Means	166
	Opportunities	168
	Reasons	169
	Expectations	174
	Total communication	178
	Behaviour as communication	179
	Bo: Building alternative communication	181
	Conclusion	183
7.	**Conclusion**	**187**
	Introduction	187
	Educator perceptions …	188
	… of children	188
	… of themselves	189
	Student perceptions	191
	Shame as a barrier to belonging	192
	The nature of discipline in schools	194
	What educators need to do	195
Index		199

Acknowledgements

Ironically, the people I would most like to acknowledge are those I'm not naming. You are all those children and adults I've come to know over the years, and your families. Without you my life would probably have gone in a different direction and been less fulfilling. Some of you I've met through work, others in my personal life. It has been such a privilege to learn from you all. My own two sons top that list; you are amazing young men and I'm enormously proud of you both.

It has been a long-held dream to write this book, and I'm indebted to Professor Stephen Joseph for help in the concept and for being an ever-encouraging mentor. Being a member of the Centre for Research in Human Flourishing at the University of Nottingham has been a formative experience and I'm grateful to all the members, particularly David Murphy for opportunities and intellectual challenge. Thank you to Debra Costley for our research collaborations and beyond, Sophie Potter, Jackie Dearden and Gerry Bailey for being amazing colleagues and providing feedback on the manuscript, and to my friend Soraya Smithson for support on the design. I've had the honour of learning from so many others over the years with a special mention to Trudi Scrivener, Anne O'Bryan, Adrienne Palmer, Andy Grayson, Sarah Riley, Max Biddulph, Jo Hancock and David Stewart. I'm also very grateful to the reviewers who exemplified constructive critique! I've had great encouragement too from the team at Routledge, with special mention to Clare Ashworth.

My life is so much richer for my friends, who have played a part in who I have become. Tanya Zybutz, Jen Holland, Dror Roublev, Tanja Bannerji, Rahila Gupta, Lena Norlen and Bridget Bunning, you are all incredible women who inspire.

Finally, thank you Jean-Jacques, for being patient with my lack of work–life balance, for never flinching at my next idea and always doing everything you could to make my dreams possible.

For Billy and Luc.

1
Introduction

Why educators join the profession

We, as educators, enter our profession because we want to make a difference to young people's lives, instil a love of learning, passion for a subject we enjoy and to have a fulfilling work life. Recruitment adverts talk of shaping lives, making a difference, no day being the same, leading to an exciting work life. There is a promise of being a role model, being able to use our creativity, develop students' talents and continue our personal learning. As educators we can look forward to going home at the end of each day knowing that we have made a difference. People considering being educators probably know that the work will be stressful and demanding, but it will be difficult to imagine fully what their working lives will be like and the toll it can take on their private lives. I imagine they have an image of them smiling and joking with pupils who show them respect and look up to them, like in the adverts. I don't imagine them anticipating feeling so stressed and out of control that they lose their temper and shout at their pupils. Yet, of course, this can be a reality, and learning to stay calm and in control will come more easily to some people than others. For most people it probably remains something we continue to grapple with and work on.

All teachers, and many other staff who work in education, want to offer pedagogical care. Some educators will be attracted to working with the most able children who learn fast, excited about the potential of building a love of maths, science or the arts in young people, knowing what a difference this learning could make to their future. Others may be motivated to support those who struggle to learn, wanting to take on the biggest challenges in schools where students face multiple barriers to learning, so that the difference they can make is even greater. Another aspect of the work, where controversy and division can arise, is within the sphere of pastoral care or what Nel Noddings, the American philosopher who wrote about the ethics of care, calls 'personal care'. Noddings (1992), and other scholars, see teaching as the practice of care, comprising empathy and support with actions. Educators may embrace this aspect of the role or feel that it is not part of their work. Whatever the motivation to become an educator, the reality for the vast majority of teachers in the UK and many parts of the world is that their classrooms will include a challenging mix of students who already have a good grasp of the topic and require enhancement activities, pupils who are trying to understand at a more basic level, alongside those who have greater challenges to even being in the classroom in a positive frame of mind. Children will require care, as will staff, and the system as a whole needs to cater for this.

The relevance of educator attitude

'Any classroom that employs a holistic model of learning will also be a place where teachers grow, and are empowered by the process' (hooks, 1994, p. 21). hooks refers to educators bringing themselves to their work and feeling able to be 'present in mind, body and spirit' (hooks, 1994, p. 21). The attitude with which educators approach their work has considerable power in determining the outcome for pupils, which might feel like an opportunity or stress factor depending on how educators view themselves and their work. Attitudes encompass assumptions and expectations, which can influence learning both positively and negatively. As educators we bring our interests, personalities, beliefs, principles and behaviours to our work; and we will impact our pupils for better or worse, consciously and unconsciously. This responsibility may be something that contributes to our sense of fulfilment or adds another burden. Educators cannot afford to have 'off' days; we have to work to our full capacity every day to fulfil the demands of our students. Alongside the expectations of the 30-plus young people looking to us for guidance, we have the demands of employers and the system in which we work that may offer more judgement than support. It takes considerable resourcefulness and resilience to work at optimum pace all day, every day, even if the holidays are longer than most professions.

Our education systems are typically hierarchical. Teachers are expected to have authority and maintain control. Pupils will often pass judgement on our appearance, teaching style, ask personal questions, crack jokes and perhaps proffer insults. Through all behaviour educators are expected to remain respectful of our pupils, even if this is not reciprocated. There tend to be considerable differences in attitudes to teachers across cultures. Some countries still revere teaching, see it as an honourable profession and celebrate National Teaching Days, with children bringing gifts and offerings to school. In the UK, and elsewhere, it can be a struggle to maintain a belief in the system, and in ourselves, when faced with critical assessment and parental demands.

In over 40 years of working with children with special needs in a variety of contexts and settings, I have had the opportunity to observe a great many educators, and to frequently work closely with them. We have discussed their pupils, and their work. I have had the privilege of learning from amazing teachers and teaching assistants, I've been impressed by their diligence and creativity, and recognised what complex and demanding work they do. Those who most enjoy their work, and continue to do it well for many years, often have a love of children, of course, and an ability to forge relationships with their pupils that builds their personal resilience. There are many ways to gain the respect of pupils: some use humour, some compassion, many are 'firm but fair', and teach their subjects with flair and passion. Yet there will remain some pupils in every class who are not finding school, or that lesson, a positive experience. Like educators, pupils bring their whole selves to school, their emotional upheavals, energy, peer struggles and behaviours that seek acceptance. Children will challenge their educators for many complex reasons. They are learning to understand themselves, to self-monitor and develop self-control, but this is work that takes the whole of their time in the education system and beyond.

My personal philosophy

I believe that working as an educator tests the character of most people on a daily basis. Maintaining equilibrium over the course of a career is a huge part of the professional challenge. Early on in my work life I chose to work with children with communication impairments, learning disability and challenging behaviour. Many educators have not made this choice yet must do this work. My own challenges with this work led me to develop a guiding belief that not only is education one of the greatest gifts that we can bestow, but also certainly can be exciting and rewarding. This is not to minimise the challenges, but to suggest they are surmountable for everyone who wishes to do the work.

This book adopts and advocates a compassionate acceptance that all children, no matter what they say or don't say, do or don't do, are doing the best that they can in that moment. With this as my guiding belief I am committed to asking myself questions about every individual I work with, to gain insight and understanding. This allows me to observe their behaviour with compassion rather than judgement, to try to keep an emotional distance where appropriate. I was certainly influenced in this by the teachings of the Dalai Lama, having seen him talk in a huge stadium when traveling in Australia. I became a super fan and when I saw that he was going to be presenting for five nights in Wembley Stadium, London, I booked two tickets for every night, taking a different friend and family member each time. On his website (https://www.dalailama.com/messages/compassion-and-human-values/compassion) the Dalai Lama says 'the greatest degree of inner tranquillity comes from the development of love and compassion'. He believes our own well-being stems from caring for the happiness of others, which allows us to overcome our own fears and insecurities, giving us strength. 'True compassion is not just an emotional response but a firm commitment founded on reason. Therefore, a truly compassionate attitude towards others does not change even if they behave negatively.'

I find this belief that children are doing their best an empowering stance with its implication that it is in the adults' power, as well as their responsibility, to understand why the child is doing what they are doing and to ascertain whether there are intrinsic and extrinsic barriers to children focusing on their learning. Education then becomes a process of working with the student to build capacity, note effort and measure success in minute increments to build confidence and self-esteem. I have been influenced by the work of pioneers in the field such as Carol Dweck who coined 'growth mindset' as a shorthand for our and our students' belief in their ability to transform their learning; the work of Carl Rogers in being 'person-centred' and the 'self-actualising tendency'; Ann Donnellan's 'least dangerous assumption' and Lev Vygotsky who coined the 'zone of proximal development' and 'more knowledgeable other' as key concepts, all of which will be elaborated on later in the book.

My initial training was as a developmentalist; I was taught to assess a child's developmental stage and then work towards the next milestone. I believe that it is still helpful to know the stages of development, but mostly in order to understand a child's behaviour and give us clues about how to break down tasks in order to better teach. Recent contributions from neuroscience suggest different models of learning, and coined the neuroconstructivist model, which places greater emphasis on interaction of inherent skills and challenges with the environment. We are also constantly gaining understanding of the role of emotions in performance at all levels. It is easy to say that happy children learn better, but it seems there are clear reasons for this in the way that psychological processes enhance or detract from neurological control.

My background and experience

My interest in disability and affinity for the work date back to my own childhood experiences. I was a shy child, I went to three different primary schools and struggled to fit in. To cope with my own loneliness and distress I would help the playground monitors look after the smallest children. This developed into a comfort with being with, and attempting to support, whoever I perceived as the 'underdog'. My uncle was physically disabled with multiple sclerosis. I would visit him in his residential care home and, while talking to peers might fill me with awkwardness, I was able to approach and offer assistance to those I perceived might benefit from my attention. When my mother and I scrutinised the 'Career for Girls' book she borrowed from the library, most pages were turned down either by me, or her, as being unsuitable. There weren't many choices at the end; I wasn't achieving highly in my state grammar school, was perceived as lazy (could try harder in school reports) and struggled with maths. This ruled out many professions that my family might consider suitable. My mother had been a physiotherapist, and she didn't consider me physically active and coordinated enough to follow in her footsteps, so we eventually settled on speech and language therapy (SALT). I remained unsure about this choice throughout much of my training, being much more interested in my social than academic life, as was noted by my tutors. I did finally qualify but did not feel ready for a serious full-time job, so I increased my waitressing hours and enjoyed myself for a while.

I was attracted, probably for fairly obvious reasons, to becoming a live-in speech and language therapist for a family in San Francisco, USA. They had one child, a beautiful daughter, who had severe physical and learning disabilities. She had no independent movement and no means of communication beyond body language and vocalisations. My year with the family was invaluable in terms of my learning in so many respects. At a personal level I had to negotiate a new culture, live within a family and spend long hours alone with my charge seeking to stimulate and engage her. It was hugely challenging, sometimes deeply frustrating and lonely, but I grew to love the whole family and understood the demands having a disabled daughter put on parents, grandparents and the wider family. This insight has remained helpful in working with parents throughout my career. At the end of my year, it was with mixed feelings that I returned to the UK. I could have tried to extend my visa, but having spent three years training as a speech and language therapist I knew that I needed to do some more formal work to enhance my skills and employability. I worked firstly in a health centre where I saw predominantly pre-school children with communication difficulties. I had a diverse caseload from which I learned a great deal, including how to offer support to, and learn from, the children's parents, and after a few years decided that I wanted to specialise in children with complex needs.

I moved to a special school for children with a range of labels, all with very limited communication skills, most of whom had been excluded from other special schools due to the challenges of their behaviour. At that time there were many schools for children with what were termed 'moderate learning difficulties'. When children measured as having low average intelligence, but who also had speech, language and communication needs, went to these schools, they would often struggle with learning and behaviour. Our very small and highly specialised school offered refuge to children who had mostly had very negative experiences in their previous schools. The inspirational headteacher had a policy of including children with different strengths and differences in each class of six students, always including one autistic child, so that all pupils would have the opportunity to learn from each other and practice interaction and social skills. The school employed two full-time speech and language therapists and had a policy of working towards inclusion of all pupils in the onsite mainstream primary. It was a highly unusual place at the time, recognised as progressive by government advisor Mary Warnock, which again provided me with amazing opportunities to learn from very gifted educators.

In the years since, I have had too many jobs and changes of career to go into in detail here, including working in retail, public relations and running an employment agency where I would hire myself out for the day! This gave me my earliest experience of teaching, to a group of African students in a scruffy 'college' set up above shops in inner-city London! This wide experience has taught me to be flexible and to think on my feet. I was driven by the desire to prove my worth, and increase my earnings, diverting from core beliefs and desires about making a difference. What I will highlight are the roles that were fundamental in my learning of what we can do to support all learners. I left the SALT profession to try my hand in other fields but continued to work privately with individuals and their families so as not to lose my skills. Support for individuals frequently took me into their schools to observe and advise. I saw examples of real inclusion, as well as trying to provide support to teachers who were struggling to teach special educational needs and disabilities (SEND) pupils in classes of already high demand. Some of the best models of inclusion were found in schools with pupils with high levels of need in terms of their family background, social status, mental health and disengagement. The skills of the educators in these challenging schools enabled them to be creative and open to including disabled students.

I moved into the voluntary sector working for a local Mencap society as a supporter to parents and families. As a speech and language therapist I had sometimes gone into parents' homes to encourage them to work on their children's communication. Now, as someone who was there to support them in any respect, I heard their perspective on the professionals they encountered. Sometimes they were full of praise and highly satisfied with the service they were offered, but they also often felt judged, misunderstood, that the advice they were given was not feasible for their circumstances. It came as a shock to me that parents were not eternally grateful for all that we offered, but I came to understand that my training had given me tools which made me an 'expert' in supporting communication, but not in listening to and understanding family needs. In fact, during my training in the 1970s I was told not to listen to parents, that they would not have good levels of insight into their children and would tend to overestimate their sons' and daughters' abilities.

The parents I worked with then also taught me a lot about grief and acceptance. The amazing women who ran the Mencap society talked about the grief of each missed milestone in their child's life; of the exclusion they felt either because of other people's attitudes or because of their own pain in having to face the extent of their children's difficulties. So many of the mothers (I rarely met fathers) devoted all their time and energy informing themselves about their child's condition, their medical care, the education, health and social care systems. They were so well informed in order to fight for their children's rights. Inclusion in mainstream schools was, as it still is, a theoretical right for all children; however, exclusion came about in many ways. Some parents were too afraid to put their children through difficult challenges in the school environment and potential bullying. Or they believed that the education in a special school would be of a higher quality for their child. Many parents were not given the school place that they wanted, so they resorted to tribunals to force the hand of the education authorities to provide a place in the parents' choice of school. Having been involved in tribunals myself as a witness I know how demanding and stressful it is for parents to have to fight for their child and hear negative portrayals of their son or daughter from the opposing side. Even when they won the cherished school place, the fight changed to needing to combat negative attitudes where educators would sometimes not provide a good learning experience, hoping that the parents might relent and place their child in a special school, which they viewed as better suited to the child's needs.

My main classroom teaching experience comes from teaching information technology in a college of Further Education (FE). Some of my work was with 16-year-old boys studying for a BTech. They were mostly first- or second-generation Bangladeshi students, with varying levels of English language proficiency. They appeared to have struggled at school and left with no or few qualifications. I had no teacher training and felt particularly lost in terms of classroom management. My first challenge was that they didn't sit down and were constantly wondering around the room and distracting each other. I asked colleagues in the staff room about what to do about this, much to their amusement, and their advice was to 'care less'. I didn't accept this and figured out my own way to increase motivation. I asked my students about their dreams and ambitions, and as a group we considered what they would need in terms of skills to make these aims a greater possibility. As bell hooks says in *Teaching to Transgress*, we need to offer students information that connects to their overall life experiences. My students' motivation increased, and their behaviour became much more engaged. Having started off rather nervous and slightly afraid of my students, I grew to like them enormously and enjoy my teaching.

As part of my FE role, I also taught long-term unemployed adults wanting a way back into work. The challenges with this group were very different. They were highly motivated but lacked confidence and were fairly easily frightened by technology and the risk of breaking something. Not only did their efforts challenge my technological skills, figuring out how they had reached a previously unseen screen, but I also improved my ability to break tasks down and explain complex ideas. They were another highly enjoyable and rewarding group to teach.

Introduction

I left that work to seize an exciting opportunity to work in India, in an Indian special school, as part of the work of a charity called Action Health. They sent medical and allied-medical professionals to India or Africa as part of ongoing development projects. My role in Calcutta was to train teachers in a special school to develop the communication of their pupils. Education was very formal; all children were expected to sit at desks and learning through play did not exist. I sat on the floor with small groups of students and developed vocabulary through games. This was very new to the Indian teachers, and I encountered resistance until they could see what the children could achieve. Teachers saw me as a potential ally and advocate with their autocratic Headteacher, a formidable woman who claimed to enjoy dismissing her staff at will. As someone from another country, viewed as more progressive, I had access to the Head, which other staff did not. She would at least listen to requests I made on teachers' behalf, before dismissing them, telling me that my lack of understanding of her actions was due to differences between 'east and west'. This was obviously an enormously formative experience, learning to live and work in a very different culture and impart my understanding of education to people who had little training themselves.

Once back in the UK I undertook further study and ultimately became a researcher, and this led me to my university teaching career, firstly teaching undergraduate psychology, and now within a School of Education. Every year we have a wonderfully diverse group of home and international students, some of whom are already teachers, others contemplating a career in education, working towards an MA in Special and Inclusive Education. In this space I have had the pleasure of teaching people with a great deal of knowledge and working to enhance my own understanding. This has led me to research and publish within the fields of pupil engagement, alternative communication, parental trauma, and anxiety in autism. As my interests moved further into the well-being of students, families and teachers, I decided to enhance my skills by completing psychotherapy training. This has been a fascinating experience, to study theories and approaches from a new discipline. I now volunteer as a therapist for a charity that specializes in providing counselling to disabled people and their family members.

I have had a varied and highly fulfilling career. In this book I am drawing on my life's work to bring ideas and understanding from multiple perspectives to help guide us all to be effective educators who feel resilient, challenged and engaged in our work.

Children others find challenging

This book focuses on those children who are often the most difficult to engage in learning, while including information that is pertinent and supportive of all learners. I have avoided using the term 'challenging behaviour' in the heading for this section, as I feel that this has become a term applied when we think the child is in the wrong. As educators we will inevitably find some students' behaviour challenging to us personally, due to the personal characteristics of the individual and our relationship with them. When working in a small team in an institution for predominantly non-verbal individuals considered to have severe learning disabilities, we each admitted that there was a particular person whom we did not feel comfortable working with. What surprised us was that it was a different person for each of us. Our reasons were individual, too. Some of the residents were prone to hurting staff through biting or hitting; my particular block was working with a woman who habitually played with her saliva. Therefore, my view of 'challenging' can be seen as individual and subjective. Obviously in a classroom situation those students who routinely disrupt the learning of others will be found challenging by the majority of educators. However, in my experience, there will be a member of staff who forms an affinity with even these pupils and will tell others 'oh, they aren't so bad'.

When we consider the needs of those 'in the margin' in our planning, we more effectively support all our pupils, as proposed in Universal Design for Learning, discussed in a later chapter. Those 'in the margin' may, or may not, have a diagnostic label due to a neurodivergence. They may have emotional and behaviour difficulties either as a sole difficulty or associated with other issues. They might have health problems impacting attendance and well-being. They might stand out from their peers for personal characteristics. For a wide range of reasons there will be pupils every day, in every class, who cannot in that moment access learning. My initial training as a speech and language therapist guides my interest in pupils who struggle with communication. They range from those who find it hard to process what is said to them quickly, who may have difficulty constructing a coherent reply when under pressure, through to those who have no spoken language and who rely on alternative means of communication if they have any effective system at all. Whatever the challenges to communication, these will impact learning. Language is the medium by which education is delivered and assessed. Classrooms in the UK contain large numbers of pupils whose communication is insufficiently developed to enable them to fully engage with the curriculum. Their difficulties in either understanding what is said, or responding effectively to it, will raise their stress levels, impact engagement and sometimes ultimately leads to a 'switching off' from school and learning. My focus on these students is partly since, in my experience, their needs tend to be less well understood by educators than some other groups of pupils, and also because the consequences of not providing effective support are often life-long and negative.

As stated above, a large percentage of pupils in most classes will have some form of communication difficulty. In areas of social deprivation primary schools can have 50% of pupils who, when screened, are found to have speech, language and communication needs (Public Health England, 2020). What has also become apparent is that teachers frequently are not aware that students have these needs, particularly when they are in such big numbers that their limited communication skills start to appear as the norm. We must address communication for all pupils, since the ability to be a flexible and effective communicator will impact on all life outcomes. We know, for example, that our prisons comprise a very large number of those with communication and learning difficulties.

Children frequently experience frustration due to their communication impairments, which may result in behaviour that those educating them find challenging. The message of this book is that when we adopt 'the least dangerous assumption', i.e. that the young people we are working with are doing their best in that moment, we adopt a growth mindset, a non-judgemental and encouraging approach, and through this we can form positive collaborative relationships with children and their families that increase engagement and learning. Adopting this stance can help the adults working with these children to reduce their own stress and enhance their job satisfaction.

The children I focus on in each chapter range from those with minor and perhaps temporary learning difficulties, through to those with life-long differences. A way of looking at the needs of all of these children is through neurodiversity, the individual differences with psychological and neurological processes that we all have. I have concerns that at times the term 'neurodiversity' has come to be used as an alternative label for those that society considers outside the 'norm'. In this book I use the term 'neurodivergent' to identify those who experience specific difficulties and differences with their development of life skills. I find it a helpful term that acts as an umbrella for a great number of labels, including characteristics that impact development, such as autism, Down's syndrome and attention deficit hyperactivity disorder (ADHD), and those with acquired difficulties, such as from head injury.

These conditions can be distinct, but also tend to have overlapping characteristics. There has been an expectation that educators learn about all the different conditions that may be present in their classroom, which is unrealistic and unnecessary. When we look at the learning differences that children present with, we can set aside the label they carry and focus on appropriate strategies for them as individuals. For example, an autistic child who has poor attention and is easily distracted may benefit from the same classroom strategies as his peer who is considered to have ADHD. In the words of my colleague Dr Gerry Bailey, 'it's the child not the label that matters!'

Our classes are made up of children whose learning is impacted by intrinsic processing differences, and those who struggle to learn due to emotional distress. Trauma is understood to impact our physiological systems and block our reception of care and learning. We cannot know who has experienced trauma, so have to build care and compassion into the system. In the UK our current system frequently relies on the identification of a child as having a learning difference in order that they can be educated in a different way. This is essentially a 'deficit' view, putting the onus on the child who needs 'fixing', and leads to the provision of extra-curricular interventions for only certain groups of children. However, much of what will benefit a child with a communication impairment, for example, will also support someone with no label but who is tired and not concentrating well. Most children, at some point in their school life, will have challenges in fitting neatly and wholly into our rigid school systems, even where they are academically able. I have personal experience of a student previously considered gifted at maths who started to find complex concepts difficult. His teachers viewed this as due to a lack of work; their concept of education appeared simplistic, i.e. effort leads to success and a struggle to learn therefore must result from lack of trying. I fundamentally disagree with this; effort is certainly to be encouraged and valued, but sometimes breaking down tasks and clear explanations are also essential. When we blame the child for their lack of success, we are not doing our work as educators. As we require children to fit into a system, that system has to offer understanding, support and compassion.

The focus of this book

This book highlights the value of asking questions of ourselves and our students. This requires reflecting on ourselves as educational practitioners and people, our settings and the children we are responsible for. It is often tempting to take behaviour at face value, yet behaviour is communicative and what it is telling us can be far from straightforward. In any moment there will be multiple forces impacting on us and the learners in front of us. We have our intrinsic challenges related to comfort, attention, concentration, memory, emotional response and motivation. There will be external challenges such as distractions, competing demands and the judgement of others. When we look below the surface, with the belief that everyone can come to school ready and keen to learn, we can uncover some of the barriers. We can improve the environment, offer appropriate support and foster positive relationships.

Many children develop patterns of behaviour for a variety of reasons, such as responses to an overstimulating environment, or as avoidance of challenging situations. These behaviours can be, and often are, interpreted as a lack of desire to be in contact with others and a lack of interest in learning. This book offers alternative views illustrated with vignettes and experiences from the author's practice. The ultimate goal of my approach is to empower students to develop and use their own strategies and accommodations, which will prepare them for happy and fulfilling lives.

Who this book is for

This book offers support to educators in maintaining their equilibrium, feeling positive about their pupils and their future, and building more positive relationships. It also systematically considers the most challenging aspects of work with children whose needs can be difficult to understand. In order to do this, each chapter looks in depth at a potential intrinsic or extrinsic barrier to learning, with suggestions of how these might be overcome. It offers multiple insights and perspectives, with a focus on relationship building as the foundation of teaching and an exploratory, reflective process to education. I invite you to consider your perceptions and understandings of all students, in their glorious neurodiversity, including those who may be considered neurodivergent.

The audience of educators for this book include practising teachers, those in training, special educational needs and disabilities coordinators (SENDCOs), teaching assistants, educational psychologists, other school staff, including school leaders; parents; and anyone else who has a role in building relationships with children in order to foster their learning, achievement and well-being. I am addressing both educators in mainstream and special schools along with alternative provision. The focus of each chapter is on using research to help foster understanding. The book draws from education, psychology, psychotherapy and neurology to build insight. My approach as an educator starts with as clear an understanding as is possible to gain in the moment. From this basis we can be flexible in our approach to children's barriers to learning. I acknowledge that sometimes we cannot get clarity for some time; instead, we have to build hypotheses and try them out. This trial-and-error approach, based in experience and instinct, along with theoretical understanding of how children learn and develop, can bring us gradually towards insight into even the most complex children and young people.

Chapters and contents

The key questions that inform the structure of the book are: 'Why is the child not attending to the learning opportunity I am providing?'; 'Why are they not engaging with the learning?'; 'Why are they not communicating effectively'; 'Why is their behaviour challenging me?'; and 'How can we improve well-being?' We start in Chapter 2 by looking in more depth at key attitudes that can be helpful to educators, based on the 'least dangerous assumption'. What is 'least dangerous' to assume about any child we want to build a relationship with is that they want to develop positively, to have choice, to reach their potential, to be fully in the world and comfortable in their chosen place. At times, with every child, young person and ourselves, our 'best' behaviour will not be what others would enjoy or respect. We might not be at our best when we are tired, hungry, agitated or upset. We might need time to cope with something that has gone wrong before we can re-engage. When we acknowledge obstacles and make provision for them, without judging or punishing, we can support young people to make good choices for themselves and others.

Chapter 3 looks at student attention. Educators want to see physical indicators that a child is listening, following instructions and making efforts. However, we all know that it is possible to look as if we are attending when our minds are far away, daydreaming or focused on what to do later. What is less acknowledged is that we may be attending when there are few visible signs of that externally. People may attend better when their body is moving, when they have their eyes shut or are fixated on something in the distance. This apparent lack of attention is challenging to educators but common among those labelled as neurodivergent. When we understand more about the attention process, we can come to accept the lack of external attention behaviours adopted by some learners and offer help with improving attention.

Attention is part of a set of skills under the heading of executive functions (EF). An understanding and awareness of EF allows us to analyse the tasks we give students and their responses to them. In Chapter 4 I discuss what are considered the core EF skills: impulse control, working memory and cognitive flexibility, relating these to learning and social interaction. EF skills are crucial for a successful academic and personal life, and research has told us that they can be trained and improved (Diamond and Ling, 2016). Much of good practice in education does just this; however, the better our understanding of processes involved, the more effective our strategies and support can be, leading to a more relaxed environment that is conducive to learning.

In Chapter 5 I consider the engagement of students and the barriers that many neurodivergent people experience. We have been learning for decades about the impact of sensory experience on autistic people. Our awareness has grown as we have heard, and listened to, autistic voices. People with the label ADHD tell us about their experiences, both when they take medication and do not. People who do not speak have been using technology to communicate, sometimes using eye-tracking, to give insight into their inner worlds. Their voices have been fundamental in our learning and enable us to work with, rather than on, people who can benefit from our support. The growth mindset is key in this work, alongside Vygotsky's zone of proximal development, and neuroplasticity, to foster positive attitudes and resourcefulness. In this chapter I tackle motivation and what we know about building students' intrinsic desire to learn and develop engaged behaviour. The least dangerous assumption here is that the vast majority of children have a will for social engagement, when the environment is comfortable for them. When this is not recognised, children are at risk of learned helplessness and disaffection with education.

The focus of Chapter 6 is more centrally on communication, introducing the Means, Reasons, Opportunities and Expectations (MORE) model I developed with my colleague Jackie Dearden. This looks at communication in total by examining the aspects of how someone communicates, i.e. the 'means'. Someone with no speech or established communication system will still communicate through their bodies and vocalisations, which those close to them learn to understand. When someone struggles to communicate clearly, their communication partners can assist by offering opportunities such as prompts, silence or scaffolding questions. Within this model, 'reasons' looks at a person's intrinsic motivation to communicate. Understanding the situations where someone has a reason to try can allow us to build on strengths and offer support where it is most likely to be effective. Finally, we believe that our expectations of what someone might be capable of are important in noticing means and reasons and the provision of opportunities. Communication is a social function and can only be learned effectively within a social setting, which classrooms provide, yet some children will still need support to access the opportunities that having peers offers.

Interspersed throughout the book are case studies of six children with specific areas of need, including giftedness and acquired brain injury, to illustrate how theory informs us of ways to design support. These cases span children who achieve at high levels academically in mainstream schools, to those who have multiple challenges with communication, interaction and engagement, and go to special provision.

A note on language and identity

I believe that how we speak to and about people conveys our attitudes and openness. It can be difficult to 'get it right' when terminology goes in and out of fashion. However, the changes of terminology tend to occur when terms that may have had an objective descriptive meaning at the outset, such as 'spastic', become a term of insult or abuse. It is recognition of the power of words to hurt and disrespect that leads to change. When I worked for Mencap I attended a meeting at their head office and complained about the inclusion of the term 'backwards' to describe people who at that time would have been better described as 'mentally handicapped', a term which has subsequently been replaced by 'learning disability' or 'intellectual disability' in the UK. Some of the parents I worked with at Mencap, particularly those whose children were already middle-aged, did not want to give up use of 'backward', as this encapsulated for them a model of understanding, describing a disrupted development. They saw their sons and daughters as children in an adult body, a concept that has lost currency in recent years. The term 'backward' was in common usage and easily understood. However, it was also inaccurate, and encompassed many people who had typical development in some aspects alongside areas of difficulty. The person who most comes to mind was a man in his 30s who attended a 'youth club' for disabled adults. He had very little useful verbal ability, needed help with most independence tasks and no sense of danger. However, he was able to name the country of any flag shown and had other special talents.

As I write, in the UK, we mostly prefer to use what is referred to as 'identity first' language. This has followed on from decades of 'person-first' where someone would be referred to as a 'person with a disability'. This is different in other countries, but something I will adopt in this book. Disability activists have told us that, although this is not a uniform view, they prefer to put their identity as a disabled, autistic, visually impaired etc. person to the fore. Their disability is not something that accompanies them as they go through life; rather, it is an integral part of who they are and impacts every part of their existence. I have used the term 'learning disability', as differentiated from 'specific learning disability', which can be used to encompass conditions such as dyslexia and dyscalculia.

References

Dalai Lama (n.d.). His Holiness the 14th Dalai Lama of Tibet. https://www.dalailama.com/

Diamond, A., and Ling, D. S. (2016). Conclusions about interventions, programs, and approaches for improving executive functions that appear justified and those that, despite much hype, do not. *Developmental Cognitive Neuroscience*, 18, 34–48.

Donnellan, A. M. (1984). The criterion of the least dangerous assumption. *Behavioral Disorders*, 9(2), 141–150. https://doi.org/10.1177/019874298400900201

Dweck, C. S. (2002). The development of ability conceptions. In Wigfield, A. and Eccles, J. S. (Eds) *Development of Achievement Motivation*. Hoboken, NJ: John Wiley & Sons.

hooks, bell. (1994). *Teaching to Transgress: Education as the Practice of Freedom*. New York: Routledge.

Noddings, N. (1992). *The Challenge to Care in Schools: An Alternative Approach to Education*. New York: Teachers College Press.

Public Health England. (2020). *Best Start in Speech, Language and Communication: Guidance to Support Local Commissioners and Service Leads*. London: Department of Health and Social Care & Department of Education.

Rogers, C. (1963). The concept of the fully functioning person. *Psychotherapy: Theory, Research & Practice*, 1(1): 17–26. https://psycnet.apa.org/doi/10.1037/h0088567

Vygotsky, L. S. (1978). *Mind in Society: The Development of Higher Psychological Processes*. Cambridge, MA: Harvard University Press.

Vygotsky, L. S. (2012). *Thought and Language*. Cambridge, MA: MIT Press.

2
Theoretical models

Introduction

In education, when we want to know how best to teach and support students, we have few undisputed facts to call on. We can look at statistics for which groups of children succeed academically, or which group of children most get excluded from our school systems. Governments utilise these kinds of figures when working on education policy; however, when we want to really understand what lies beneath the statistics, we need to turn to theory and research. Our statistics might tell us, for example, that students whose parents have had a university education are more likely to go to university themselves. When we want to ascertain why this is, we theorise, and then test this with research. In our field, the answer to almost all inquiries is equivocal; there will be evidence in support of a number of possibilities, but typically nothing definitive. We nearly always end up saying 'it depends'. Take a long-debated issue – whether it is better for children with special needs to be educated in mainstream or special schools. Some research has suggested one of these in particular, but most has ended up saying 'it depends …' on the child, the school, etc. What is helpful for us to know is that the area of agreement in this debate is that good-quality teaching and a positive relationship with educators are the more important factors than where these are found.

This lack of clarity is very much the case when setting out to ensure all students feel a sense of belonging to school, including neurodivergent learners, i.e. those who have learning or social challenges. As our systems have been designed principally by neurotypical people who do not struggle to access learning, as far as they work for anyone they work for this group. Neurotypical children who have supportive families are likely to be resilient and adaptable to school systems. They may not like everything about their school, but they can probably cope with the demands without too much cost to themselves. Neurodivergent children and those with social and emotional difficulties are likely to have multiple challenges with our systems that mean that even if they succeed in managing the school day there will be a price they have to pay. Families see this with some children who go home and have a 'meltdown' where they express all the built-up frustrations of the day. This can apply to staff, too; we don't know how we will respond until faced with the experience. Teacher educators try to prepare trainees for the reality and how they will manage the pressures they face, but this does not stop new staff feeling overwhelmed. The support that they receive from mentors and colleagues is fundamental to their flourishing in the role.

I consider myself to be a predominantly intuitive practitioner. Only when I decided to study for a master's degree did I come fully to appreciate theory. Many of the aspects of children and my practice that I had felt puzzled by had already been addressed by some of the great thinkers in the education field. They provided me with ideas to explore and terms for my experiences. It was gratifying to find that I was not alone in many of the ideas I had come to, or that my own thoughts and reactions were not too far-fetched! This chapter therefore offers some theories, models of understanding and concepts that I continue to find helpful in my practice. This is not an exhaustive list by any means, so at times I might point you to further reading. This is the case with fundamental educational theory. Many of you will already have a grounding in this, having studied the work of Piaget, Montessori, Skinner and most importantly for me Vygotsky, whom I discuss in Chapter 3. These thinkers formed the basis of much of the way that we currently teach and manage children in the UK.

Understanding of difference

In considering the needs of all students I start by looking at those who are perceived as the most challenging to teach or support, those identified as having 'special educational needs and disabilities' (SEND). Much of what we learn from these students, who often sit at the extreme of a continuum of difficulty, can be applied to all learners. When we learn to educate and include those with SEND, we are better able to make learning accessible for all. When we start to consider the education of disabled students, we are focusing on those who traditionally have been the least included in our provision. In the UK, schooling until the age of 18 is compulsory for all children, including those with the most profound disabilities who actually qualify for educational provision until the age of 25 to give them time to reach their potential. Policy across Europe varies, with most children in Portugal attending mainstream provision, with former special schools being transformed into resource bases (UNESCO, 2020) and most children with special needs in other countries such as Sweden and Belgium being in special schools. Even where education is legislated for all, those with disabilities are at the highest rate for non-attendance. Historically, some students were perceived as less likely to benefit from education and this was used as a reason for segregation into provision that focused on keeping children comfortable and happy. This attitude has largely changed, and it is accepted that children with special needs can not only benefit from education but need increased levels of support. We can see that the way in which we perceive disability, and how it impacts on human potential, therefore becomes part of decision-making when resources are scarce.

The history of perceptions and behaviour towards people who are seen as different from the norm has a troubled path. People who behaved in ways that were not 'typical' have been viewed as inferior, subjects of pity or even dangerous, e.g. thought of as witches. Our responses have frequently been cruel, making people the targets of jokes and stereotypes, or more benevolent when people were locked in institutions ostensibly for their own safety and protection. What we have not yet done is found a way to fully value and include everyone.

The patriarchal view of disabled people as needing protection, for themselves, and protecting society from them, is the basis for what is now termed the 'medical' model of disability. In this perception, people's differences are seen as something that require fixing, or making well. In the medical model we seek for what is 'wrong' about a person, so that we can find an appropriate intervention to cure the problem. We have developed classification systems, such as the Diagnostic and Statistical Manual of Mental Disorders (DSM) or the International Classification of Diseases (ICD), which seek to reach agreements on the appropriate term to apply to someone with a specific set of characteristics. Psychiatrists tasked with 'diagnosing' someone will look at their 'symptoms' and do a matching exercise to find the nearest possible label. Some people acquire multiple labels since their characteristics don't fit neatly into a single category, while others have changes in diagnosis over time. We make these attempts at fitting people into boxes in order to find the best 'treatment'. The DSM is now in its fifth edition, and the ICD its 11th; since our view of each label changes over time, diagnosis can be arbitrary, imprecise, and some people may never reach the threshold for a particular diagnostic label despite encountering significant learning and behavioural challenges.

Disability is often seen as an individual tragedy, something to be avoided, with a stigma attached, which can lead to individuals and their families feeling a sense of shame. It is very difficult for parents to celebrate the birth of a disabled child in the same way they would a non-disabled baby. In some cultures, disabled children are hidden away as they may bring hostility or discrimination to the family. Micheline Mason, a disabled writer and activist, tells us about the difficult start in life that disabled babies often have due to the impact of negative expectations from society on families (Mason, 2000, 2008).

There is generally a strongly held assumption that disabled people can benefit from expert intervention. Although this can be true to some extent, it is also a problematic position where typical parents and educators come to feel de-skilled and dare not risk trusting their abilities and instincts. Much research, to this day, is focused on either seeking ways to eradicate difference occurring, or working out how to make people behave more 'like us'. We have inflexible systems in our societies and education, which require people to make adjustments and amendments to their behaviour. When they do not do this, we turn to assessment to find out why. This is considered appropriate when people have an illness; we need to look at 'symptoms' to find a 'diagnosis' and then a 'cure'. I place these terms in inverted commas since they are specifically medical terms for conditions that can be changed, and that often threaten life if not addressed. However, we then also apply them to people who are not sick or diseased, but who function differently from what we are used to. The medical model has led to a lot of the separation and segregation disabled people have experienced, and their voices have not typically been heard until recent times.

In response to the insult of this medical model, disability pioneers, such as Mike Oliver, offered an alternative way of thinking. When someone uses a wheelchair, they cannot get into a building by going up a set of steps. When there is a ramp, they can enter and do their job. The ramp does not affect their physical impairment, but it does remove their disability – when they can enter the building, they are able to fulfil their ability. This is the basis for the 'social' model, which sees disability as situational. When we adapt society, our buildings and our thinking, people with impairments can join us fully. A more recent example is the increased valuing of autistic people in the workforce. Some employers have recognised their particular strengths in the ways that they perceive and think, and have found that they bring considerable talents to the companies they work for. Autistic employees remain autistic – they often require accommodations from their employers, particularly in terms of making their environment comfortable (see Chapter 5) – but this does not reduce their abilities. In other words, when we can listen to what someone needs in order to be comfortable, we can usually make adaptations that mean that we benefit from their inclusion.

Both models of disability have met with critique, the medical because of its lack of understanding of disability and exclusionary actions, the social because it may minimise the impact of someone's impairment. Campaigners such as Tom Shakespeare suggest a more middle ground, where the challenge of living with impairment is recognised as potentially debilitating, alongside the negative attitudes and lack of provision in society. Disabled people may have conditions that bring them pain or discomfort and need regular treatment for physical issues, which can impact their lives. It is important to recognise impairment and its impacts, alongside removing barriers to participation. As educators we need to think about these polarised positions to help us to ascertain what barriers someone may be facing, to open the conversation about impairments and to talk with the child and parents about how to minimise the barriers and make our classrooms as inclusive as possible. School cultures need to ensure that children are comfortable having accommodations made to support them, whether this is wearing a hearing aid or ear defenders to protect themselves from sound.

Consider this example: Jodi is 8 years old and moving to a new primary school as he was unhappy in his previous placement. He was perceived negatively in his original school because he would regularly become distressed, covering his ears and asking to leave, sometimes even running out of the classroom due to his sensory sensitivity. As his anxiety about what might happen during the day rose, his behaviour deteriorated, he sought regular reassurance from the adults in the classroom and didn't engage in his work. His school was unwilling to keep him in school, as they argued that they could not meet his needs within their provision, and his parents, distressed by the deterioration in their son, agreed to move him. His new school invited his mother to tell them about her son. She explained that although he was a very sociable boy, he found noise, lots of people and movement distressing. Once an environmental stimulus had caused him to feel discomfort, he became increasingly tense, which in turn increased his sensitivity, setting up a cycle where he either showed his distress in class and upset other children, or went home in a shocked and exhausted state. The school were able to put certain supports in place. He sat near the door and could ask to leave the class with his TA for a short time if he started to feel his anxiety rise. He was encouraged to notice and warn his TA when he began to feel upset so that preventative measures were put in place. It was explained to his peers that Jodi's ears hurt when they were noisy, and the class became a quieter place, beneficial for his peers too. Situations where there was likely to be increased noise and movement were planned for and he was supported to avoid or cope with them. What might have been considered his 'symptoms', i.e. sensory sensitivity and anxiety (referred to as 'characteristics' in more social model terms), remained a challenge for him, but adaptations to the environment meant he could better cope and learn. He remained in this second school for the rest of his primary education, a happy child with lots of friends.

Alternative views of disability to the medical and social models focus more on capabilities and strengths. The capability model focuses on the choices or 'freedoms' that people have in their lives and how these lead to 'functionings' (Terzi, 2005). This model sees people as diverse in three ways, in terms of inherent characteristics, their circumstances and the ability to turn resources into valued functions. Returning to Jodi as an illustration, his inherent characteristics were heightened sensory awareness with resulting high levels of anxiety. His circumstances in the first school, which held a view that they were not the right place for him, were averse to him developing resourcefulness. In the second school, adaptations to the environment allowed him to learn to advocate for himself in order to cope better with school. To fully support a child, we therefore need to understand their strengths and barriers to learning, to adapt the environment to their individual profile, and to support them in developing effective strategies.

Our traditional approach to working with children who show poor progress or behaviour has been to assess their development and find out their areas of weakness. Many children will have uneven or 'spiky' profiles, where some skills are appropriate for their age and others are ahead or behind. There has been an assumption that this is not ideal, and that in order to access the curriculum and become a fully functioning person, the emphasis should be on getting all skills to an appropriate level. In this way we seek to eradicate difference. In this model support takes the form of focusing on the things that the child finds difficult in order that these improve, with the aim of them functioning more like a typical child. When this approach is applied, a child can become 'stuck', year after year, trying to gain skills that they cannot master. Conversely, a focus on strengths looks for areas of competence, and works on building these to compensate for areas of difficulty. This approach encourages us to see potential, and to acknowledge that typical development is not a necessary masterplan that everyone must follow. For example, children who do not process sound well may struggle to learn to read. When children with Down's syndrome, who often have poor auditory processing, were provided with the opportunity to learn to read through visual methods, even before they could speak, they were able to acquire skills similar to those of their peers, although by a different route (Buckley, 2001). Recognising a weakness in learning through phonics, but a strength in learning visually, meant that children were provided with more appropriate support. It was also discovered that learning to read helped develop their language. Children who acquire early reading skills may continue to have problems with processing spoken language, but they will have reading as an alternative to information gathering, increased self-perception as readers and those around them will have greater awareness of their abilities.

What we can take from current thinking about models of disability is that we always need to look both at the individual and the environment they are in; whether someone experiences disability is determined by the relationship of these factors. For example, someone with Down's syndrome who cannot read who lives in a city in the UK may be disabled in terms of living an independent life. The same person, living on a farm where they are part of a team of workers looking after livestock, may have only limited disadvantage. Of course, they need to want to live and work on a farm in order to gain this benefit!

In another example, it has taken many decades for schools to adapt to dyslexic students. For many years the focus on dyslexia was whether it actually existed. Now, in the UK, dyslexia is better understood, although often only partially, and provision has improved. In many schools, numerous adaptations are routinely made, such as avoiding strong contrast of black text on white paper, or printing on coloured paper. Students have access to technology such as screen readers to support their rate of taking in information, and adaptations are made to exams. Our understanding of the differences a dyslexic person may experience when attempting to read has given us a toolkit to support their learning. The students are still dyslexic, and likely to be so for the rest of their lives, but in a setting where accommodations are made to their particular difficulties, they are not disabled, and increasingly there is awareness that the difference of dyslexia can result in strengths such as creativity and innovative thinking.

Neurodiversity as a concept

The term 'neurodiversity' was coined by autistic advocates in the 1990s (Botha et al., 2024) as an essentially political term that proposes that what have traditionally been labelled as disabilities, 'neurotypes' such as ADHD, autism, dyslexia and developmental coordination disorder are part of the infinite variability within people. This is in the response to the frequent 'othering' that people who are given or who adopt identity labels experience in society. Neurodiversity therefore sees 'difference' rather than 'disability' and is political as it challenges exclusions from any aspect of life for anyone. As with biodiversity in nature, neurodiversity needs to be welcomed in contributing unique perspectives. The term neurodiversity has become synonymous with seeking full human rights for all, and as a way of developing neutral attitudes towards difference, rather than trying to force people into being the same as the majority. It sees societies that fully include everyone as ultimately stronger as a result. This obviously fits with strengths-based approaches and suggests that all schools should be fully inclusive for everyone's benefit.

The concept of neurodiversity is helpful in focusing on a child's individual characteristics rather than the label applied to them. Each disability label is a very broad umbrella encapsulating highly diverse people. A label such as 'autism' or even 'severe autism' tells us very little that is helpful about the person with that label. We might anticipate that the child will have communication and social challenges, which could be a starting point to inform our approach and avoid overwhelming them. Assumptions are less helpful when they lead us to see characteristics that might not actually be present, just because we have learned that they accompany that label. A case study I published with Jackie Dearden in 2013 called for a change in the automatic use of 'minimal language' with autistic children. We told the story of a boy of 10 who attended a special school and had a very restricted curriculum. He had little effective communication beyond being able to shout and push people away when he didn't want to do something. His educators followed what was then 'best practice', assuming his behaviour was determined by limited understanding, and speaking to him in single words or short phrases. Through our work we were able to show that he could understand and respond to full sentences, something that the school had not ascertained since they were not expecting it to be the case; his comprehension appeared to be an anomaly, given the rest of his behaviour. We adopt an approach such as using minimal language to avoid overwhelming someone, so as an act of care, but this needs to go along with continuing to offer scaffolded opportunities to demonstrate ability once a supportive relationship has been established with the child. We must not let our assumptions about what someone might be capable of be governed only by how they currently behave. There have always been examples of inspirational educators who were able to instil a love of learning and higher attainment in previously disaffected students, mainly by showing a belief in their ability.

As educators, we may feel anxious about our ability to meet everyone's needs. However, I believe that the neurodiversity concept, along with a deep understanding of essential skills for learning such as attention and executive functions that are discussed in later chapters, will equip us to support every child to learn. We do not need to be an expert on each label that a child in our classes may carry, but we do need to understand individual strengths and challenges in order to teach them strategies. Strategies should be helping a child to utilise their abilities, and interests, to find solutions to areas of challenge. For example, children with various labels, including those with developmental or acquired difficulties, along with those considered 'neurotypical', can have difficulty with focus and behaviour for learning at certain times of the day. This lack of focus might stem from having stayed up late playing video games, having had an argument with parents before school, having fallen out with friends during break time or being told off by an adult; it might stem from trauma or neglect, or it might be a typical characteristic for the individual child. Planning for this eventuality means that we address the difficulty for everyone in the class who requires support with attention at that time. This is the basis for Universal Design for Learning (UDL), an approach based on educators routinely planning for all the neurodivergences that may occur in the classroom. When we think about who might not be able to smoothly access everything and make provision for them, we ensure that we cover everyone's needs. This concept originates in building design, where, by thinking about the needs of wheelchair users, we make accommodations that benefit parents of small children, the elderly, people with chronic fatigue, etc.

UDL divides learning into three broad functions of the brain: recognition, i.e. what we learn; skills and strategies, i.e. how we learn; and caring and prioritising, which relates to why we learn. From this understanding educators build a flexible curriculum with three main aspects. To support representation, we need to offer multiple forms of content, recognising that some children will benefit from listening, some from looking and, ideally, they will be able to engage with content in the form of their choice. Students can be encouraged to learn through physical action and communication, where these are strengths they possess. UDL recognises that students who have some autonomy and ability to choose will have stronger engagement with learning and greater persistence. The CAST website provides detailed information about every aspect of UDL along with suggestions and tips.

Development and assessment

Our school systems are dominated by assessment. We seek reassurance that our students are learning by checking their grasp of content. We measure the success of educators and schools by examining learners and making comparisons of results. We measure the aptitude of students against their progress and ultimate gains. Assessment can be used in a positive sense to ascertain individual areas of strength as part of valuing and building on these. However, this has not been the typical approach; rather, our assessments look for deficits and areas of weakness in order to try to make good the gaps. Rather than being a positive experience where we help students know themselves, assessment is typically a dreaded and anxiety-making process, where people will be compared to each other and potentially shamed. I know of a school where an assembly of upper school students were segregated according to those who had reached their target in mock exams, and those who had not. The names of the 'successful' students were read out and they were allowed to leave the assembly; everyone else had to stay behind. This very public 'outing' of less successful learners was presumably designed to promote them to work harder at the risk of causing harm through humiliation.

It is relevant at this point to look at what underlies much of our assessment. We work to a notion that some people are more able than others, and that we can therefore expect more of some students than their peers. This greater ability is typically seen as 'intelligence'. The dictionary definition of intelligence is 'the ability to acquire and apply knowledge and skills' (Oxford Languages, n.d.). The way we think about intelligence tends to be more complex than this, particularly as we try to measure and compare individuals.

We might look at speed of processing and answering a problem, or emphasise finding an innovative solution or remembering detailed information. The ongoing debate about how to understand intelligence is highlighted in interest in Howard Gardner's (2000) theory of multiple intelligence, which gained wide appeal. By suggesting that intelligence is made up of many aspects, such as linguistic, interpersonal, logical and musical, we can appreciate and value a broader range of people than those who are able to show high academic performance in tests. Educators are fully aware that students bring different approaches to their work, show varying speeds of processing information, a range of skills and levels of interest. Seeing intelligence as a form of broad ability is part of a strengths-based approach. What matters is the end result of supporting students to be self-regulating and self-determined individuals with resilience as essential life skills that will underpin learning.

However, in the field of special educational needs, intelligence can be seen as a more limiting concept in that it frequently governs our expectations of what an individual can achieve. Students bring with them their assessed IQ in terms of the category of learning disability they are placed in. The originators of IQ tests, Binet and Simon, were initially tasked with distinguishing between those of average ability and below in order that the latter be given additional support in school. IQ is a calculation of the mental age measured by the test and chronological age, with 100 being average. Binet's concept of intelligence was that it was not fixed and that those who scored lower on IQ tests needed more teaching than other students in order to reach the same level. Over the course of the 20th century, IQ came to be seen as something that was immovable; whatever score someone achieved at a point in time would be stable, and this was used to place children into schools designed to meet that level of intelligence. Children scoring at the lowest levels were placed along a continuum, with labels that would no longer be thought acceptable given to each group who scored below average. These ideas of intelligence as fixed formed the basis of decades of discrimination and the eugenics movement, where some people's lives were considered to have less intrinsic value than others (Bhimani, 2022). Intelligence was also thought to be hereditary, leading to forced sterilisations of women with low IQ (Rowlands and Amy, 2019).

IQ tests are still widely used, particularly in research, as they have been found to be fairly reliable indicators of school performance. This is perhaps not surprising given that they mainly assess verbal/linguistic and mathematical/logical skills, which our educational practices are founded on. As educators, when we have access to a test that has been administered by an educational psychologist, we can benefit by looking at the profile of the student, rather than the overall score. Considering sub-tests to find areas of strength is a useful entry into supporting a child. However, it is imperative that we dismiss the notion of intelligence as fixed, which is essentially ignoring the value of education. Neuroscience has been able to provide us with information about how brains can adapt and benefit from practice. When we spend a lot of time on a skill this tends to lead to structural changes in relevant parts of the brain. This accords with theories that the special abilities of some autistic people arise due to their limited focus on perhaps only one thing that they engage in continuously until they become expert.

It is important to note at this point that the scores a student gains on any test says nothing about how they attained it. A student may score at average or above, yet we cannot know whether this is a true reflection of their ability. They may still be facing obstacles to their learning, and actually have potential for even higher marks. Despite seeming to do well they may feel frustrated and disappointed with themselves. Similarly, we cannot see the amount of work a student may have to put in to achieve an average score. If we, as educators, have decided on what we expect a student to be capable of, our 'target', and they achieve this, we can feel confident that we have provided efficient support. Yet some students will have unidentified learning obstacles that with a huge amount of work they overcome, thereby masking their struggles. Parents can help to alert us to this, but their concerns are sometimes dismissed. A teenage girl getting good results was spending virtually all of her time outside school studying, at the cost of her mental well-being. Her school, focusing on her results, did not believe that she could have any learning difficulties and therefore refused to refer her for assessment. We need to focus on student process as well as the end result.

Growth mindset

When considering how we best support learners of all levels, Carol Dweck promotes the power of 'not yet' over the 'tyranny of now'. Children who embrace the mindset of 'not yet achieved but I'm on the way' over 'I failed this so I can't ever do it' have better achievement and greater self-confidence. Children with what Dweck has called 'growth mindset' are those who believe that they have the potential to learn and who know that their work and effort will make a difference. Dweck's (2002) research focused on children's own self-concepts, including how keen they are to face a challenge or the extent to which they are frightened of failure due to a complete lack of confidence and self-belief. Students with fixed mindsets have a sense that, if they are intelligent, everything should come to them easily, that they should not have to work at something in order to achieve. Needing to apply effort is then seen as not being intelligent or capable. Similarly, in the fixed mindset making an error is seen negatively and as evidence of a lack of ability. This leads children to want to cover up their errors and avoid help-seeking. These children are at risk of giving up trying, becoming defensive and adopting behaviours that help them hide their learning struggles because they are frightened of looking unintelligent. Our competitive classrooms and focus on grades contribute to this belief. Our schools frequently perpetuate fixed mindsets. For example, we group children into tables at the beginning of the year and give each group a cute name to disguise how this relates to our assessment of them, although children quickly figure this out. The children on the 'top' table may feel proud and it can reinforce their self-belief, but with this also comes pressure and anxiety: 'what if they can't stay there'? Their efforts are concentrated on maintaining their high grades at the expense of developing a love of learning and persistence. Conversely, the children on the 'bottom tables' will think they are seen as less able than the rest of the class. Although some teachers argue that this can spur on a child to try harder, it is more likely that it will instil a sense of shame and hopelessness, which leads to lack of effort.

Dweck's research also considered how children develop these mindsets and found a link with parental praise in early years; in fact, a study of how mothers praised infants showed in children's mindsets at age 5. Praising children's abilities was found to have harmful effects of turning them away from learning. In one study, telling children that their high test score meant they were clever, followed by giving them tasks that were too hard for them, resulted in a failure at the third set of tasks, which were at a comparable level to the first set. In this example their measured intelligence went down over the course of the test as they were first told they were able, then made to feel less so, and their deflated self-belief led to a lack of effort in the final stage. We need children to value finding something difficult, as it presents an opportunity for learning without worrying about failure. Part of developing a growth mindset in children is to present them with the evidence from neuroscience that working their brain will grow it, just as working a muscle does. When children understand this, they are keener to keep trying, setting them up in a cycle of success. We have long known the power of limiting beliefs, and understanding mindsets helps to explain how they have impact.

To foster growth mindsets in our pupils we need first to understand them ourselves. We need to believe that children can learn with our support. In our interactions with our pupils, we will then offer praise for their learning process and approach to a task. We can comment on the effort they made and the strategies they adopted. We need to avoid praising intelligence and skill as this inevitably makes children vulnerable. They can feel that these aspects are things outside their control that may disappear. Their fragile belief in their ability to overcome obstacles will limit their learning. Dweck's team has gone on to look at how mindsets relate to children's behaviour, finding a reduction in bullying and aggressive behaviours when growth mindset is fostered. Educators need to adopt 'not yet' over any other form of negative feedback, with feedforward that shows learners how we will help them succeed. As Dweck says, this is a human rights issue, with this knowledge it is untenable that we continue to assess children at one point in time and set limiting expectations based on this information.

I see how the mindset plays out with my students at university and myself as a learner. Some students, within a month of starting the course, will explain that they 'must get a distinction' in order to satisfy their own expectations or those of other agencies. This is obviously a highly stressful and distressing situation for students whose funding may depend on their grades. They have often already achieved highly in order to get a scholarship for the course but have high anxiety about whether they will be able to do the same at a higher level of study and different educational system. For some of these students the anxiety they feel, and their lack of confidence in their abilities, negatively impacts their learning. Others arrive with their focus on what they will learn and how it will be of use to them in furthering their ambitions. High grades may still be important, but not the main focus. These students pay careful attention to the feedback they achieve and often have a rising profile of grades across the course.

None of this is to deny that some students find acquiring knowledge and skills more difficult than others; however, when we understand why, as discussed in later chapters, and offer appropriate support, along with growth mindset, they will learn and feel better. All our pupils deserve to develop a growth mindset along with passion and persistence for their long-term life goals, what Angela Duckworth (2017) terms 'grit'. They will do this when we give them challenge with modelling and reassurance.

Person-centred approach

Carl Rogers, the originator of the person-centred approach, was interested in how people become what he termed 'fully functioning' (1963). Effective learners will be open to experience and self-organised to follow their individual meaningful goals. Rogers saw people as naturally curious with inner resources, who, with the right social environment will be intrinsically motivated to learn. He believed that students should learn experientially, rather than being taught, as the latter tended to lead only to inconsequential learning. He suggested (Rogers, 1969) that a focus on exams and grades was detrimental and measured only the wrong kind of learning, for example awarding a degree suggests a final point, whereas actual learners are interested in continuing the process. Rogers saw people as having a natural potential for learning, when they are intrinsically interested and see a relevance to themselves in material presented. However, since learning requires self-organisation, it may be resisted and experienced as a threat. For Rogers, significant learning occurs through doing and in relationship with other people. We need to bring our whole selves to our learning, including emotional responses. Within a person-centred pedagogy, teachers are facilitators, who provide and organise a wide range of resources, and meet their students as people. Within the facilitator-learner relationship, trust, respect, and warmth are crucial as the conditions for growth. The implication of his theory is that if we want learners to fully engage and benefit from what we provide, we must give them freedom, autonomy and trust. It is obvious that these conditions are encountered infrequently in our schools in our current systems either for staff or children.

Rogers saw the wider environment as a facilitator of learning through experiencing. Part of this is how learners are perceived by educators; when we offer empathic understanding and make time to know our students, they will be more ready to learn. A key concept of the person-centred approach is 'unconditional acceptance'. Being valued for who we are, with the whole of us accepted as an authentic part of ourselves, allows us to grow and thrive. Our teacher- and curriculum-led, competitive and judgemental systems are the antithesis of what Rogers advocates. Acknowledging the similarities between person-centred education and more modern positive psychology, Joseph et al. (2020) make the case for the former having a clear theoretical position, i.e. that within a positive relationship our pupils will be self-determining, make their own decisions and work constructively with others. This does not mean that our students will automatically make good decisions, but they will learn from every decision they make if given autonomy to adjust and try new responses. This will support flourishing as a learner.

It is Rogers' belief in the resources a person intrinsically has that is in contrast to the way in which we typically attempt to support learners. For educators to work in a person-centred way we have to relinquish our traditional control and directivity of students and surrender to an attitude of not knowing what is best for the child. The approach I advocate in this book is Rogerian in promoting deep understanding of individuals to foster our unconditional regard and acceptance of them. When we can offer empathy, rather than judgement, we show genuine compassion towards our learners, maintain our composure and offer support within a positive relationship. We honour the wisdom of the child and their goals, offering assistance in helping them achieve them. When we can demonstrate the benefits of what we are teaching to their ultimate goals, we will increase engagement. I believe that although our current educational systems run counter to a non-hierarchical and non-directive approach, we can still espouse much of Roger's theory as a way to build positive relationships and inclusive cultures. When we provide non-judgemental acceptance of children's behaviour, we foster peer acceptance and kindness. This is not to suggest classrooms where 'anything goes'; rather that making clear expectations for the well-being of the group, and offering support to meet these expectations, avoids shaming those who err. There is a huge difference between shouting at a child to stay in their chair, and offering a gentle reminder that that is what is required, or empathising with a child in order to try and understand why that task might feel impossible in that particular moment. Our emphasis on some of the strategies offered through positive education, such as a focus on mindfulness, then sit within a sound theoretical base and are likely to be more effective, compared to when they are teacher-led add-ons to the curriculum.

Positive education seeks to improve well-being of learners. One of the first steps to this can be through children having a positive relationship with the adults around them, where they feel safe, known, understood and cared for. Ideally, we will like our students, but where this is not an immediately available sentiment, we can still adopt caring and understanding. Within supportive relationships young people are able to learn about themselves, which is beneficial in itself and is supportive of learning:

> success in learning about oneself is integral to success in learning about the world, and in life's achievements. Education can be understood as being about the full development of the person and not merely the functional acquisition of facts or the use of memory to recall these facts. In the person-centred approach, one is not at the expense of the other as both are so closely intertwined.
> (Joseph et al., 2020, p. 558)

School well-being, emotions, stress and trauma

An increasing focus on the extent to which schools can, and should, support well-being in pupils has led to many initiatives. Practices such as mindfulness are now widely adopted in schools in the West. However, the debate about teacher responsibility for well-being is ongoing, and many schools delegate pastoral care to non-teaching staff. When I read the first draft of the latest UK government policy for SEND, I noted that teachers were given responsibility for pupil well-being, although this disappeared in the final published document. Some of the focus on well-being comes from the increasing number of reports about the rates of mental ill-health found in today's children, sometimes related to bullying, which can be more pervasive now that it happens online. In addition, neuroscience has taught us that children who are highly anxious, stressed or traumatised have structural changes in their brains which impact healthy development. We can be sure that children focused on survival cannot learn to the best of their ability.

We know that many children struggle to cope with the demands of school, both academically and socially. The UK Children's Society, and many other organisations, suggest that in 2022 1 in 6 children aged 5–16 have a mental health problem, and the rate has increased over recent years. Many of these children, although not exclusively, will be those who have increased vulnerability due to their disabilities or differences since they have higher levels of particular difficulties with fitting into established systems. Research has suggested another vulnerable group, those who have experienced neglect, abuse or violence, make up almost one-third of the school population in England and Wales. All children will be experiencing varying rates of stress and distress at different times according to internal and environmental factors. We cannot always recognise or know what pupils are feeling or dealing with, so our schools have to be responsive to everyone, at all times. Being responsive, in this instance, refers to educators building trusting relationships with young people and being open to sensitively discussing emotions, something which is included in governmental guidance in England as a whole school approach (Long, 2022). This approach is essential in ensuring that children feel safe at school.

Young people experiencing emotional distress, or who have been traumatised, typically struggle to regulate their emotions, which often results in challenging behaviour. Some children may be withdrawn, others aggressive, both leading to decreased engagement with school and negative long-term outcomes. Anxiety, a condition found in high numbers of pupils, and particularly those who are neurodivergent, can manifest in myriad ways. Pupils may not want to go to school, feel physically unwell, have poor sleep, fail to do their schoolwork or become perfectionists, leading to being introverted or angry and upset. Many children having these experiences may find explaining what they feel, or why, impossible. A teacher responsible for behaviour in a number of schools recently told me that since the Covid-19 pandemic they have encountered a new phenomenon, that of children being present in school but refusing to go into lessons. They appear unable to explain their inability, which presumably stems from a form of anxiety. This creates enormous challenges for schools who feel ill-equipped to support the mental health needs of these children but where services that could offer help are overstretched and frequently unavailable. Our efforts need to start by trying to give them the language they need to talk about their feelings, to help them develop insight. It is best to avoid questions such as 'what's wrong', which put the child under pressure when they may not be able to articulate an answer. The UK charity Young Minds suggests drawing an 'anxiety iceberg' with the child. On the top write or draw what can be seen, such as a child fighting with their friends, or refusing to go into their classroom. Then support the child to consider what might be going on under the surface, either at school or at home.

Signs of anxiety, or other emotional disturbance such as trauma, can manifest in many different ways that may also be signs of a learning difficulty. It is imperative that we support the emotional needs of every child, in order to be clear about their learning support needs. Children experiencing emotional distress find it harder to learn, and the learning support needs of neurodivergent students can lead to them having increased anxiety and emotional distress. Many autistic children, for example, may dread the noisy corridors they encounter as soon as they enter the school. Children with ADHD may awake each morning with a sinking feeling that they will be misunderstood and not liked at school.

Difficulty with emotional self-regulation tends to impact behaviour holistically, leading to lack of attention and organisation, and poor memory and planning, areas discussed in Chapters 3 and 4. Children with high levels of anxiety, or who have been traumatised, are frequently hyper-vigilant and may be in a continual state of 'flight, fight or freeze', meaning that they come to school in a heightened state where the smallest challenge can tip them into disruptive behaviour. We might think we are seeing a child going from 0–100 as an over-reaction, not being aware that they always function at around 80 so only a small obstacle can tip them into extreme behaviour. As educators we need to avoid labelling them as 'over-reacting', and show understanding that their constant anxiety leads to them being easily triggered. Traumatised children may have greater difficulties in trusting adults and our efforts may therefore take longer to promote change. This is another part of the argument for a whole-school approach; children's dysregulation can continue for many years but ultimately be helped by a long-term consistent approach from all their educators. In his hugely helpful book *When the Adults Change Everything Changes*, Paul Dix (2017) discussed the importance of consistency across all staff.

Training for staff supporting traumatised children covers recognising signs of trauma being present. Although this would be helpful, it is not necessarily required if staff adopt 'trauma-informed' and 'trauma-responsive' approaches for all pupils. The first step in being 'trauma-informed' is the ability to observe children's behaviour without becoming absorbed within it. A more distanced view, which allows us time to reflect and consider what the student is showing us, then gives us time and space to consider why that might be, rather than rushing to a response. Of course, we need to manage this very quickly so that we are still responsive to situations to prevent escalation. As adults we too are 'triggered' by student behaviour and it can be enormously difficult not to react negatively, particularly when we feel threatened, stressed and exhausted. We need to look after ourselves in order to look after our pupils. Dix suggests a whole staff agreed script to deal consistently with unacceptable behaviour in the classroom. This helps avoid teachers having to make impromptu responses that risk escalating a situation. However, there is a risk of these scripts being used in a performative manner and as a way of not listening to children, so they need to be used in the most authentic way and preferably designed for an individual.

A reflective attitude in staff can be seen as an opportunity to 'reframe' our views of student behaviour, which leads to a more compassionate response to them. In this way we maintain our self-regulation, which is better for us and supports the child in regaining theirs. What is perhaps even more challenging for educators is understanding students' needs to feel a sense of control. There is so much emphasis on adult and particularly educator control being necessary to manage groups of students. However, being trauma-responsive means recognising children's inherent autonomy and how to use this to everyone's advantage by trusting them to make choices for themselves. Of course, the choices they make will not always be what a school hopes for, or what is best for the child, but this is part of learning. I am not advocating complete freedom, but rather children being given the sort of choice that comes from a question such as 'I can see you are struggling to concentrate; what do you need to do to get back to your work, take a 5 minute break to look out of the window, stay in your chair but do nothing until I can help you, or can you manage this yourself?' With children who would struggle to understand these options, or to choose, we can offer 'I don't think you are ready yet, I'll try again in a minute'. When we show trust in our pupils, their trust in us will increase. The noting of their behaviour is an important part of these types of comments and questions, as it helps students develop insight and ultimately independent self-management for learning. It is also key that how behaviour is commented on is non-judgmental.

Ensuring a safe and effective trauma-responsive provision requires understanding on the part of staff, which includes knowing how to avoid becoming traumatised themselves due to listening to pupils' experiences and understanding that some re-telling of trauma can re-traumatise young people. A whole school approach will be more effective for adults and pupils, providing a strong care base for everyone. However, I argue that there is still much that can be done by individual educators, within their own practice, which can support their pupils and serve as a model for colleagues, helping to promote a wider approach. Where educators identify a child as having experienced trauma, they still need to make a referral for specialist provision. However, in the meantime there is much that their appreciation of the origins of what schools consider unacceptable behaviour can offer to the child. This starts by viewing all of a child's behaviour as communicating something about their emotional state, which can benefit from care and support for self-regulation. To quote Andrew Curran (2008), 'Twenty-five years of neurobiological research tells us that children learn best when they feel loved'.

Summary

To summarise what has been discussed so far, we can adopt the following tenets for our practice:

1. See children as individuals who will have patterns of strengths and challenges, and focus our attention on the former as ways of overcoming barriers.
2. Avoid having expectations of a child based on any label they have been given.
3. Recognise that emotions are key to learning, that our schools can be inclusive and supportive places that allow children to safely bring their whole selves.
4. Support staff in maintaining their own well-being so they can effectively self-regulate and make more supportive relationships with their pupils.
5. Adopt a growth mindset; our efforts in teaching and supporting children will reap benefits, although at varying pace across individuals.
6. Communicate our interest in our students and evidence belief in their autonomy and ability to make the best choices, with our guidance.

Least dangerous assumption

While all the theories discussed here have been formative in my practice, the one that I repeatedly use as the basis for my work is the least dangerous assumption (LDA) (Donnellan, 1984). I learned about this initially when having the privilege of working with Anne Donnellan and her colleague Martha Leary, but her ideas are clearly articulated in a paper that has formed the basis of many calls for more inclusive practice. Recognising that so little in education can be presented as fact, and even strong evidence is missing for the most part, the LDA reminds us to consider where our assumptions about an individual arise from and what their consequences could be. Thinking back to the 1970s when I first trained as a speech and language therapist, I was taught that children with spastic cerebral palsy (CP) could not develop literacy skills, that this was part of their condition. At that time many people with severe spastic CP did not have effective communication skills, so our knowledge of their ability to generate language was limited. Our assumptions about people with no or very limited movement control impacted our view of their cognitive capability. This has long been the case and is considered by many contemporary activists as part of a history of discrimination, which continues in our present society. Christopher Nolan, a pioneering author with CP, had to fight against many negative views that he was not actually the originator of the words he wrote until finally receiving recognition. As medical interventions, and technology, provided people with increased opportunities to overcome physical limitations, many more people have demonstrated what were previously unexpected communication abilities. These pioneers have helped to change our assumptions, and people are generally offered more opportunity to demonstrate their inner world, mainly because we acknowledge that they are likely to have greater awareness than they can easily demonstrate. However, in the intervening years people have faced severely restricted lives because of the assumptions made based on what we could observe. We have had to learn that not being able to move, or speak, does not mean that someone has nothing they would want to say should we offer the opportunity. Donnellan argues that in the absence of evidence, assuming that someone is not interested, or is not capable of having ideas and thoughts, is the worst assumption, i.e. one that does the most harm should the assumption be incorrect.

According to Donnellan (1984), the criterion of the least dangerous assumption 'asserts that in the absence of conclusive data educational decisions should be based on assumptions which, if incorrect, will have the least dangerous effect on the student' (p. 142). She concludes her paper with a set of questions that acknowledge that as our long-term goal for all students is to acquire skills for independent living as far as possible, and that we have multiple educational strategies that we can select to meet this aim, we will be making assumptions in order to decide the appropriate intervention. When going through this process we will weigh up factors about what might be effective, least time-intensive, best value, etc. However, what is imperative to consider is 'which assumptions will have the least dangerous effect on the likelihood that the goal will be attained' (p. 148). For Donnellan this is a call for students to be educated in inclusive schools where they will have the opportunity to forge relationships with a wide variety of others and learn from their more able peers.

What this looks like in reality can be seen if we return to the example of someone with CP who has not developed spoken language or effective non-verbal communication. We could assume that they will not understand what is said in a classroom, based on their inability to demonstrate comprehension. From this we could assume that there would be no point in them being in an inclusive classroom, and in fact that this might even be detrimental since they would not receive, in that setting, the expertise that they need in terms of physio, OT, speech and language therapy, and specialist teaching. But if we consider that they may actually have been able to understand at least some of what was going on in the classroom, and that this would have provided them with a rich social environment in which to acquire more skills, and to feel part of a community, the least dangerous assumption would be to include them. Adopting the LDA in this instance places the child in a mainstream classroom, believing that they will learn much from the environment, as we are all social learners, and that this opportunity will ultimately help with long-term goals of relationship building and belonging. Placing them in a segregated environment, in contrast, may give them some valuable teaching and support, but less experience of being with diverse peers who offer the opportunity for learning through interaction and observation. Making decisions about where to place a child will often need to be an individual process, considering the child and choice of environments, and this is a dilemma that parents typically face. The ideal would appear to be to have inclusive environments that could meet all a child's support needs while offering rich social encounters.

When considering an autistic child with sensory sensitivities our thinking process is likely to be different. Again, mixing with typically developing peers will offer opportunities for learning and developing friendships. However, alongside this is likely to be an overwhelming environment where individuals may become so distressed and dysregulated that they are not in a state to encounter others in a positive way. In this instance it would be possible to argue the LDA would be for the young person to attend a specialist unit where the environment could be kept more comfortable, with opportunities for mixing with other students for shorter periods, rather than full immersion in a mainstream school.

Another example would be whether we attempt to teach literacy skills to non-verbal children with intellectual disability. We might consider the resource of the educator's time to be wasted in trying to teach literacy where there is no evidence that the child will be able to acquire it. However, I would argue that the LDA is to offer the opportunity, bringing literacy in any form to a child with significant disadvantages would be the most humanitarian option. In my work with children with no effective communication the access to technology depended on their being able to demonstrate what were considered prerequisite skills. This was due to the limited resources available within health and education systems. In contrast, in the United States, where services would be paid for, policy suggested that all non-verbal children be given the opportunity to use electronic communication aids, with no prerequisite skills required. Since that time the easy and relatively inexpensive use of computers and tablets has brought communication technology to many children, who benefit significantly.

To illustrate this further, I will tell you about Nihal, whose story has been made public through a moving play written by his mother, *The Ballad of Nihal Armstrong*; hence I am using his real name. Nihal was born in the 1980s, a time when the law gave parents the right to choose their children's school. Nihal had severe CP, which meant that he had little independent movement and so needed support with all aspects of life. As a young child he was assessed as severely visually impaired, although as he got older, he was able to demonstrate that he could see adequately well. This perhaps reflects an assessment made in the absence of evidence to the contrary since he did not initially have a means of demonstrating vision. To communicate he used body movements and vocalisations. His mother, Rahila, wanted Nihal to attend a mainstream school with typically developing peers. For this to happen she had to find a school willing to take him. This was by no means simple and much of Nihal's primary school education was spent moving between mainstream and special schools. The mainstream schools rejected him on the grounds that he could not fully participate, despite Rahila attending classes with him and demonstrating how he could answer questions, when given time, by turning his head. Schools wanted 'proof' that he understood, but Nihal was not able to respond sufficiently consistently to convince educational professionals of his capacity. They constantly relied on their modes of assessment and reiterated their assumptions that he would be better supported in a special school. When Rahila was forced into accepting specialist provision, her views that this was not where Nihal needed to be were confirmed. Rahila had observed her son in multiple settings and knew that he was benefiting from being part of groups of people interacting around him. In the special school he was spoken to by adults, but there was no opportunity for him to socialise with peers, as they were all as disabled as he was. The least dangerous assumption for Nihal was that given a rich language and social environment, being part of a lively and exciting community of peers, he would feel happy and more able learn from his environment. Ultimately, Rahila found a secondary school that accepted Nihal and welcomed him as a part of their community. Ironically this was a school with a great many challenges in terms of its demographic and Nihal posed less challenge to the teachers there than many of their other pupils. Nihal settled into this school, developed more consistent communication and was working towards taking part in standardised assessment when he tragically died.

There is much awareness and criticism of current schooling systems for being factory-like (see Ken Robinson's TED talk), where all the emphasis is on exams and competition. Curricula leave no space for pressure-free interaction; teachers are overloaded with paperwork and education is measured with spreadsheets. The majority of children survive this system, although we do not always know at what cost. Those who struggle to survive frequently cause their educators and parents a great deal of anxiety and sense of failure. Yet, in most cases, these children are doing their best but reacting to the pressures they feel. My version of the least dangerous assumption, for every child, is that they are always doing their best in that moment. I believe in the intrinsic goodness of everyone, a desire to be happy and part of society. What gets in the way is a society that does not welcome or even accept our differences. We all know the experience of walking into a group of people who stop talking and the discomfort this brings. Our response might be to walk away feeling lonely and rejected or to conclude they were talking about us and become defensive. On a day when we feel full of confidence we may join the group anyway and make conversation. If we have just experienced something negative, we might move swiftly away. We cannot know in any given moment what the person we are encountering is dealing with. Any individual may be bringing with them pain, discomfort, anxiety, hope, excitement. When we meet them with openness to what they are dealing with, they may be able to move out of their state and join with ours, although this involves some form of transition. When they cannot move with us, we experience them as blocking and challenging. If our response to this is authoritative and judgemental, it may bring us into conflict. In contrast, if we meet them with what I believe is the least dangerous assumption – that they are doing their best and trying to join us – we will then start to look for ways to understand and support them. If that is too hard today, it may be possible tomorrow.

Conclusion

As educators we are joining children on their journey towards greater levels of understanding and self-regulation. Children are not fully formed smaller adults; they are 'works in progress' who need nurturing. We all learn at different rates, and better at some times than others. In our education system, not progressing and failing to learn engender feelings of shame, which is a block to progress and takes us on negative paths of embarrassment and defensiveness. For optimal learning we need to be in a positive state, feeling confident about our potential, willing to make mistakes as opportunities for growth. When we hold this in our minds our view of every child can be more positive. Instead of going home feeling dejected and a failure, we can acknowledge the 'not yet' for us and our pupils. This is not to say that believing that children are always doing their best in that moment makes it easy for us to deal with extreme and challenging behaviour or repeated minor disruptions. Most of us have been 'schooled' into our responses and often have some 'unlearning' to do. However, in my experience it does give us space to think and reflect on our own behaviour and that of our pupils. When we believe the child was doing their best, although it was causing chaos, we can stop and consider what was happening to them that led to their response. We can show compassion and empathy, and work with the child for a long-term positive outcome.

References

Bhimani, N. (2022). Intelligence testing, race and eugenics. Wellcome Collection. https://wellcomecollection.org/stories/intelligence-testing--race-and-eugenics

Botha, M., Chapman, R., Onaiwu, M. G., Kapp, S. K., Ashley, A. S. and Walker, N. (2024). The neurodiversity concept was developed collectively: An overdue correction on the origins of neurodiversity theory. *Autism*, 28(6), 1591–1594. https://doi.org/10.1177/13623613241237871

Buckley, S. (2001). Reading and writing for individuals with Down syndrome – An overview. Portsmouth: The Down Syndrome Educational Trust.

CAST. (n.d.). Universal Design for Learning. Accessed 18 September 2024. https://www.cast.org/impact/universal-design-for-learning-udl

Curran, A. (2008). *The Little Book of Big Stuff about the Brain: The True Story of Your Amazing Brain*. Wales: Crown Publishing.

Dix, P. (2017). *When the Adults Change Everything Changes: Seismic Shifts in School Behaviour*. Wales: Crown Publishing.

Donnellan, A. M. (1984). The criterion of the least dangerous assumption. *Behavioral Disorders*, 9(2), 141–150. https://doi.org/10.1177/019874298400900201

Duckworth, A. (2017). *Grit: Why Passion and Resilience Are the Secrets to Success*. London: Vermilion.

Dweck, C. S. (2002). The development of ability conceptions. In Wigfield, A. and Eccles, J. S. (Eds) *Development of Achievement Motivation*. Hoboken, NJ: John Wiley & Sons.

Gardner, H. E. (2000). *Intelligence Reframed*. New York: Basic Books.

Joseph, S., Murphy, D. and Holford, J. (2020). Positive education: A new look at Freedom to Learn. *Oxford Review of Education*, 46(5), 549–562. https://doi.org/10.1080/03054985.2020.1726310

Long, E. (2022). The future of pastoral care in schools: Exploring whole-school trauma-informed approaches. *Pastoral Care in Education*, 40(3), 342–351. https://doi.org/10.1080/02643944.2022.2093958

Mason, M. (2000). *Incurably Human*. London: Working Press.

Mason, M. (2008). *Dear Parents…* Nottingham: Inclusive Solutions.

Montessori, M. (2011). *The Montessori Method*. Blacksburg, VA: EarthAngel Books.

Oxford Languages. (n.d.). Accessed 2 November 2003. https://www.google.com/search?q=intelligence+meaning&rlz=1C1GCEA_enGB1042GB1043&oq=intelligence+meaning&gs_lcrp=EgZjaHJvbWUqEAgAEAAYkQIYsQMYgAQYigUyEAgAEAAYkQIYsQMYgAQYigUyDQgBEAAYkQIYgAQYigUyBwgCEAAYgAQyBwgDEAAYgAQyBwgEEAAYgAQyDQgFEAAYkQIYgAQYigUyBwgGEAAYgAQyBwgHEAAYgAQyBwgIEAAYgAQyBwgJEAAYgAQyATSAQgyOTc0ajBqBqN6gCCLACAQ&sourceid=chrome&ie=UTF-8

Piaget, J. (2002). *The Language and Thought of the Child*. London: Routledge.

Rogers, C. (1963). The concept of the fully functioning person. *Psychotherapy: Theory, Research & Practice*, 1(1), 17–26. https://psycnet.apa.org/doi/10.1037/h0088567

Rogers, C. (1969) *Freedom to Learn*. Columbus, OH: Charles E. Merrill.

Rowlands, S. and Amy, J.-J. (2019). Sterilization of those with intellectual disability: Evolution from non-consensual interventions to strict safeguards. *Journal of Intellectual Disabilities*, 23(2), 233–249. https://doi.org/10.1177/1744629517747162

Skinner, B. F. (1986). The evolution of verbal behaviour. *Journal of the Experimental Analysis of Behavior*, 45, 115–122.

Terzi, L. (2005). Beyond the dilemma of difference: The capability approach to disability and special educational needs. *Journal of Philosophy of Education*, 39(3), 443–459. https://doi.org/10.1111/j.1467-9752.2005.00447.x

UNESCO. (2020). *Europe Fact Sheet – Global Education Monitoring Report*. https://unesdoc.unesco.org/ark:/48223/pf0000373718

Vygotsky, L. S. (1978). *Mind in Society: The Development of Higher Psychological Processes*. Cambridge, MA: Harvard University Press.

Vygotsky, L. S. (2012). *Thought and Language*. Cambridge, MA: MIT Press.

3
Attending

Introduction

To be included in society we all need a set of skills that allows us to follow rules, avoid upsetting people or getting into trouble with the law. To be successful in our work, to be able to hold on to a job and get promotion we need to be able to organise, stay on task and collaborate with others. Family and friends will value our trustworthiness and reliability, and ability to share, take turns and arrive on time. Many of us take these attributes, in ourselves and others, for granted – this is just what it is to be 'normal'. However, all of these are skills that we learned as children, smoothly, with little awareness or painstakingly with help, and which we may start to lose as we age. They are skills that are mainly governed by the frontal lobe of our brain, which serves as a conductor and coordinator for the other parts, and can be considered as 'survival skills'. This and the following chapter will look in detail at what are referred to as 'executive functions', as they are fundamental to knowledge acquisition and learning to fit into social groups. An analogy sometimes used is that they are the 'air traffic control' system of the brain. They oversee and coordinate all the other parts to ensure smooth and effective behaviour.

The reason for educators looking in detail at these skills is that they are also, for the most part, things that we may not observe. When we look at a child who is not behaving as expected, there are myriad potential reasons. What is clear is that there will be a cause, as all behaviour has a purpose. What we can observe is often the consequence of something happening internally for the child. This may be at an emotional or neurological level; most likely there will be components of both, since emotions impact body control, and vice versa. What is essential is that we ask questions about the root of the behaviour in order to build children's self-insight since, as discussed later, this is the first step towards children regulating their emotions and having control over their behaviour. Educators can be wary of delving into territory that they may feel ill-equipped to deal well with. We have a model of delegating to 'specialists' when we identify a student as having a particular problem. Of course, the advice and support of a specialist can benefit both child and educator, but in a climate of scant resources and limited personnel there is also much that we can do.

When we see a child get into line, keep silent, attend to their name being called and obedient when given an instruction, what we are actually seeing is a child who has mature executive function (EF) and is hopefully feeling happy and confident in their abilities. Conversely, the child who keeps moving out of line, pulls the hair of the child next to them, fails to hear their name being called or to do what is asked, may be someone who has yet to develop effective EF, or whose performance is being negatively impacted by emotional distress or trauma at that moment. Our perceptions of what we see in the latter child is someone being 'naughty', 'challenging' or 'defiant'. When this happens, we risk setting up a downward spiral where the child, who struggles to control themselves, feels shame and develops a negative self-image, which puts them at risk for further EF difficulty. The least dangerous assumption for the child is that they are trying to manage their attention as best they can in that moment, that they will welcome strategies and support to cope better, and it is therefore imperative that educators understand EF skills and offer understanding to the child to help them develop a growth mindset.

This chapter looks at attention as necessary for effective learning and coordination of EF skills. Attention can be a reflex, such as when you hear your name mentioned even when in discussion with someone else. Teachers have many ways of gaining, or attempting to gain, class attention. I think we need to go beyond this automatic type of attention towards something more intentional that might be called 'attending', i.e. something a student can decide to do, have some control over and gradually learn to master.

Paying attention

This chapter, focused on our perceptions of students' ability, challenges us to look below the surface, as I will suggest throughout the book. We start by considering the ability to direct and maintain attention. Attending is the foundation of all learning, yet as we can all recognise, challenging at times. Our ability to attend to the task at hand is likely to vary, by time of day, levels of comfort, the task and distractions. If you are reading this book, it is likely that you have naturally good levels of attention or have worked hard to achieve it. It might be that you struggle to attend for some topics or occasions, but when truly interested or motivated it becomes easier. However, our schools are full of children who struggle to attend, or to attend at the right time and in the right way. Some of these would be considered neurodivergent, but includes all students at times, since attention is governed by multiple factors. We need to be able to identify common blocks to attending before we can find ways to teach our pupils to find their own strategies for success.

Much time in teacher education is spent on advising how to gain and hold the attention of pupils. In the UK, there is pressure on teachers to move away from more social learning environments, with a return to focus on sitting separately and facing forward. This is a response to perceptions of increased disruptive behaviour, and despite evidence that students will learn better through doing than listening. Most schools require students to attend to instructions and rules and show respect through attentive behaviour. No one wants to talk to groups of people who do not appear to be listening and are perhaps obviously engaged in different activities. In my university teaching I have become accustomed to international students who appear to be active on their tech devices while I talk. At first, I was put off by this behaviour. Once I understood that they were trying to help their own learning, it was easier to tolerate. Now I have to trust that they are using dictionaries or translation programmes to support their understanding, although this is probably not always the case. After all, distraction is real and common, as I keep finding as I write this book!

When I have worked with young people, particularly those considered learning disabled, from a stance of assuming their interest and desire to communicate with me, I have often had someone in their lives explain to me that 'they don't understand' or 'they can't do that' or even something like 's/he just likes to chew books'. This has usually been based on that person having overtly attended to only a limited range of activities or objects and appearing not to have understood their purpose. Attention in this situation is perceived as directed interest and rewarded and reinforced by carers. This can lead children to continue to play with toys that they had as infants, as these are the things that appear to attract attention and offer enjoyment and comfort. A 10-year-old child I worked with 'chose' to spend her free time sitting on the floor surrounded by plastic baby toys. What could be observed was her randomly selecting a toy, bringing it to her mouth and chewing it. It looked like a preference. I wanted to bring in books to look for areas of interest, but her carer said this would not work as she just tore books and didn't like them. What we found was that when I held the book beyond her reach, but where she could see the images that I pointed out to her, she started to look. I would slowly read a simple story, waiting until I had seen her glance at the book. She would reduce her other movements, stop chewing the toys and gradually learned to raise her hand and touch the book as indication that she was ready to move to the next page. My interpretation of what was going on for this child was that she was stuck within repetitive movements and actions which she could not inhibit (see Chapter 4). Her picking up and chewing of toys had become reflex actions but were perceived as interest and preference. This led to limited opportunities to attend to anything else. My interpretation of her tearing books was not that she did not like them, but that she was unable to control her hands sufficiently to prevent herself from doing that.

Parents and educators of children who apparently have a narrow range of skills and interests can easily believe that the children are making choices to only engage in limited ways. We struggle to believe that someone might do this, yet still be open to trying something different. As I will continually comment, one of the big challenges in working with neurodivergent pupils is our perception of limitation, based on what someone appears to choose to attend to. In my experience this is typically not the case. As discussed in the next chapter initiation can be a huge challenge, meaning that people get stuck in familiar patterns of behaviour that they struggle to escape from without help. An example that comes to mind is when I went to visit an autistic adult who had a very narrow range of words and phrases that she could say. Something that she said repeatedly throughout the day was 'cup of tea'. I noticed that she didn't actually drink the tea that the kind and responsive carer made for her. I placed in front of her the word 'tea' written on a slip of paper and told her what it said. On another piece of paper, I wrote 'coffee' and read this. She immediately pointed to 'coffee' and drank this avidly once it had been made. Her carer expressed considerable surprise; they had been under the impression that she didn't like coffee since she never said it. In reality, she was using a phrase she could say easily i.e. 'cup of tea' to stand in the place of 'I'd like a drink' or 'coffee please'. We have to open our minds and offer alternatives before we can conclude that what someone appears to want is actually their choice, and not a blocked repetitive form of behaviour. Even where children are not considered neurodivergent, we may observe resistance to change and children wanting only to attend to what is familiar as a way to feel safe.

It is so easy to make an assumption that someone cannot attend when faced with a person who appears to be occupied in their own world and not interested in, or perhaps not even aware of, ours. This applies very often to autistic children, or those described as severely learning disabled. It may also apply to children labelled with attention deficit hyperactivity disorder (ADHD), and we cannot afford to only take it at face value. In my personal life I find it very difficult to maintain what I am saying to someone if they do not look at me. In my working life I recognise that if I want someone to listen, I must respect their need to look away. I once answered the phone to an autistic writer who, having introduced herself, said 'don't talk just listen'. This relates to being 'single-channelled' or 'mono' (Murray, 2021). Some autistic people need to focus on only one perceptual channel at a time, i.e. if they need to listen, it helps them not to look, or if they are speaking, they may struggle to switch to listening.

Eye contact

Making eye contact with another human being is a fundamental aspect of communication in the Global North. When looking into someone's eyes we get glimpses of their emotional state, their level of interest and liking for us, or an idea that they might be lying; as the saying goes, eyes are the 'windows to the soul'. Eye contact is about connection and is a foundation for social skills. When someone fakes a smile, it is the eyes that don't join in. There are cultural differences in how we might use eye contact to show respect, insult or distress, or to express aggression. People who are in a state of emotional distress will often look away from other people, and eye contact is likely to be reduced in people with depression. In the UK we often associate the ability to 'look me in the eye' as a sign of honesty; however, in parts of Asia this might suggest anger. The length and intensity of contact makes a big difference to the meaning and the amount given can signal self-belief or a lack of confidence. This means that something so automatic as making eye contact in the way appropriate for your culture is actually a complex skill. You have to know how long to look, how often and where to look, if not at the person.

We use eye contact as part of our non-verbal communication. It is important in a conversation where we can use our eyes to welcome and include (or exclude) others, offer opportunities for a conversational turn or signal that you would like to say something. Eye contact is a critical aspect of joint attention. When I ask a challenging question in class, many students will avoid eye contact with me so that I don't choose them to provide the answer. All these nuances of behaviour mean that errors are easy to make, and people with different ways of making or avoiding eye contact will stand out. We can also make people feel uncomfortable with our use of eye contact. An anxious person may feel scrutinized and even judged if we look at them, adding to their nervousness and decreased eye contact. This might feed our negative perceptions of the person.

Eye contact starts with mothers and infants gazing at each other. This can impact the development of blind and visually impaired children who make deep connections with others through different senses. People with limited vision may develop abilities in a different order to sighted people by practising their eye gaze towards simple objects and images before attempting to look directly at others, since faces are animated, complex and full of information, which can be overwhelming to process. People avoiding eye contact for other reasons may adopt similar approaches.

An intense focus on the importance of eye contact has particularly come to the fore in autism research (see Stuart et al., 2023). A lack of eye contact was included as a characteristic of autism by both Kanner and Asperger when they first described the condition. The young boys Kanner assessed notably avoided looking at him, contributing to the view that they were deliberately retreating into their own world. Since then, huge amounts of time have been given to both researching eye contact in autistic people, and attempting to teach it, mostly with limited success. Even when someone has been taught to make eye contact, it can appear unusual, forced and insincere. Since eye contact is a way that we signal our interest in others, autistic people's avoidance of it is a key aspect of the perception that they are unaware of others or are seeking to avoid them. Autistic advocates have now taught us, from their insider experience, that making eye contact can be an uncomfortable thing to do, or at worst intensely painful (Trevisan et al., 2017). There are competing theories about why this may be, but it seems that many autistic people feel overloaded if they look directly into someone's eyes and perceive the communication there.

Many autistic people say that they would like to be part of the social world but find it highly challenging. The neurodiversity perspective on this is that those of us who are neurotypical and need eye contact to feel in communication with someone must adjust and trust that someone can be fully present with us, despite not showing it conventionally. When we allow an autistic person to not meet our gaze, accepting their difference, we may have richer conversations and help them find greater comfort and confidence. Think of how some very difficult personal conversations happen in cars when neither party is looking at the other! Autistic children should never be forced to make direct eye contact; whether they decide to look directly at someone should be their choice. An emphasis on eye contact, including commenting positively when it happens, could encourage people to go outside their comfort zone or even learn to 'mask', a trait found in many autistic people where they adopt behaviours in order to fit in socially, rather than being free to be their authentic selves. This can be a conscious effort to fit in, or develop unconsciously, and lead to late identification of challenges. This tendency has been identified as potentially damaging to people's well-being and associated with serious mental ill-health. We should not waste our time, and autistic people's, on direct teaching of eye contact, and to show respect for their needs we might choose to sit next to a child when we work with them, rather than sitting opposite, so there is no pressure to make eye contact. Some autistic people adopt their own accommodations such as looking at someone's face to meet social conventions, but actually not focusing on their eyes; however, ideally we would not force or encourage people to have to meet social conventions.

Eye gaze

Eye gaze is different from eye contact. This refers to where we are looking, so it can include objects, people, a screen or outside a window. Where someone looks can also be a form of communication. Either deliberately or unconsciously we can signal our interest in something or someone; think of detectives solving mysteries by seeing where the guilty party looked! Most students will be able to take control of their eye gaze much of the time, and particularly when prompted. This is a foundational skill for learning and social behaviour. The most obvious example is the need to look at the teacher, what s/he is indicating, what is written on the board. Part of learning to read includes looking at images in picture books to support word recognition and decoding. Children develop their eye gaze incrementally: in the first months of life babies start to be able to fixate, then gradually become able to follow, or 'track', something they have previously fixated on. This forms some of the earliest developmental tests that health professionals do to check whether a child is keeping to expected milestones. The ability to be able to track salient objects continues to develop and plays an important role in being able to read, looking at print from left to right in English, right to left in Arabic and vertically in Korean, for example. However, there will be some children for whom even this skill is challenging either all or some of the time, or who even when directing their gaze struggle to make sense of what they perceive.

Eye gaze is a key part of joint attention where we focus on something with one or more other people, in a triangular relationship where all parties are aware of the other's attention (Siposova and Carpenter, 2019). In the example of eye gaze this requires eye control to look between a person and the object. Joint attention can also be of non-visual aspects, such as enjoying music together or mutual revulsion at a bad smell! We can join our attention either through reflex when the stimulus draws our attention, such as a loud noise, or as deliberate action with a particular goal in mind.

However, differences in eye gaze have long been noted in autistic people and are some of the earliest indicators of someone being on the autistic spectrum. Some research (Jones and Klin, 2013) has found difficulties sharing someone else's eye gaze as an indicator of autism that appears from as early as 2–6 months. When children are unable to follow and share where someone else is looking, either because of lack of awareness or difficulty with eye control, or even because they are fixated on looking elsewhere, they miss important learning that helps develop social skills. There are different and competing theories seeking to explain difficulties directing eye gaze, such as people not paying sufficient attention to the salient point or finding paying direct attention to it overwhelming. What is clear is that some autistic people have developed different ways of looking to take in information. For some this is through peripheral vision, or through very fast glances rather than fixations, which leads to reports of remarkable visual skills and differences in perception. For those of us trying to communicate with someone who does not use the eye gaze that we are used to, we often 'read' this behaviour as lack of attention or interest.

Pointing

Another way in which we share information with young children, and discover their interests, is through their ability to point. Adults model this behaviour, by pointing to books, people, aeroplanes in the sky, etc., and this forms the way interactions are typically delivered for pre-verbal children. We teach the names of objects by pointing and saying their names. We are also very responsive to the gestures of children: when they point, we frequently reinforce with 'yes, it's a plane', thereby teaching them vocabulary. It is evident, therefore, that a child who struggles to direct their gaze to where an adult is pointing will again potentially miss out on important learning. It is usually very difficult for adults to persist with consistent input, e.g. saying 'look, it's Grandma', when the child fails to follow the instruction. Similarly, when a child does not point themselves, the adult will have much less information to draw on to see where a child's interests lie. In both scenarios children are at risk of becoming more isolated and with reduced possibilities of developing typically. The purpose of considering these potential areas of difficulty is both to suggest how some children's learning is different despite greater levels of potential, and to understand that behaviour, although communicative, can be misleading if we jump to conclusions without investigating further.

There are two different forms of pointing that a child can use. As children start to communicate, it is typical that they will point at the thing that they want, and maybe attempt to say its name. Since the adult has a gestural clue to what they are wanting, they will name it and help refine the child's speech, through modelling. The sort of pointing that children do when they want something, frequently combined with vocalisations and hand movements, is called 'proto-imperative'. In other words, this form of pointing replaces the phrase 'give me …'. This is highly successful communication; even if adults refuse to give the item pointed to, children will generally receive a response, even if a negative one. The other form of pointing means 'let's look at this together' and is called 'proto-declarative'. A child will typically look and point towards something, and then switch their eye gaze to check back to the adult to see if they are looking at the child's item of interest. Again, adults will typically be very responsive to this, saying, 'it's a dog, you like the dog'. If the first step to reciprocal social behaviour is a parent and child looking at each other, the second step is looking together at something else. As you will realise, a child who cannot point for shared attention is going to develop differently, as they will usually receive a lot less attention and language modelling from the adults around them, who may well report that their child isn't interested in anything beyond what is put right in front of them. As with eye contact, a lack of proto-declarative pointing has been identified in research as an early indicator that a child is at risk of autism (Gabig, 2013). However, children who have experienced neglect, trauma and other emotionally based challenges may also have barriers to learning social interaction, and a lack of feelings of safety can result in eye contact and eye gaze being withdrawn. We are all used to young children who appear shy and refuse to look at a stranger, although they may gradually feel confident to engage in joint attention. As adults, when we are upset we may avoid looking directly at someone as a way of not displaying our emotions. We can support all students by reducing pressure to look at us, or at what we are sharing, but still maintaining connection to show we are interested and present for them when they are ready.

Attention and distraction

Up until this point I have been considering early years communication, where there is a highly stimulating source for attention, such as an animated adult or object of interest that suddenly appears. We help babies to develop their attention skills by hiding and appearing, such as in a game of peek-a-boo. We hide our eyes, or look away, and when we return to look at the child, they experience a surprise and react, hopefully by laughing. This activity also helps develop an important early concept, that of object permanence. We show them their teddy, then hide it behind us. Very young children won't look for it, a literal 'out of sight, out of mind'. Once they are around the age of 4–7 months, they will move their body to try to see where it has gone and get excited about its return. By playing these games with adults, children learn to initiate, perhaps hiding themselves, maybe playing with strangers on a bus. Being an exciting and responsive adult joining in the child's frame of reference helps to grab the child's attention so that they don't have to consciously direct it. Games such as these also develop the important skill of turn-taking. Children who struggle to wait for their 'turn', in a conversation, game, in class, will tend to be unpopular with teachers, and sometimes peers as well. Young people and adults who cannot wait, interrupt conversations and find queuing highly stressful will struggle to fit into society and experience rejection.

There are stages of attention that children are expected to follow, as they grow and develop. Up until the age of 1 we expect infants to be easily distracted, their attention pulled away by a 'pre-potent stimulus', i.e. something noisier, more colourful or less static than what they were looking at. Between the ages of roughly 1 and 2 years, they will select a place of focus and attend only to that; at this stage they may appear to have 'selective deafness' when it can be difficult to pull their attention away from what they are doing. The next stage, between the years of 2 and 3, is a time of learning to switch attention. They will develop the ability to respond to their name, stop engaging with what they were doing to listen to an instruction, for example, and then return their attention to their activity. A greater degree of control of self-directed attention develops between 3 and 4 years, and in the following year they will be able to give attention to more than one thing at a time, helping them to be school ready.

When a child does not show us apparent attention, we tend to increase our volume and movement. This helps to make us more dominant in the environment, and in turn this assists children to focus on us. For example, when we want to play with a baby, but perhaps they are fixated on their fingers, or something they are chewing, we will make sounds, talk and move, so that we become the most dominant, or salient, part of the environment. However, for some neurodivergent students, including those labelled as autistic or having ADHD, this may still not be enough. It can be very difficult for adults to persist in trying to gain attention when their efforts have little impact. It becomes a tiring and thankless task, and our tendency is, again, to interpret behaviour as lack of interest, despite our best efforts. For some children to attend we need to be the most dominant focus to facilitate their disengagement from something that has initially commanded their attention. Our perception of a child where this is not a successful strategy is to assume that they are not motivated to interact with us, and this leads to them receiving less stimulation and opportunities for learning.

Once an older child has developed as someone who rarely interacts with others, we cannot observe or know how this behaviour developed. For example, children who were provided with little stimulation as babies and infants might have reduced attention compared to others. There are concerns that young children being given access to mobile technology, possibly in place of interaction with adults, will inhibit their development. Research suggests both that children can learn important skills by using tablets and mobile phones, but also that some will receive fewer opportunities for skill development (Radesky et al., 2015). It is certainly possible to observe parents in public places who spend most of their time looking at their phone, with their child either trying to get their attention or with a device of their own, where in the past they may have been interacting. Parent training courses focus on the importance of parent–child interaction as a crucial part of learning in the early years, since it has a huge impact on language acquisition. The primary mode by which development happens in the early years is through having a stable and consistent model to follow, within a securely attached relationship, usually differentiated for the stage the child has reached.

In recent years there have been multiple concerns expressed about a lack of skills in children starting nursery education, many of which can be ascribed to a lack of appropriate environmental stimulation. The political discourse can focus on more mothers going to work alongside the rise of children's access to technology, particularly where it is used as a 'babysitter'. There are current concerns about the impact of reduced socialisation during the Covid-19 pandemic. With every child, therefore, there may be multiple reasons for what we observe as poor attention. Understanding more about this attention, what may have led to it and what can help improve it will be an important step in helping the child. Most importantly, we cannot afford to easily jump to an assumption that the child has limited capacity or is not wanting to be in contact with us. We need to believe that we can build a relationship with a child and that this will be the foundation of growth for them. Improving attention may be through providing guided opportunity to do so, by selecting something a child is highly motivated by and supporting them to maintain focus a little longer than they would instinctively do. For other children, a more systematic approach might be setting a time target on a clock the child can see and supporting them to gradually increase the time spent on a specific activity alongside building independence in managing their focus.

To help you reflect on a child's attention, consider the following:

1. When is the child most still and focused?
2. What are the features of this time; is it for a particular activity, with others or alone, at a particular time of day or in a specific context?
3. If the child focuses better with certain people, can you identify the nature of the relationship and any support that is provided?

Listening

Children need to be able to attend before they can listen, although they can listen without actively demonstrating attention. Think of the child who appears to be engrossed in playing but overhears some of an adult conversation not directed at him. Listening refers to being able to focus attention on a sound, in order to make sense of it. That might be identifying a familiar object or taking in words to understand their meaning. Listening is not the same as understanding; the words heard have to be processed, as discussed in Chapter 4. Children can have good listening skills but still struggle to make sense of what they have heard, similar to adults listening to someone speak in a language they don't know.

Active listening is a key skill for all children; those who can't hear will need to learn differently. Attention to what is heard can waver and we all have the experience of daydreaming but coming back to the situation when someone says our name. For young children to actively listen it helps if we ensure we have their attention before speaking. As educators we use strategies such as asking the class to be quiet, look forward, put down anything they are holding, and give all their attention to what is about to be said. Even then, some children, particularly those with poor processing of sound, will struggle to listen to an entire instruction. As they hear the first part, they may fixate on a particular word trying to grasp its meaning, by which time they have missed the latter part. This is why good practice with young students and additional language learners is, having gained their attention, to speak slowly, segment instructions and provide something visual that is related to the message. Having something to fix their eyes on can help some children to attend, but depending on what this is, other students might prefer to look away as they listen, as this limits the amount of information they are trying to process at any one time, i.e. not having visual input leaves more cognitive space for listening. We have to allow for both possibilities in our classroom.

Observable lack of attention

There are multiple characteristics of lack of attention that will be familiar to all educators. As we have already discussed, many students may fail to look intently at us, which may or may not indicate lack of attention. We will see children not following instructions, which could be because they were not attending at the time they were given. Similarly, when asked a question they may not answer, perhaps through lack of knowledge, but equally because they did not attend to the question. Students of all ages will have varying ability to withstand distraction. Poor attention will lead to losing personal items, forgetting where they need to be and failing to complete tasks. They may fail to look at the detail of a problem and so make errors and show poor organisational abilities. These difficulties are likely to lead to particular behaviours, even in the more resilient students. They may avoid activities that require sustained attention or give up quickly when they anticipate finding something difficult. An example in my own life is when listening to people speak a language I have some knowledge of but a lack of fluency. If I focus very hard, I will be able to gain the main points of any message; however, I may also need to clarify meaning. I can do this for a certain amount of time, but then my attention tires, and I find I haven't been listening to what was said. A similar experience is likely for pupils who have English as an additional language, as well as those who are tired, distressed, hungry, have communication or hearing impairment, or learning disabilities. Teachers require expect active listening for increasing lengths of time as pupils get older, and not all children will be able to match their development to requirements.

Sustained attention is the basis for executing the other EF skills. As discussed in the next chapter, this is challenging for young children and is a major factor in many neurodivergent students. All teachers will be familiar with signs of hyperactivity: children who constantly squirm in their seat and fidget; who might run in the corridors, despite being constantly reminded not to, perhaps climbing where it is not appropriate; who are constantly very active, noisy, over-talkative and who frequently leave their seat in class. The behaviours of these children are a big challenge to teachers since they tend to attract attention and disrupt the learning of other students. Children who behave this way may or may not be given the label of ADHD. This group of children, who are predominantly boys, are at high risk of exclusion from class and school because of the effect their challenges with attention bring to their own learning and that of others. As educators we may try hard to remain patient with a child who we understand has difficulties controlling their active behaviour, but the constant disruption, if not managed, can become overwhelming to our efforts to educate others. As I will discuss later, understanding of ADHD within schools can be somewhat superficial and it is possible to underestimate the extent of difficulties a child is facing, when what we are presented with is primarily someone who jumps around too much and calls out answers in class. We can easily perceive this as deliberate behaviour and miss the efforts the child may be making to exercise control. When we approach a child who behaves this way as doing their best in that moment, we can ask questions and make suggestions towards building their insight, with the long-term goal of gradual improvement.

A child who did not have other aspects of ADHD found remembering to put up his hand before answering mostly impossible. This made him very unpopular with a particular teacher who liked to maintain a quiet and orderly class. His behaviour disrupted the calm, and he felt negatively judged and disliked by the teacher. When his teacher changed to someone with a personality that enjoyed lively initiations and overt enthusiasm for learning, he felt appreciated and started to enjoy school more. I relate this as an example of the power and influence of educator perception. As we know, when a child gains a reputation in the school for being bright, or unruly, this can stick, and can be internalised as a message by the child, which therefore impacts their school career. This will apply to all children, but very particularly to neurodivergent children and those with emotional regulation difficulties, whose greater challenges put them at higher risk for negative self-perception.

Giving or not paying attention are two poles on a continuum with infinite shades. We encounter children who always appear to attend well, and those who rarely do, but the majority of students will attend to a better or worse degree throughout the day and across the week and term. What we cannot observe is how hard a child is trying at any point; those with naturally easy attention may be working much less hard than someone who only grasps half of the task, another reason why we should offer the benefit of the doubt and notice all attempts at effort to encourage children to keep going. Being attentive is very tiring and the expectations of our systems put huge strain on the majority of children and their educators.

How we support attention

In any interaction with children, we need to start by building rapport and trust. Their attention and response to learning tasks will improve when they are feeling supported and optimistic. We can hold in mind what the child may bring to the interaction with us, depending on their previous experiences. Children will very early develop a self-perception as themselves as a learner. They might have been told they are clever by parents and may find it a shock to realise that some learning is not yet easy to acquire. Conversely, they may bring with them many unsuccessful interactions with adults that lead them to feel suspicious and wary. Since we are unlikely to know what the child is bringing, how they are physically on that day, what has been happening prior to our meeting with them, we can work from the least dangerous assumption that they will need to find us calm, attentive to them and willing to listen. We may often feel pressurised by time and competing demands, but bringing these to our interactions with students will inevitably impact negatively on them.

Building rapport with some children is easy, particularly when they are already effective communicators and perhaps share our sense of humour or common interests. It is so much harder when the child does not appear to be attending to us, is distracted by something else, does not speak or respond, and seems hostile, and we struggle to find any common ground. But there are still ways to build rapport that will work for most students, even if this will take longer with some than others. In my experience with non-verbal autistic adults, developing rapport could take many hours, and the extent to which I would feel in interaction with them would fluctuate. It would often not be possible to know what was impacting their level of attention that day. My work with Mike was particularly challenging; for several months he would arrive in my room and then fix his gaze on a corner of the ceiling. I would have the sense that he wanted to look at what I was sharing with him, but he could make only fleeting glimpses towards me, and then turn back to the corner. I verbalised that he seemed to be stuck and that it was difficult for him to direct his eyes, and he made sounds that seemed to signal agreement. When he was in this phase there appeared to be little to do other than to have a consistent approach, to let him know that we were not going to give up on him, that we would keep trying, and to verbalise what we could see and our interpretations of what was happening internally. In this way I and my colleagues maintained our rapport, so that once Mike was more able to respond, we could continue to build his communication skills.

For me building rapport starts with following the child's interest. They might bring something to you that they are interested in or would like to share. They may be willing to discuss something they have created, or a game they like to play. When working in a special school for autistic non-verbal children I took in a children's magazine as something that was unlikely to be a part of their school experience, in the hope of gaining their attention. This was highly successful with James, whose teacher had suggested that he did not communicate other than by selecting a few familiar symbols, pointing to something he wanted, and lots of refusal behaviours such as shouting and pushing adults away. I held the magazine and a couple of books in front of him as options and allowed him to take the magazine and start turning the pages. I made a few comments as he looked, to see if he would respond, but stood to his side and didn't make many interventions until he had gone through every page of the magazine and turned back to the beginning. As he went through again, he paused on some pages, and I started to suggest that there might be something on that page that interested him. I pointed at what I could see, and over the space of the next few minutes as I modelled pointing, he joined in, and we started to share attention. He began to turn his head to look at me to check whether I was following his gaze and finger as he pointed initially to images and then to letters, prompting me to say each letter he pointed to and then the name of the character he was interested in. When I said the letters and names he smiled and made happy vocalisations. He also let me move closer to him, although I still exercised caution regarding moving into his personal space. This was the start of a piece of work that went on for several years, as I gradually came to know James. His early interest in letters developed, and when I met with his mother to let her know what we had discovered she commented that she had always known he could read because he would take the TV page of the newspaper to his room and come down at the right time for the programme he wanted to watch. However, his school was not aware of any reading ability or even interest in phonics; they were working on his recognition of symbols and images and on basic conceptual tasks. Their work was founded on how he presented in the classroom and his level of resistance to the tasks they gave him. For all educators in a busy class it can be difficult to find the time to build rapport, to find out what someone is motivated by, and to put aside the demands of the curriculum. However, it is possible to offer this opportunity to children within the school week, perhaps as a group activity involving peer sharing and staff engagement.

Going back to the self-perception of the student in relation to their abilities, it is important to build rapport through tasks they can be successful with. In the early stages of getting to know any child I will typically use 'no fail' activities, i.e. where there is no 'correct' answer, and the purpose is to elicit a response. By giving the student the opportunity to participate in something where pressure to perform is minimised, I signal that I am interested in them, and not there to judge or test. I have frequently used a set of cards from LDA called 'What would you do', which are actually intended to develop critical thinking skills. These cards comprise eight sets of images. In each set there is the main image and then five smaller cards that provide options of possible responses. One image (in my old set) is of a crying boy standing outside a shop with a box of broken eggs at his feet. If the child is willing and able to describe the picture, I will ask what they see and what they think has happened. When working with a non-verbal or reticent communicator I will model what I see and that I think he was sent to the shop by his mum to buy some eggs but dropped them when he came out of the shop. I then present each 'answer' card and discuss what is happening. In one he goes into the shop and talks to the manager, presumably asking for another box of eggs. Other options include stealing a pack and hiding it under his shirt, going home and confessing to his mother, and going to a neighbour's house to ask for eggs. I ask the child to pick what they would do, and whatever their choice we celebrate and talk about that. If they don't select, I model my choice, offer encouragement and comment on where I see their gaze directed, suggesting they might choose that one. The message of this activity is usually conveyed very effectively, i.e. I am interested in them and their ideas, and whatever they choose is an interesting and valuable selection. I can also demonstrate an emotional response, such as surprise or delight with their choice, showing pleasure in my interaction with them as further encouragement.

Part of the 'no fail' approach is the language we use. For as long as possible I will try to avoid using the word 'no' in relation to something they have done. Many educators are highly effective at offering feedback such as 'I see why you chose that, but here's why I would select something different', or 'I'm interested in your answer, it isn't the same as mine, do you have any other ideas?' Children with low self-confidence, who may perceive themselves as poor learners, are frequently quickly put off when they hear 'no'. It is always imperative, even with adult learners, to show that any contribution is welcome even if not correct. We need to be careful not to offer a routine 'good try', which soon becomes a replacement for 'no', but at the same time praise effort and participation. In their study of training adults in rapport building for working with autistic children, Ensor et al. (2023) found that although training can be effective, maintaining the skills was difficult, due to the responses of the children. Their study also found that the overall engagement of children improved when adults took time to develop rapport before adopting a behaviour programme.

Another aspect of trying to ensure that students are successful in their activities is scaffolding. Most educators will be familiar with the concept of the Zone of Proximal Development (ZPD), suggested by Vygotsky. From his research (Vygotsky, 1978) and work with young children he developed the idea that there are three levels that any of us have for any specific task. If we take driving a car as an example that many of us have tackled in adult life, we can see that we start from the position of very limited knowledge beyond what we may have observed others doing. We are likely to have a concept of ourselves already, ranging in terms of thinking it looks easy and we will be good at it, to seeing it as frightening and difficult. Knowing that we are developing a skill that is crucial for everyone's safety, we have an apprenticeship model for how we become competent drivers. When we have had a few lessons, hopefully developed a level of trust in our instructor and tried out some basic manoeuvres, we are in the ZPD, i.e. we are able to go on the road, knowing there is someone with us who will guide, explain and, if necessary, hit the emergency controls. This is the zone where we can achieve with the right support but would not be able to do so independently. We gradually move towards independent competence, pass our test and in the UK are legally allowed to drive alone. In other countries people have to drive for longer with an experienced driver alongside them, in recognition that passing the test is just one step along the way of being a safe and competent driver. Going back to children and any skill they need to master, or any material they need to learn, they constantly move through these three stages, from limited awareness, to being able to accomplish the task with the aid of a 'more knowledgeable other' (MKO), or scaffolding, to full independence. Vygotsky suggests that when working with children we should aim our attempts within the ZPD of that individual at that time. When we offer tasks that are either too easy, or too difficult, we risk losing the rapport, attention and engagement of the student. This obviously presents a huge challenge to classroom teachers who cannot know the ZPD of every one of their pupils for every task. In the UK they will typically tackle this through in-class assessments providing information about individuals, followed by grouping children so that they can differentiate the work to hopefully match the level of the students to make the learning accessible to them. Even with this approach it is likely that there will be students who are more advanced for that task and may find it too easy, and therefore disengage, or who will still struggle. The UK response to this is frequently to use teaching assistants (TAs) to work with individual children or even smaller groups within the class or for a separate 'catch-up' session.

From the concept of the ZPD comes 'scaffolding' as a way to teach that limits the risk of a student failing. The term 'scaffolding' was first used by Wood et al. (1976) to describe the breaking into small accessible tasks anything that the child needs to learn. This forms the basis of the UK National Curriculum, where information is provided at different levels at different times so that the foundations of understanding and knowledge of a topic is gradually developed into more advanced levels.

Scaffolding is a key concept for special educators and being able to analyse both the task and the student's response is a key skill. Take the child learning to write their name. Firstly, we need to think about the aspects involved: knowing how to hold a pencil, knowing how hard to hold it for optimum control, remembering the letters within the name, thinking about where to place it on the page, how big to write, alongside ignoring any potential distractions. Each one of these aspects can be broken down further. A pencil has to be held in an appropriate place not too near or far from the tip, it has to be held firmly enough to ensure it doesn't wobble, but lightly enough that we don't make tears in the paper. To remember the letters, a child can have something to copy, but if not, they have to remember the shape and order of the letters, then think about the start point for writing that letter legibly. When a child does not write their name successfully it may be difficult to know why, based on what you can observe, which is why awareness of components is key. In the ideal situation the adult will ask or make suggestions to the child of what aspect they need support with and break the task into component parts to ensure success. To find out whether the child knows the letters in their name, they can be given a selection to choose from, ranging from just a small number to the whole alphabet. To see if the child knows the order of the letters, they can be written by the educator on separate pieces of paper for the child to put in order. By taking the physical aspect of writing from the task we can better examine the cognitive components. Once we are sure that they are in place, we can offer support with writing.

Educators wanting to explore these issues in their own students can reflect on the following:

1. Is there a common task that some children find harder to master than others; how might this be broken into segments, i.e. 'scaffolded'?
2. What activities can you introduce into your classroom that are low pressure, high enjoyment to encourage participation?
3. How might you build time into the week for relationship building between you and pupils and the children with each other?

Kim: Persistent disruptive behaviour

As with the other case studies in the book the portrait below is an amalgam of real people to illustrate how challenges with attention frequently manifest in the classroom. Since starting in reception class Kim's educators have found her behaviour challenging. She arrived in school in a chaotic state, clumsy, uncoordinated, with a tendency to trip. It was very difficult to get her to sit down for any length of time, and she ignored the other children and adults, flitting from one area of the class to another picking things up and putting them down in different places. When the teacher was talking to the children as a group, she often looked the wrong way, would start to fiddle with the hair of the person in front of her or pick at the carpet. She sometimes got up without permission and started to walk around the room. She sometimes forgot to ask to go to the bathroom and had several 'accidents' in the classroom, although would then deny that it was her. In a one-to-one with staff, it was very difficult to hold her attention even to play with a toy that she had chosen.

Her teacher spoke to her mother, who was a single parent coping with two older sons identified as having ADHD. Kim's mother described herself as possibly having ADHD too. She described Kim as being a difficult child who did not sleep well and was often irritable and hard to sooth. She was willing to consider that Kim might have the same condition as her brothers but did not see any urgency in seeking confirmation of this, as she thought that it had made little difference with her sons who were always in trouble at school and had no respect for their mother. Kim's mother had many challenges to deal with, finding it impossible to work herself, and struggling to survive on benefits. She had no close family members to support her and insecure housing. She explained that they had had to move multiple times, on one occasion due to her eldest son being reported to the police and social services. He had 'fallen in' with a crowd of teenagers who took drugs and committed petty crime to fund their habits. She was very concerned about protecting her second son from going down the same path. She did not have the same fears for Kim due to her age and that she was a girl, which her mother thought meant that she would be more sensible.

After a couple of years at school, following structured interventions, Kim showed slightly better attention in class, although this was still only sustained for a short while. She made many careless errors in her work and did not pay attention to details, for example when given an instruction, or she would not directly answer a question, instead fixating on a particular word and guessing what she needed to do. When she made errors, she would become distressed and defensive, start to get agitated and even run out of the classroom. Her fine motor coordination for writing was poor so her work looked messy which was a constant source of frustration for Kim. Staff found it hard not to become irritated with her as she rarely appeared to listen when spoken to directly and even after considerable explanation would not follow an instruction. She also tended to make the same errors repeatedly. She frequently left activities unfinished and was easily sidetracked. She was often distracted by something in the environment or daydreaming. Kim was constantly forgetful and poorly organised, often losing items. When she did hear a question and know the answer, she would call this out, despite being warned not to, and would be told off. Sometimes this led to her shouting about it not being fair and causing more disruption.

Kim regularly fell out with her peers. Friends would ask her to keep quiet as she would distract them, but she would continue to want to talk, or would fiddle with their things. Her constant fidgeting and restless movements irritated those around her. Her peers got annoyed when Kim would interrupt when they were explaining something or answering a question. She found waiting for her turn in a game too difficult, which again set her apart from her peers and meant they did not want to play with her.

Kim's school, following specialist advice, adopted a range of strategies to support her. Acknowledging that her body needed to move and that fiddling helped her to concentrate rather than preventing her from doing so, they supplied a range of items that she could hold in her lap and manipulate in a subtle way, not drawing attention to herself. These were offered as a whole class approach with other children in the class being allowed to choose a fidget toy, although after the initial novelty only a few continued to use a fidget toy. Kim's work was broken into time-bound intervals, clearly demarcated for her. In between each she was given a classroom task to do which involved movement. This both satisfied her need to move and gave her responsibility to help build her self-esteem. Breaking work down was accompanied by reminders to slow down her approach to getting something done, as her tendency to rush increased her errors. The school was also advised that children with ADHD respond to immediate reward and 'quick wins'. When tasks were broken into small stages, she could be immediately praised for making a start or completing one stage, helping her with motivation. As attention is better for something that interests the child, particularly something novel and exciting, Kim was frequently encouraged to learn through areas of her own interest.

Another approach that was found to be beneficial for Kim was Forest School, where a group of children were taken once a week for two hours. The health and safety rules of Forest School were explained and reinforced each week, but as long as children obeyed these, they were free to join in activities with the teacher or their peers or spend their time alone. Kim took to swinging in the hammock looking up at the trees, seeming to respond to the rhythm of the movement. At Forest School she was calm and quiet, she loved the space and freedom and after a visit would have a more productive afternoon. Her mother recognised the value of Forest School, reporting that Kim got up more readily on the days she was due to attend.

Kim attended a homework club at school, as her mother found it very difficult to support her at home; when she tried, they soon had a big argument since Kim could not stay on task and strongly resisted doing the work. In the homework club, unless an adult was sitting with her and providing regular prompts, she fiddled with materials and made no progress. Kim's primary school saw some progress with the support they provided but remained concerned about the impact her behaviour had on her peers. Some parents made appeals to the school to exclude Kim, on the grounds that she was a bad influence on their children whose learning was negatively impacted by being in the same class. Parents' perceptions were that Kim took up too much of the teacher's time. The school did not want to exclude Kim, but they sought support from their educational psychologist and reorganised funding to provide some one-to-one support for Kim with a TA. This took place out of the classroom, so that Kim's peers could focus on their English and Maths lessons without interruption. During these sessions Kim managed to make some progress, particularly as the TA was skilled at building her self-confidence and reassuring her that she could learn. However, this approach also further isolated her from her peers and led to her feeling embarrassed.

In secondary school Kim continued to find maintaining appropriate focus in the classroom very difficult and got bored quickly. To her educators she often appeared sullen and withdrawn in lessons, seemingly lacking motivation. She had little sense of time, often arriving late in lessons with no explanation for what she had been doing. Teachers were irritated with her apparent lack of focus and care of her work and concerned about her poor academic achievement. When faced with multiple pieces of homework she felt panicked and overwhelmed, not knowing where to start. She tried to make friends but even maintaining focus for a conversation could be difficult for her. She was inclined to talk more than listen and would not recognise when someone was looking bored or frustrated. Sometimes she said things that seemed rude or hurtful without awareness. When people said unkind things to her, or complained about her behaviour, she became instantly defensive and aggressive. Once she had become upset, she found it very difficult to self-regulate, although once she had calmed down, she would not hold a grudge, even appearing to forget having had an argument. When she was agitated, she found it harder than usual to express herself, which increased her frustration and anger. Some peers avoided her due to her mood swings and unpredictability.

Kim had been good at art in primary school and started to flourish in art lessons. She formed a strong relationship with the art teacher, who appreciated her talents. She allowed Kim, and a small group of other students, to use the studio one afternoon after school and helped Kim to prepare for an art show in school. Kim found an increasing ability to focus when painting; in fact she would often be unaware of the time and reluctant to finish when it was time to leave. At times this brought her into conflict with the teacher, who maintained calm and enforced clear boundaries. Kim gained greater self-confidence and motivation by showing her work and receiving notice and positive regard. She decided that she wanted to study art at college and understood that to do this she needed to improve her English and Maths to gain the required grades. This led to working harder to engage with these subjects, although it was still a challenge. She also gradually formed a friendship with another girl in the art group and this became very important to her.

Although Kim remained without a formal identification of ADHD, her schools worked from the assumption that this was the nature of her difficulties and made accommodations for her. It did not make her educational journey a smooth one but did ensure that despite the challenges she presented to her educators, she was not formally excluded from school as so many others with the condition are. Although the debate about the reality of ADHD as a condition is resolved, there remains lack of understanding of the full picture in some educators. Observable differences in the brain of people with ADHD show the impact is mainly in relation to EF and emotional processing. The neurological differences can lower brain efficiency, children can have slower brain maturation and may never achieve the same levels as non-ADHD peers. Their differences make it difficult for individuals to gain control over their behaviour. Given our understanding of this, schools need to adopt flexible responses to behaviour, even when this appears to be a deliberate flouting of rules. Children with ADHD still need boundaries, but our responses need to be about future learning rather than punishment.

ADHD is a genetically based set of characteristics, which can be impacted negatively by environments that are low in structure and sensitivity. Kim's household, with its multiple challenges, meant that Kim was at higher risk for the condition developing; her mother was unable to provide protective structure or have full insight into her own and Kim's difficulties. This gave Kim a double difficulty to manage: the inherently different way her brain worked, making it very difficult to fit within the constraints of a classroom, and the lack of emotional and material stability at home.

The prevalence rate for ADHD is considered to be around 3–5% (Russell et al., 2024), suggesting at least one child in every class will express an aspect of the disorder. Although ADHD occurs in both genders, the presentation tends to vary, with girls experiencing particular problems with attention. Boys with ADHD may show more hyperactivity and impulsivity, although all children can demonstrate aspects of all of the triad of difficulties. It is thought that around 60% of those with attention differences have difficulties that last into adulthood, impacting their occupations, finances and relationships. Adults often continue to have difficulty with timekeeping and organisation. ADHD adolescents, particularly those who have not been formally identified, are at particular risk for substance misuse, unsafe sex, risk taking, truancy and criminal behaviour. Research (Young and Cocallis, 2019) estimates that around 25% of prisoners in the UK have ADHD, possibly due to their poor impulse control and lack of success in school. I know of a teenager who brought his father's knife into school to show it to his friends, unaware of the potential danger of this and how it would be perceived when seen by staff. The behaviour policy of the school meant that he had to be permanently excluded, having put other people at risk. Of all adults being treated for alcohol or substance misuse, around 25% have ADHD (Smith et al., 2002); it is thought that they may be using drugs to self-medicate in the absence of standard treatment. ADHD can lead to difficulty recognising what people want or need, making people vulnerable to abuse and depression, with three times the rate of teenage pregnancy being one consequence. Additionally, poor coordination and behaviour control lead to risky behaviour: people are 4 times more likely to be injured or poisoned, have 2–3 times higher chance of road accidents and be 3 times more likely to die early.

Although ADHD can bring benefits such as increased energy to achieve and a drive to accomplish, many people with the condition find managing in a restrictive environment such as a school very difficult. To reduce the potential negative consequences of ADHD, it is imperative that schools are alert to signs that a child may be experiencing difficulty with at least one aspect of the condition, in order to ensure they receive the best education and support. Current thinking is that a combination of medication and behavioural treatments are the most successful form of intervention. There are two types of medication, either stimulant or non-stimulant, both of which have unfortunate side effects such as insomnia and appetite suppression, which can lead to people being reluctant to take it. Whether a child is medicated or not, there is still a lot that a school can offer to help them develop greater behaviour for learning. Our awareness of particular aspects of EF skills will support us with understanding individual needs and providing helpful strategies. Some of these were used by Kim's educators, such as routines, prompts to stay on task, breaking down and structuring tasks, and allowing for regular breaks. Praising effort will be very important, and giving regular positive feedback, pointing out specific things they have done well, will help. It is important to understand that some children will need to move their bodies regularly, and many of those with ADHD benefit from exercise and relaxation. Perhaps most importantly of all is a compassionate attitude that continually supports the development of self-insight and the building of autonomous skills for life.

Technology can be utilised to support learning. Since children with ADHD can struggle with time and keeping attention, breaking down tasks into clearly indicated time segments, and providing a clock so that they can monitor how they are doing, can help with focus and build success. A highly structured procedure can be written to follow for each set of instructions. Unlike with autistic students, it can be helpful to maintain eye contact with the student when talking to them, bearing in mind that many students have characteristics of both autism and ADHD. We need to check the student's understanding of a task before they begin it and be willing to repeat if necessary. Avoiding multiple commands and breaking down tasks will help to make them manageable and build student success. We need a classroom climate where all children are comfortable in asking for help and clarification since the shame and stigma of difference can be felt acutely by older ADHD children who are often reluctant to indicate difficulty. Many neurodivergent children will find transitions of topic or place difficult, so we always need to anticipate this and provide support. When providing written documents, we need to use large type and highlighting to make important points stand out. Children with attention differences have a particular need to understand the purpose of what they are learning or doing, which will be helpful to the whole class, so we need to ensure that they have registered that something is important.

With the recognition of ADHD as a difference in brain function comes awareness of some of the strengths of the condition, such as the ability to develop multiple skills and accomplish at a high level, utilising their high levels of energy. In many TED and TEDx talks people with ADHD talk about their personal experiences of ADHD and what it feels like on the inside. Jessica McCabe suggests that 'attention deficit' is a poor term since people do not lack attention, but rather they have difficulty in directing their attention, which is pulled in multiple ways at once. Stephen Tonti's experience is of being hyper-focused once something has attracted him, so he suggests he is 'attention different'. However, since the essence of 'attention deficit' is not being able to direct attention to where someone else has decided you should place it, such as is the case every day in school, children with this experience are frequently seen as problems by their teachers.

How to increase attention and focus in class:

1. Be aware of your assumptions about children and set out to check them.
2. Avoid placing students under pressure to meet social norms but rather focus on acceptance of difference.
3. Notice where attention is directed as a way of making contact with a student, even if they are not attending to what you have asked.
4. Make a plan for extending attention using the child's own interests initially, helping support greater independence of focus management.
5. Practise deconstructing tasks into elements that can be taught and practised separately before being put together.

Conclusion

As educators we are already skilled at teaching content. To support our understanding of teaching skills, and specifically here, attention, we need to do a number of things. Firstly, we need to keep an open mind about what obstacles the child may be experiencing when they do not succeed in successfully completing successfully complete the task. We need to try to avoid simplistic interpretations, such as 'he just isn't trying'. Holding the least dangerous assumption – that the child is always trying and doing their best – will help us to maintain our patience and perseverance. We will think about task components and offer scaffolded opportunities to enhance success and comment positively on it.

Educators need to build rapport with students in the knowledge that this will give the children positive self-concept and build their resilience as well as allowing them to work on their skills and behaviour. Much of early education is actually practising putting into action attending and other EF skills. Missing developing effectively at this stage puts children at high risk for negative social and educational outcomes. It is what educators have understood and worked on throughout history, but without always having names for the processes or awareness of how to separate skills in order to support children's development.

References

Ensor, R., Riosa, P. B. and Yu, K. H. X. (2023). Evaluation of a rapport-building intervention for early interventionists working with children on the autism spectrum. *Behavioural Interventions*, 1–16. doi:10.1002/bin.1983.

Gabig, C. S. (2013). Protodeclarative. In Volkmar, F. R. (Ed.) *Encyclopedia of Autism Spectrum Disorders*. New York: Springer. https://doi.org/10.1007/978-1-4419-1698-3_1117

Jones, W. and Klin, A. (2013). Attention to eyes is present but in decline in 2–6-month-old infants later diagnosed with autism. *Nature*, 504(7480), 427–431. doi:10.1038/nature12715.

Murray, D. (2021). Monotropism: An interest-based account of autism. In Volkmar, F. R. (Ed.) *Encyclopedia of Autism Spectrum Disorders*. New York: Springer, pp. 2954–2956. doi:10.1007/978-3-319-91280-6_102269.

Radesky, J. S., Schumacher, J. and Zuckerman, B. (2015). Mobile and interactive media use by young children: The good, the bad and the unknown. *Pediatrics Perspectives*, 135(1), 1–3.

Russell, S., Hinwood, C. and Fuller, C. (2024). *Attention deficit hyperactivity disorder (ADHD) Programme update*. NHS England. https://www.england.nhs.uk/long-read/attention-deficit-hyperactivity-disorder-adhd-programme-update/

Siposova, B. and Carpenter, M. (2019). A new look at joint attention and common knowledge. *Cognition*, 189, 260–274. https://doi.org/10.1016/j.cognition.2019.03.019

Smith, B. H., Molina, B. S. G., Pelham, W. E., Jr. (2002). The clinically meaningful link between alcohol use and attention deficit hyperactivity disorder. *Alcohol Res Health*, 26(2), 122–129.

Stuart, N., Whitehouse, A., Palermo, R. et al. (2023). Eye gaze in autism spectrum disorder: A review of neural evidence for the eye avoidance hypothesis. *Journal of Autism Developmental Disorders*, 53, 1884–1905. https://doi.org/10.1007/s10803-022-05443-z

Trevisan, D. A., Roberts, N., Lin, C. and Birmingham, E. (2017). How do adults and teens with self-declared autism spectrum disorder experience eye contact? A qualitative analysis of first-hand accounts. *PLoS ONE*, 12(11), e0188446. https://doi.org/10.1371/journal.pone.0188446

Vygotsky, L. S. (1978). *Mind in Society: The Development of Higher Psychological Processes*. Cambridge, MA: Harvard University Press.

Wood, D., Bruner, J. S. and Ross, G. (1976). The role of tutoring in problem-solving. *Journal of Child Psychology and Psychiatry and Allied Disciplines*, 17, 89–100. doi:10.1111/j.1469–7610.1976.tb00381.x.

Young, S. and Cocallis, K. M. (2019). Attention deficit hyperactivity disorder (ADHD) in the prison system. *Current Psychiatry Reports*, 21(6), 41. doi:10.1007/s11920-019-1022-3.

4
Executive functioning

Introduction

So far, we have thought about how we perceive, or take in, information from the environment and our bodies. Most children will be sensing visual, auditory, olfactory, kinaesthetic and tactile stimuli in every environment. They will also, to varying degrees, be processing sensations from within their bodies. The extent to which children are aware and able to name their internal sensations will depend on their upbringing and experience, since applying the label 'hungry' or 'tired' is a learned process. Once this baseline of attendance to stimuli, both external and internal, is established, even if only as an intermittent skill, another set of cognitive processing skills come into play, referred to collectively as executive functioning. They are a set of interacting processes that are essential for social interaction, learning, managing behaviour and becoming an independent person. There are many categorisations of EF with some degree of variation, but with a consensus that the core EFs are inhibitory control, working memory and cognitive flexibility.

EF skills are of key importance for a child starting school and are found to be better indicators of social and academic success than measured IQ. Development of EF starts as an ongoing process from birth and refinement may not be until a person's mid-20s. For some adults, difficulties with EF persist throughout life, leading to them being at increased risk for lack of academic success, poor work history, social isolation and even criminality.

It is essential that teachers understand EF skills in order to select appropriate strategies to support their learners, yet it seems instruction about EF is rarely included in educator training programmes. We have instituted this where I work at the University of Nottingham. I see an understanding of EF as crucial to working with all children, and particularly those who are neurodivergent. For example, if we consider a child who, while listening to the teacher read a story, is constantly moving, looking around the room and distracting the other pupils, we need to consider a range of explanations. Perhaps he does not find the story interesting, or it could be triggering an uncomfortable emotional response. Maybe the problem rests within the child, e.g. he finds concentration difficult. He might be being deliberately 'naughty'. Another explanation is that there is a smell in the room that is making him uncomfortable, and he is struggling to draw his attention away from this to focus on the story. He could be demonstrating difficulties with comprehension of language that makes the story incomprehensible, so he isn't trying to listen. He might have a poor working memory that makes following a story auditorily too difficult, or even an undetected hearing problem. My point is that there are a great many assumptions we can make, and we won't know the answer until we investigate, but what often happens in this scenario is that educators offer prompts or reprimands for his poor attention without finding time to look beyond the behaviour. In this example, a child with poor hearing could be provided with hearing aids. Similarly, a child with poor working memory can be told the same story in a different way, with more picture cues and reminders, and a slower pace, addressing the root cause of the visible behaviour.

When we can see a neurological explanation for a child's behaviour it can help us to maintain our tolerance and keep viewing the child positively, as well as giving them self-insight and identifying an effective strategy. When we can break down the components of a task to identify a specific block to learning in a child, we can improve our teaching. We can also more effectively support our pupils to develop self-regulation and self-control, skills that are just as important as their academic success for their life opportunities. Research indicates that emotions and EF skills are inextricably linked and children who feel a sense of hope and school belonging have better EF than those who feel alienated and unsuccessful (Dixon and Scalcucci, 2021). As educators we therefore need to be aware of the continuous cycle of positive emotions promoting learning and difficulties with learning reducing well-being.

EF skills have been studied by neurologists for centuries. Many of you may be familiar with the nineteenth-century case study of Phineas Gage who sustained a severe head injury at work. The damage was in a specific area of his brain, the left frontal lobe, enabling those who studied him to ascertain the specific changes the location of the damage made to his personality and behaviour. This work was part of learning that certain skills are located in particular areas of the brain, and the role of brain function in personality.

Current understanding of the brain is that although skills may be localised to certain parts of the brain, the organ works as a whole, through complex interconnected networks that build through experience. The concept of neuroplasticity is highly encouraging for us as educators, as neuroscience has demonstrated that people can change their brain structure and neural connections with the correct forms of practice. As we explore the various EF skills, a picture will emerge of how our ability to resist impulses, plan what we need to do, think flexibly and self-monitor will all lead us to interact with others in specific ways. What we see when we are in relation with someone is the final stage of the cognitive process, and it is then challenging to ascertain how the individual components of any interaction are involved. In other words, we can see when a child is unsuccessful, but it is very difficult to determine why without a knowledge of the processes involved and a specific investigation. Obviously, we can ask students for their experiences, but they may have limited insight, with a frequent response of 'don't know' to our 'why' questions!

Impulse control

Impulse control takes the form of either inhibiting the initiation of an action that has formed in the mind, or stopping an unwanted action that has already started. It is an active state that implies the ability to process information about rules applicable to that moment, drawing on past experiences, potential consequences of the action, the context and the ability to consider how these interact with longer-term goals. A decision must be reached to either not respond to the impulse, or to alter the initial impulse towards a more appropriate response. The ability to exercise inhibition is likely to vary according to the circumstance, level of tiredness and amount of available energy. As adults we may be familiar with the difficulty of controlling the impulse to eat something we love but that is bad for us, to stop playing a game when we should be doing something else or to stay in bed when it's time to get up. Our impulses can be very strong, verging on compulsions, and for each one we are making active decisions about whether to indulge or restrain ourselves. It will be helpful to bring this to students' attention and to focus on this as a way to comment on behaviour. So rather than 'I've told you already three times not to do that', we might respond with 'I can see you are still finding it difficult to resist doing that, what will you do to help remind you'. Rather than a reprimand, a child then gains insight along with the responsibility to take action themselves.

Our ability to not act on an impulse is a key part of fitting into school and society. It gives us the opportunity to think about consequences before we say or do something. Inhibition of our responses allows us to resist temptation and consider choices. Much of our work with very young children focuses on teaching this skill, often through gentle physical reminders, such as placing our hands over theirs as we place something on the table, and verbal reminders to wait. In any group of children, it will quickly become evident who does, and does not, have good levels of impulse control. Ability will be determined by both a child's background experiences and their level of neurological maturity. For example, children born prematurely have been found to have reduced EF skills (Bohm et al., 2004). The typical characteristics of children with poor impulse control are blurting out answers before a question is complete and without raising their hand, interrupting and intruding on others, difficulty awaiting their turn, reckless behaviour, being accident prone and making important decisions without considering the consequences. In young children these behaviours may pass as irritating but not of particular concern, and of course we want to provide children with opportunities to learn better impulse control in their first few years at school. However, once we are in later primary school years, when children are 9 and 10 years old, they are the sort of behaviours that consistently bring them into friction with teachers and lead to sanction. It is very difficult to ascertain from the outside whether children are being wilfully challenging, or are fighting, and sometimes failing, to gain control over their impulses. The least dangerous assumption would be to always assume that children want to do what we ask, but their brain and body are not sufficiently under their control in that moment to do so. Many children will show puzzling behaviour, where something they manage well at one moment they fail to do at another. This sort of pattern often leads observers to believe they are in control and deciding to be disobedient, and of course skills vary with degree of motivation for a particular task. There can be a big difference in our reactions to children who are acting impulsively; we can criticise and punish, or we can comment that we can see they are struggling to have good control in that moment and suggest a strategy that may help them going forward, as will be discussed in more detail later.

We need to develop effective teaching of impulse control, since a lack of development has been found to have dire consequences. In a large-scale study, Ahmed et al. (2021) found that children with poor executive function skills at age 4 typically had poorer educational attainment and impulse control in adulthood irrespective of their social class, home environment and parental level of education. In other words, it is possible to ascertain the EF of very young children and identify those who have not developed to typical levels despite the opportunity to do so by the time they start school. Ideally, once identified, educators would focus on teaching strategies to support inhibition, although current teacher training and the National Curriculum do not support this. Ahmed et al. (2021) also examined reasons for the relationship between early EF and later poor outcomes and suggest that children with good EF when they enter school are in a better position to take advantage of the education offered. Those struggling with all EFs, and particularly impulse control, have the double impact of trying to develop appropriate behaviour for learning alongside the demands of the curriculum. Impulse control is the EF that is most likely to bring children into conflict with others, leading to a downward spiral of poor self-image and unaccepted behaviour. We need to recognise how frustrated children who struggle with their impulses are likely to feel. They may experience reprimand as unjust when they are not intending to do anything wrong. Being told off, especially repeatedly, is likely to lead to them feeling hurt, misunderstood, angry and perhaps defiant. This suggests that the best support for many children, and certainly a wider group than just those identified as neurodivergent, is the deliberate teaching of strategies to improve EF skills in order that children are more ready to take advantage of the learning opportunities at school. The opportunity to play with peers and accept the need to share is a good foundation that can be offered in early years education.

Impulse control will be a big factor for educators in managing any group of students. It is enormously difficult for most of us to maintain calm and composure when faced with a child who constantly interacts with us or others or attends to non-relevant stimuli. A school's typical response to poor impulse control is seen in behaviour policies. This may set out a reward scheme where those who operate self-control are given points, stickers or some other tangible and often public reward. Those children who do not control their impulses will either receive no reward or be sanctioned. Either of these options tend to bring about feelings of shame and embarrassment in the child for actions they may have little control over. This system rewards those who are fortunate enough to have intrinsically mature control levels, whose appropriate behaviour may come with no effort, and punish those who may be working hard to govern their responses even if unsuccessfully. We only see that they have failed, not that they are trying. Very early in a child's school career these neurologically and psychologically defined characteristics set them up to be seen, and responded to, in a certain way, that has long-term negative consequences. Educators need to be able to set up boundaries within groups and classes to ensure a calm and supportive environment where all children can learn; however, this should honour the differences that children bring, and all responses should be educational. Punishment is only a short-term and ultimately unsuccessful response, which does not teach a child with poor self-control the strategies they need to improve. Shame for natural behaviour may lead to greater levels of unacceptable behaviour, or helplessness and lack of agency.

> To help you think through challenging issues within your students, you can consider the following:
>
> 1. How do you respond emotionally to a child who persistently disrupts by doing things they shouldn't?
> 2. Is there something you could adopt to give you thinking and analysis time when feeling frustrated with a student's behaviour?
> 3. What could be happening in the environment that forms a barrier or enabler to self-control for that child?
> 4. What might be happening within the child and/or your relationship with them that impacts their self-regulation?
> 5. What feels comfortable to you as a way of talking to a child whose behaviour is not desirable, to help them to reflect on their own behaviour in that moment without inducing shame?

So far, I have used the example of children who may otherwise have typical development. Poor impulse control can appear differently in non-verbal children considered as severely learning disabled. The behaviour of these children tends to give others the impression of a lack of understanding. In fact, this may be the case for all students, where our first compassionate response to a child not following our rules is to assume they have not remembered or understood what they are supposed to do and reminding them. When they fail to follow rules, we often remind them that we have already told them many times what acceptable behaviour is, suggesting that we think they have forgotten. However, this misses the struggle they may be having with control and can be a frustrating response that undermines them. They are likely to know the rule but be unable, at that moment, to follow it. For example, when supporting a non-verbal autistic man to participate in the community, I wanted to take him out of his residential home for some exercise. I was warned that if he walked past a food shop he would run in and grab what he could reach. The staff presented this as him not knowing that he wasn't allowed to run into the bakers and grab a cake. Taking a different view, that he was highly likely to understand, and his behaviour was actually a difficulty with impulse control, I talked to him about how we would manage going to the bakers to buy something of his choice. We first discussed what he would like to choose, using visual choice boards. I then slowly described arriving at the shop, walking in together, standing in the queue and making the purchase. As we reached the street where the shop was located, I paused and reminded him again of what we would do. On reaching the shop I continued to talk to him, slowly and calmly, saying 'we are going to go in, there are two people in the queue, we are going to wait behind them, I will be with you and help you wait'. I repeatedly reminded him that he could stay in control and buy what he wanted. The calmness of my voice, even if in reality I was nervous of him not succeeding, and my reassurance allowed him to restrain his impulse to grab the food. My intervention was successful for a number of reasons: firstly the rehearsal element instilling a belief that he could restrain himself and painting a picture of what this would be like for him; secondly, my at least outward confidence in his ability, and assurance of support; and lastly, it was key that I understood the nature of his difficulty and accepted that he would want to manage acceptable behaviour if given the chance. This example highlights that even for those who have the least apparent self-control our support can be effective and can be applied to any student who persistently fails to follow rules. We need to demonstrate our confidence in their ability to gain greater self-control and through this help instil self-belief.

Lack of impulse control in learning disabled people can mean that basic expectations are still being explained to them when they are in their later years of education, with no alternative explanation for their unacceptable behaviour explored and the assumption that they have a lack of understanding, put down to limited learning ability. This then misses an educational opportunity that would support learning to control behaviour and often leads to underestimation of potential ability. An alternative, to remind them of a helpful strategy, rather than providing a focus on poor behaviour, would feel more collaborative and show compassion. Many educators know that it is more effective to say 'walk in the corridor' than 'don't run', since the latter can actually be processed in the brain as a suggestion of running. Children need to hear what they need to do, not what they have done wrong. This suggests that educators should try to routinely repeat what the child is supposed to be doing, rather than focus on a sanction for poor behaviour. How this is done, i.e. with a smile, or frown, will vary by educator and their relationship with the child, but hopefully we can inhibit demonstrating our frustration and concentrate on supporting the child to follow instructions. Children might be taught a particular action, such as placing a card in front of them, when they self-identify as not being able to follow an instruction, as a way of helping them to develop insight and independence.

We commonly make the erroneous assumption that impulse control equates to greater levels of intelligence. Students who struggle to control impulses not only act in ways that are not their choice, and not considered acceptable, but they also miss out on demonstrating their ability to respond appropriately. A minimally verbal autistic adult with cerebral palsy was being assessed by a psychologist on a test that required him to listen to a word and select the correct image from a choice of four (the British Picture Vocabulary Scale). Instead of waiting to check each image, he pointed randomly at the pictures and was therefore scoring at a very low level, indicating a below average IQ. When I placed my hand gently over his and reminded him to scan all four pictures before responding he was able to demonstrate his true understanding and gained a much higher overall score. His random points suggested a lack of understanding that was not actually the case. When I supported him with greater impulse control, he was able to scan, consider and then answer correctly.

Early proficient EF allow greater levels of learning from the start of school that set children on a positive cycle of self-belief, supporting resilience and a mindset that enables growth and learning. People with poor self-control experience more stress than people who find it easier to inhibit.

Executive functioning

The knowledge that they may make a poor decision can lead to anxiety and lowered self-confidence. Research led by Baumeister (e.g., Baumeister et al., 2020) over many years has examined the phenomenon of energy depletion when exercising impulse control. People who successfully inhibit inappropriate behaviour for an initial task are less likely to be able to do so for the following one, even if this task is different. Current understanding of this is that we unconsciously start to conserve our energy for future tasks. We may be able to successfully complete a second task if the motivation is strong enough, but there will then be even less energy available for the next. In this research the metaphor of self-control as a muscle is used as a way of thinking about this energy use, suggesting that exercising the muscle, i.e. practising, can lead to improved function.

To support development of impulse control, to 'exercise the muscle', we can start by giving positive feedback, acknowledging that the child is trying hard. Bearing in mind Baumeister and colleagues' research, acknowledging that a child did well earlier in the day, and that they may have run out of energy, can be supportive and give the child self-insight. The end goal of all strategies that we give to children should be insight and independence. To build insight we need to use our understanding of what might be going on. Since the child probably can't tell us, and we may not have access to psychological testing, we can form hypotheses and work with the child to test them. In my work I will often say 'you did really well earlier, but now you seem to be struggling, even though I can see you are trying hard. I'm wondering whether you are feeling tired, you've run out of energy and may need to do something different for a few minutes.' I might then offer a different and fun activity or allow them some quiet time. When they are ready to try again, I will scaffold the task to ensure success. This can be in the form of a set of visual instructions that they can reveal one by one that take them through a logical process. I will tell them how long they are likely to need to spend on the task and what success will look like. I might help them with motivation by reminding them of what they will achieve. If the child still struggles to succeed, I will take that as my responsibility, and apologise for not finding the right way to help them. I can then form a different hypothesis and try again, either at the same time or later. Obviously, this approach requires an individual, or small group, approach and can be time-consuming. However, once an area of difficulty has been understood, and appropriate supportive strategies identified, we can teach the child to follow what works for them independently. The intensive support will not necessarily be something that continues long-term, although of course other difficulties may arise.

A whole class approach can also be helpful, where part of what we teach is insight into our individual processes and behaviours. This approach needs to identify strengths and areas of difficulty, showing that we all have unique patterns. Schools that offer a strength-based approach can build strong communities of acceptance and understanding where all students feel included. This is imperative when discussing EF, since we know that emotional factors impact performance. When children develop self-insight, they can support each other to be successful. They will be able to identify areas of potential difficulty and avoid or prepare for them. They might ask their peers for help when competition is reduced, and everyone is acknowledged as bringing their particular gifts. Of course, we need to ensure that identifying areas of difficulty do not become self-fulfilling prophecies for the children, where they come to easy acceptance that they find something hard. This is where an emphasis on a growth mindset and a 'not yet achieved' is very important.

An example of effective peer support was an autistic primary school child who usually had a teaching assistant with him, to guide his work and maintain his focus. He was easily distracted and needed frequent redirection to the task. The teacher chose other children who were often distracted to be his buddy and remind him to do his work when he stopped. This not only helped the autistic student but worked wonderfully with the buddies. In helping their peer to focus they remembered that they needed to as well! Alongside making the student less reliant on adults and gaining some independence, it also fostered the development of friendships so that he felt more included. This helped build a positive spiral that meant he was happy and learning at school.

Remember how often some of these EF challenges are seen in adults among your family or friends. The people you know will always be late, so you tell them to come earlier than you want them. The person in the queue in front of you may only take their purse out and start to sort their change when they are ready to pay. Some people ask you the same question on multiple occasions and don't retain the answer. These are traits that we see as just a part of how someone is, not related to their ability or lack of consideration of others, although we may be less tolerant when similar behaviour is exhibited in children we are trying to educate.

Some points for further reflection include:

1. To what extent are you seeking to build self-control in your students, and how might it be for you to relinquish some control in order to offer students the opportunity to fail or succeed?
2. How comfortable are you in supporting students who have failed in a way that gives confidence that this is part of a learning journey?
3. How could you introduce impulse control as a concept that everyone needs to learn, and what games or classroom activities could you include to help students investigate this for themselves?

Working memory

Although definitions can vary, what we usually mean when talking about working memory in education is the ability to hold verbal or visual information in mind while we complete a process or guide our behaviour. This can also refer to keeping information in mind while trying to ignore a distraction. For example, we give the child an instruction, they attend to their peers having an argument, but still remember what the instruction was and can complete it. Working memory is also involved in making choices, when weighing up options. It requires the taking in of information from the environment and being able to draw on knowledge or previous experiences from long-term memory and to hold in mind the immediate goal. However, for everyone, working memory is limited in capacity, duration and focus; we tend to remember around four things for a few seconds unless we do something with each, such as talk to someone, process and act on the information. Life is very fast-paced with so much information constantly coming at us, and we need to process this immediately; we value speed. People who can manage the pace, with good working memory, tend to be good at writing and reasoning. Conversely, poor working memory impacts learning and can lead to children being seen as unengaged and unresponsive, and perhaps as lazy, unmotivated or lacking intelligence because they do not respond appropriately in the expected time. Working memory is important in developing mathematical skills, such as needing to hold numbers in mind while thinking about what operation to use. It is a key skill in learning to read, as children need to be able to hold in mind individual letter sounds for long enough to link them together into a word. Working memory difficulties are recognised as contributing to dyslexia for some people. Working memory helps children remember what they need to pay attention to in order to complete an instruction so children with poor working memory may struggle to complete tasks and appear disobedient.

Given that the goal of education is to store information in long-term memory, the process by which that happens, i.e. working memory, is key. It is thought that around 10% of children have working memory problems (International Dyslexia Association, 2020), and they are not usually identified unless specifically screened. Gathercole et al. (2006) found that what teachers observed in these children was a lack of attention. They may adopt or be given the label of ADHD, or dyslexia, or may not have any identified neurodivergence. Yet as they go through school, they are likely to fall behind in maths and reading and come to the attention of teachers for additional support. They fall behind in their learning because they are unable to process information fast enough for the environment, their working memory becomes overloaded so they cannot access the information they need to complete the task. Once information has been lost from working memory it is not retrievable, meaning the task has to be restarted from scratch. Where there is no time for that, the student is forced to guess, which may lead to errors, or giving up, often in the form of 'zoning out', where their mind wanders from the task. Frequent loss of learning opportunities will be increasingly detrimental to the child.

Slow processing speed is related to classroom behaviour. What teachers notice about a child with poor working memory can be behaviour that results from the challenges the child is having. When a task heavily relies on a skill the child finds very difficult, they can persist, which takes an enormous amount of energy, give up, leading to the appearance of lacking motivation, or distract themselves and potentially others from the task to cover up their difficulties. Poor self-confidence and high anxiety are likely in children who constantly face these difficulties, particularly when no one notices or wrongly attributes them to a lack of effort. Routine within an activity, or across the day, can support children who struggle with working memory as tasks then include an automatic element. Many of us feel unease or distress, including lack of control when our familiar routines are disrupted. The children we work with may protest or become distressed when the safety of routine is taken away.

When children struggle with working memory they can benefit from some key strategies. Firstly, we can reduce the amount of information we deliver at any one time. Once educators have gained students' attention, they need to speak slowly, segment each aspect of an instruction, and be concise and precise. You might give the child an idea of what they should listen out for before giving the instruction. Information can be repeated, either using the same words to assist the processing of some students, or with different phrasing to simplify or state a different way to make it more accessible. Children's understanding can be checked by asking them to repeat what they need to do; this helps them process what is otherwise only in their working memory and may be lost. Some children may benefit from repeating the instruction to assist their memory. The most effective strategy of all, however, is to use visual aids. When we show an image, or words, that supports understanding, we provide time for processing and lessen the cognitive load in the working memory.

Good teaching practice usually involves recapping previous learning and locating new information in previously understood content. The more we use these techniques, the more accessible we make material for those with poor working memory. When we are able to show students how what we are teaching relates to their own lives, we increase motivation and make concepts more meaningful. The more enjoyable learning is, the more students will feel confident in their skills, and this in turn will impact EF. Within our classrooms we can play memory games with young children, such as showing a number of items, hiding them under a cloth and removing one that they have to identify. Games where people have to repeat and add to a list are popular with all ages. Singing and rapping are also good stimulators of memory.

> To bring greater awareness to the importance of working memory, you can reflect on the following:
>
> 1. To what extent is working memory part of a task that a student is finding difficult?
> 2. Are you aware of strategies that children use for themselves, such as self-talk, as they carry out an activity?
> 3. How might you use children's own strategies to give them self-insight and further support?

Cognitive flexibility

Being cognitively flexible means we can shift our focus when appropriate, change perspective to see something from another view, and alter and adapt how we think about something. Cognitive flexibility enables us to learn from our mistakes, try new things and switch from doing one task to another. Lack of flexibility might manifest as repeating mistakes, struggling to see other people's view, requiring time to adapt to change and struggling to understand abstract concepts. Children with poor cognitive flexibility, such as many autistic students, may prefer concrete and literal subjects and set routines. Cognitive flexibility allows us to find alternative solutions to problems, make adjustments and be resilient in the face of change or unexpected events, because we are able to quickly see a way around a problem. We all might experience a lack of cognitive flexibility when we struggle to pull ourselves away from an activity we are doing, such as playing an online game. Part of learning is the flexibility to apply knowledge gained in one arena to a different one in order to be creative and offer critique.

A typical cognitive flexibility challenge for young children is a sorting task. When given a set of coloured shapes, they might first have to sort by colour, then by shape and perhaps then by size. For an older child, cognitive flexibility might be seen in a game encouraging them to think of novel uses for a particular object. The need to be cognitively flexible is present throughout the day for all children in school. They need to move from classroom to playground, adapt how they talk with friends to how they talk with adults and work on tasks in groups with people who see things differently. There is a strong focus of research on the need for cognitive flexibility in the development of maths and reading skills (Nunes de Santana et al., 2022).

Having poor cognitive flexibility can lead to behaving in ways that may be misperceived as wilfully disobedient and challenging. A child may insist on doing something in a certain way despite the evidence that it doesn't work. They may become very upset when they make a mistake as they don't see a solution. They may be resistant to trying something new and become distressed when they cannot control what is happening. From the outside it will be difficult to understand the causes of these behaviours. People who lack cognitive flexibility may be intent on keeping their worldview, seeking information to fit what they believe. It is unlikely that students acting in these ways will have self-insight; their actions will be driven by their lack of flexibility.

Since cognitive flexibility matures throughout childhood, building in ways to develop it for all pupils is important. A structured classroom schedule is a good starting point, since this alleviates some of the cognitive load, i.e. the amount of information that can be held in working memory at any time. We all have our individual capacities, and routine reduces cognitive load by bringing in familiarity that requires less active thought. Take time to explain and support students with changes and transitions; give warnings and ample time. Provide visual information and schedules as a concrete reminder of what will be happening. When children feel secure in the predictability of a routine, we can then encourage them to try novel tasks, or to try tasks in a new way, with scaffolded support and recognition of attempts.

Many classroom games, for all ages, can support cognitive flexibility, so children feel relaxed and are having fun as they learn. For young children we might ask them to alternate finding an animal in a picture, then finding an object. Word games are helpful to show how one word can have multiple meanings, or a game to find different links between a group of people. Stories can involve discussion about different characters' perspectives. Show students an image and ask them to give a couple of different descriptions about what is happening in it. For older students the challenge of saying the colour a word is written in, when the word itself says a different colour, will practise a number of EFs. There are many helpful websites that offer numerous ideas for different age groups.

To help you reflect on this topic consider the following:

1. Are you aware of who your highly flexible thinkers are? Do you tend to see them as typical or exceptional for their age? Do you equate this with their learning capacity?
2. What might support you in seeing pupils who are typically lacking in flexibility as able in other ways that might be used to help them?

Organisation and planning

It will be apparent that the three core EF skills already discussed – impulse control, working memory and cognitive flexibility – along with attention, are fundamental for all learning. On the foundation of these rest other EF skills. Educators will have observed students who are well organised and always arrive prepared for the lesson. They are likely to be even more aware of those with poor organisation, i.e. the child who doesn't remember what they need for that day, who leaves their PE kit at home, who turns up late and generally has poor time management. These are typical behaviours of children with poor EF, for which schools frequently reprimand or sanction. There remains a wide range of organisational ability amongst adults, and people may be successful in certain job roles due to their strength in organisation. However, it is very common to see children who don't keep track of information, forget to give notices to their parents and frequently lose their belongings. Thoughts can be disorganised as well, as you might see when asking a child to relay a familiar story or give an explanation of what they did at the weekend.

Although poor organisational skills are more easily identified than other EF skills, a lack of understanding of the nature of these difficulties frequently leads to a school perception that a child is not trying, or even choosing to be difficult, particularly as difficulties persist over time and children appear not to be learning. Schools may offer support to improve organisational skills, but for this to be most effective it needs to be delivered in a way that respects that the child may be trying their best even when the outcome is poor. Learning to be better organised, when the difficulty arises in brain structures and systems, will be a slow and gradual process that requires constant gentle prompts and reminders from educators and carers along with structured teaching programmes. It will be important that attempts to improve organisation are set within a more holistic programme that focuses to a large extent on psychosocial support and an attitude of 'not yet' achieved. As educators we need to notice any success and bring this to a child's attention. Dixon and Scalcucci (2021) found a link between improved hope and sense of school belonging and increased EF. They suggest that schools running programmes aimed at building hope and school belonging would require less time to make an impact, and be more effective, than direct work on EF. Many schools already have these sorts of programmes, frequently for specially selected children. I suggest that all our schools should adopt a holistic culture, where ensuring inclusion and belonging for all is at the heart of their ethos.

Alongside organisation, students need to be able to plan and prioritize, which is considered another EF. They will need to hold information in their working memories to remember a goal, either short- or long-term, in order to decide on what steps they need to take next, and possibly resist an impulse.

Part of planning is the awareness of how long a task may take and therefore how much energy to expend or conserve at various points, in a similar way to the way we might approach a challenging exercise class. Another EF is task initiation, which can be an enormous challenge for anyone setting out to do something that we anticipate being onerous or difficult. Students need to think of their long-term aims in order to access their motivation to start a task. Task initiation requires the directing of behaviours and actions while holding goals in mind. Thinking back to those students who struggle with impulse control, this is likely to impact their ability to start tasks as well. When they follow their impulse, this gets in the way of their planning a goal-directed task, and not being good at task initiation may make them more prone to giving into impulses.

Self-monitoring and emotional control

The remaining EF skills are also of great importance, in their own right, as the means of living in a social society, but also because of the way they support or detract from the other skills. We all need to be able to control our emotions in order to have a smooth passage through life. Children start by learning to identify their emotions and then to select how to manifest those in any given situation. As children get older there are increasing expectations that they will maintain their equanimity, even under pressure. Of course, this frequently goes wrong, ending with the ubiquitous playground squabbles and broken friendships. Again, children who struggle to control their emotions will be seen negatively within schools and social groups, impacting their ability to connect with others and to maintain appropriate behaviour in the classroom. The inappropriate display of any emotion is likely to draw comment, usually negative, and the sort of persistent disruptions that unregulated children cause lead to sanctions and even exclusions. Given this, it is imperative that children are surrounded by adult models who demonstrate their own ability to self-regulate and stay calm. As Dix (2017) points out, we cannot teach students to behave the way we would like by showing anger and shouting.

Children who are distressed for whatever reason are likely to show this in their behaviour, although not necessarily in the most obvious ways. A child experiencing family disruption started to urinate more frequently than usual, as a way to feel a sense of control over his life. A girl of 7 whose grandmother had died stole pencils and rubbers from her friends. A boy whose parents divorced became verbally aggressive to the adults in his school. Unless we look below these behaviours, we may just react by trying to stop them rather than viewing them as important clues to what support a child needs.

Part of maintaining emotional control is self-monitoring. Children need to have self-awareness, to know the extent to which they are behaving appropriately in any moment. They will have to use this monitoring to make adjustments to their actions and behaviours by assessing what is needed in the situation they are in. When control is determined by external factors, such as strict school rules with resulting punishment, we limit the extent to which children have to learn self-discipline. Adults in schools can model the skill of self-control in their interactions with students. When we show gentle compassion and understanding, it may become easier for the students to offer the same to each other and themselves. Frustration with their own poor behaviour may lead to a child being more stressed and increasing the likelihood of further unaccepted actions. Anxiety about 'getting it wrong again', anger at being reprimanded and feeling misunderstood, increases stress. It becomes easy to see how children may be in a daily downward spiral, but this is not inevitable. A trusting and compassionate relationship that reassures that a bad day today still offers hope for tomorrow can, over time, improve outcomes.

General approaches to improving EF

Following a large-scale review of studies that measure the impact of particular interventions on EF functions, Diamond and Ling (2020) identified a set of characteristics that were likely to lead to success. They suggest that students engage in real-world activities alongside a 'more knowledgeable other' (MKO) who expresses belief in both the task and the student. Minimising stress, increasing self-belief and building social connections are also important. EF skills need to be continually challenged in different ways. The most successful programme identified in their study was mindfulness practices with a movement component such as T'ai Chi or Taekwondo, but straight-forward exercise was less effective than other approaches, such as cognitive training. However, regardless of the actual programme, a key factor appeared to be the trainer's ability to make the task fun and personally meaningful. School is often a serious business, and the pressure of material to cover can make it difficult for educators to find time to play, yet the good news is that when we can, this is going to benefit students in multiple ways.

Carol: Giftedness as a mixed blessing

Being different, even in a way that may please your family and teachers, such as showing high academic ability, can be a mixed blessing. Any student who is singled out by their classmates as not being like them is likely to experience some negative consequences. Schools are complex social settings where being too clever, or not clever enough, brings what may be unwanted attention and focus. In the book I have mainly focused on those who experience barriers to learning. Conversely, Carol has learning as a strength; she absorbs information readily and easily. She is able to draw on her excellent working memory and cognitive flexibility to attain and retain information at a rate and level higher than most of her peers. However, she struggles with inhibition and is frequently in trouble for her lack of self-regulation. She also demonstrates high levels of sensitivity, particularly to sound, finding the classroom over-stimulating. At times, as a young child, she would cover her ears and cry when the noise level became too much. She also reacted to smells in the dining room and so her parents arranged for her to bring in packed lunches, which she eats in the classroom alone. Since her abilities originate in the way her brain works, she can be considered as neurodivergent.

Carol attended a small primary school with just one class per year and 30 children in the class. This was in an area of economic deprivation where around half the class had free school meals. In primary school Carol's highly proficient use of language made her sound different from her peers. She frequently used words they were unfamiliar with, leading to teasing by classmates. Carol didn't understand why she was the focus for their unkindness and would lose her temper with them, leading to further verbal attacks and complaints to the teacher about her behaviour. Carol excelled in all subjects, completing her work quickly and asking for more. She was seen as the class teacher's favourite, increasing her alienation from peers. She received glowing reports from the teacher and her parents told her how proud they were of her achievements and her being so clever.

Carol found friendships challenging; she wanted to impress people with her knowledge or grades, which made her unpopular. She liked to ask her peers what score they got on a test and told them that she achieved more. When children reacted negatively to this, she accused them of bullying her. Instead of persisting with establishing friendships Carol was allowed to avoid the playground and spend break-times in the library pursuing her love of reading. This made life for the school community more peaceful but meant that Carol's behaviours became more rigid. The time that she put into reading and homework meant that her academic ability continued to grow and outstrip that of her peers, but her social skills remained poor. Spending so much time alone increased her isolation and reduced the opportunity to learn how to socialise in an acceptable way. As an only child she didn't have the experience of having to share or negotiate at home either. Her parents, trying to be supportive, reinforced how well she did at school and showed pride in her achievements. They also recognised that she was limited in her interests and focus and so organised music lessons outside of school in the hope that this would give her a less academic focus. Both parents and school were proud of Carol's achievements, moving quickly through piano grades; she was celebrated in assemblies for this and for her performance in spelling competitions. Unfortunately, this became another skill that she would talk to others about in school, trying to connect with people but appearing to be boasting. The message from the adults in her life was positive reinforcement of academic and musical skills and the allowing of lack of development of social skills.

These issues continued into secondary school, where her differences were increasingly visible and led to her feeling isolated and anxious. Carol comes from a bilingual French-English background and understands both languages well, although as she has never lived in France, and she is not proficient in French expression. She has a wide vocabulary in both languages and when she entered secondary school, she was keen to learn Spanish. Her teachers persuaded her to study French, as she was likely to achieve a high grade in this subject despite Carol's motivation being stronger for Spanish as something new and more challenging. In French lessons she was often bored: the teacher worked at the pace of the others who were mostly beginners and offered 'enrichment' to Carol by asking her to support her peers with their learning; however, she showed no understanding of why they did not understand or retain their learning and instead belittled them. This led to her being told to study through an audio tape on her own at the back of the class.

Carol continued to demonstrate rapid rates of learning; however, this left her bored and frustrated in many of her lessons. Her anxiety impacted on her inhibition control and when frustrated in class she frequently argued with peers and teachers, appearing defiant and challenging. She was competitive with staff, looking for errors and correcting them. Carol found self-regulation difficult; she easily took offence at something said or even a look from a peer and would shout and swear, leading to sanctions. She did not fit in and told her parents that the other students excluded her. In an effort to help, some teachers suggested that Carol cover up her ability, implying it might make her more popular and avoid making other pupils feel bad about their lesser abilities. Carol tried this approach for a short while, but the frustration of not being her authentic self overtook her and she reverted to previously learned behaviours. The negative perception of Carol and her behaviour mean that staff avoided any confrontation with her, often leaving her to her own devices rather than pressing her to do the advanced work they gave her. She became increasingly unhappy and sometimes missed school, telling her parents that she was feeling ill.

As awareness of her difficulties grew, and her behaviour deteriorated, the school started to consider what they might do to support her. To enhance her cognitive development and provide Carol with peers more similar to her in ability, she was invited into some classes at a local private school. This also proved challenging for several reasons. Carol found coming into the group daunting, as she had only one established way of relating to peers, i.e. wanting to demonstrate her achievements. This started her off badly, making her instantly unpopular. Her social background being different to the other pupils set her even more apart. Alongside this, Carol found, in this group, her abilities were less exceptional, and this led her into a crisis of confidence and a loss of identity, further compounding her distress.

Given that her academic abilities were prized by both primary and secondary schools, there has been little focus or understanding of Carol's holistic needs. She has been perceived as being in a privileged position in finding academic work easy, so not recognised as needing support until patterns of behaviour had become fixed. The school system is more geared to support those who struggle to learn, and less so those who are academically able. She was seen as having an advantage over other pupils and no one recognised the level of distress, which was masked by her aggressive exterior. Carol was referred to the school counselling service but showed resistance to forming a relationship with the counsellor, possibly as a defence, using intellectual skills to mask the feelings beneath. Her identity was both that of someone who is highly able, but also not liked or welcome in school. She was confused about the judgements she encountered, which, as a mix of positive and negative, were conflicting.

Research suggests that some very high achieving students, unless they are supported with clear understanding, can have above average rates of mental health difficulties (Luthar et al., 2020). In Carol's case the lack of understanding of her need to develop social skills in primary school missed a point at which she may have been able to develop differently. Instead of allowing her to escape her social struggles by hiding in the library, ideally, she would have been supported into the playground and helped to learn to relate to other children. This could have been through a buddy system, but also within a culture that promoted many ways of doing well, not just academic success. The school needed to work with her parents to increase their awareness of Carol's social needs. A child like Carol, whose academic abilities exceed their social development, has an uneven and atypical profile. They are often not equipped in terms of emotional maturity to cope with their differences. Rather than staff being relieved that their class included a student who would not need much additional support with learning, they needed to be aware that she would have her own challenges. Greater focus on Carol as an individual, helping her to reflect on her capacities and perceptions, would have better supported her emotional development.

Carol's story highlights the complex interplay between what is valued in schools, and wider society, against the well-being of the student. Educators can get caught up in what is referred to as the 'performativity agenda', where the main focus is on academic achievement as a measure of everyone's worth. Students and their families celebrate success, and teachers are praised and valued when their pupils do well. In this culture, how someone feels about themselves and how they experience education often receives less attention and may even be ignored. Carol wanted to learn Spanish, but the motivation of the staff in persuading her to do French may be serving the needs of the school to have as many high grades in national exams as possible, since this is how they will be measured by the government. As someone who learns easily Carol may feel incongruence; she is feted for something for which she puts in little effort. This can contribute to 'imposter syndrome', where people fear being 'found out' for not deserving of the position they are in. When schools value effort, we place children on a more level playing field and help build their resilience. Carol is at risk once she leaves school. She does not have the requisite skills, despite her high grades, to form friendships at university, or to work as part of a team.

Conclusion

Throughout this chapter I have emphasised that although EFs are essential for all aspects of a successful school life, they are not generally understood by educators. Of course, teachers and other professionals are constantly offering children opportunities to develop their EFs, even when unaware of deliberately targeting EF skills. Educators remind students of expected behaviour, patiently ask they why they are late, again, and scaffold and differentiate their schoolwork. Staff working in the playground and at lunch times chat with children who don't have friends or have had an argument and support them to get back into friendship groups.

Despite all this good work it is inevitable that the behaviour of some children continues to challenge, and that staff have their patience tested. Ideally schools would be quiet, calm places where people did not have to raise their voices or express frustration, where adults present as models of the behaviour they want to see in the children. However, it is often the case that as the children get tired and their performance reduces, so do the staff. When we, as educators, understand the challenges our pupils are facing, can access our own EFs and stay composed, we can instil confidence and a desire to learn in our students and build positive relationships. We need to recognise that EF fluctuates within the day, from day to day and even minute to minute. Children are impacted by their internal states, such as hunger, and the external environment constantly making demands. Knowing that someone completed a task well in one situation can lead to us being frustrated that they won't repeat it. We can feel irritation and assume that the child isn't trying, since they could do it before. This is not inevitable. When we use our observations, but look below the surface, utilising our understanding of EF, we can offer students understanding of themselves and support that makes a difference. We can do this in the knowledge that strong EF is the best foundation we can give them for a successful life.

There are a multitude of ways in which we, as educators, can support the development of EF skills in our pupils. Many are outlined in the pages above, and summarised in these points:

1. Make time to investigate barriers to learning for specific pupils – do the detective work yourself or refer to specialists where there is no evident explanation. For example, when you have had a difficult day with a child, make a note of what happened, including the time, day, context, who

was there and what happened – use this information over time to build a picture of a child, which can be shared with colleagues and other professionals.
2. Analyse typical class tasks in terms of the working memory involved and develop a way to provide support within the task.
3. Make use of classroom tasks that help build cognitive flexibility and offer emotional support to students who find this difficult.
4. Use frequent scaffolding of tasks to ensure success to build confidence and self-belief.
5. Talk to children about their energy levels, helping them to manage this themselves.
6. Talk to children about the need to manage impulse control; that this is a gradual learning process and that making mistakes is not a problem when we use them to help our learning.
7. Encourage children to record and measure their own progress rather than comparing themselves to peers.
8. Where possible, favour discussing behaviour to build understanding in the child and ourselves, rather than relying on the short-cut of reward and punishment.

References

Ahmed, S. F., Kuhfeld, M., Watts, T. W., Davis-Kean, P. E. and Lowe Vandell, D. (2021). *Preschool Executive Function and Adult Outcomes: A Developmental Cascade Model*. Washington, DC: American Psychological Association.

Baumeister, R. F., Vonasch, A. J. and Sjåstad, H. (2020). The long reach of self-control. In Mele, A. R. (Ed.) *Surrounding Self-Control*. New York: Oxford University Press, pp. 17–46.

Bohm, B., Smedler, A-C. and Forssberg, H. (2004). Impulse control, working memory and other executive functions in preterm children when starting school. *Acta Paediatr*, 93, 1363–1371.

Diamond, A. and Ling, D. S. (2020). Review of the evidence on, and fundamental questions about, efforts to improve executive functions, including working memory. In Novick, J. M., Bunting, M. F., Dougherty, M. R. and Randall, W. E. (Eds) *Cognitive and Working Memory Training: Perspectives from Psychology, Neuroscience, and Human Development*. New York: Oxford University Press.

Dix, P. (2017). *When the Adults Change Everything Changes: Seismic Shifts in School Behaviour*. Wales: Crown Publishing.

Dixon, D. D. and Scalcucci, S. G. (2021). Psychosocial perceptions and executive functioning: Hope and school belonging predict students' executive functioning. *Psychology in the Schools*, 58, 853–872. doi:10.1002/pits.22475.

Gathercole, S. E., Lamont, E. and Alloway, T. P. (2006). Working memory in the classroom. In Pickering, S. (Ed.) *Working Memory and Education*. London: Academic Press.

International Dyslexia Association. (2020). *Working Memory: The Engine for Learning*. https://app.box.com/s/6e5w2a89hkssyzaawzpmc5vkbq18aiae

Luthar, S. S., Kumar, N. L. and Zillmer, N. (2020). High-achieving schools connote risks for adolescents: Problems documented, processes implicated, and directions for interventions. *American Psychologist*, 75(7), 983–995. https://doi.org/10.1037/amp0000556

Nunes de Santana, A., Roazzi, A. and Cabral Nobre A. P. M. (2022). The relationship between cognitive flexibility and mathematical performance in children: A meta-analysis. *Trends in Neuroscience and Education*, 28, 100179. https://doi.org/10.1016/j.tine.2022.100179

5
Helping children to engage

Introduction

Schools are increasingly concerned about the well-being of their pupils, particularly given the high rates of children experiencing poverty, trauma, abuse or neglect (Bilson and Martin, 2016). The topic of engagement is central to well-being, as engagement in school both promotes and derives from well-being. Engagement is related to school belonging, a predictor of academic achievement, which is fostered by the school climate, as part of a cycle that also promotes well-being. When we foster engagement, we are also providing students with protection for their mental health, which flourishes within supportive relationships with educators and peers. Schools with reduced levels of competition that avoid making comparisons between pupils help to provide feelings of safety.

In my experience schools engender different feelings when we enter them. Some have more welcoming entrances and reception staff than others. I've seen pupils warmly greeted by staff who then proceed to talk to them about why they are late, whereas other schools show only disapproval for late students. Receptionists have to focus on safe-guarding, meaning that visitors are required to go through a procedure, but the degree of friendliness with which this is managed varies. At one point I worked in a school which I found so hostile that I would stand outside and steel myself before going in. Ideally, staff of primary schools will warmly welcome all pupils into their classrooms, but this is also possible in secondary schools, where the head or senior leaders stand at the entrance greeting pupils, preferably by name. These are all immediately evident aspects of a school culture, indicating some of the values they hold, along with their framework for understanding pupils and their behaviour. There is much that every school can do to build a positive climate that promotes well-being, high aspirations for all and engagement in learning. As children enter the building, they should feel like they are welcome there, and every day starts afresh regardless of previous tensions.

Engagement refers to the skills and enthusiasm a child brings to their learning, or extracurricular activities. This obviously involves attention, as discussed in Chapter 3, but then considers what a child does with that attention, and how long it is sustained. Engagement includes the effort and energy a student employs, which is influenced by relationships, learning activities and the environment. Engaged students will ask questions, share ideas and collaborate. Educators of engaged students are able to measure understanding and promote discussion to lead to deeper learning. To channel energy into learning, students need to feel a sense of belonging and empowerment. Engagement is part of a positive cycle of behaviour; conversely, lack of engagement sets up a different and downwards behavioural spiral.

Engagement can be seen as contrary to fleeting attention, such as when a child might wander around a classroom, picking up objects or looking at something momentarily, but then moving on to the next item. An engaged child will often be physically immobile, with their eyes directed at what they are attending to, with evident focus. Jensen (2005) defined engagement as a 'state of being'. A state is something flexible, different from a trait that is a more permanent aspect of a person. Engagement is on a continuum, and, as it is a state, it will tend to vary throughout the day and week. Even students who engage in many of their lessons may not do so to the same degree in all, since contextual factors are important and influential. Both engagement and belonging are variable states that are highly influenced by the environment, meaning that educators have some degree of control over them. Some research has found higher levels of engagement in female students, who, although they may not enjoy school more than the male students, have been found to work harder and have higher achievement goals, although there is evidence that this varies by subject studied (Wirthwein et al., 2020). Engagement is also seen to diminish in some pupils in the final years of school. When we support a child to engage, we are therefore helping them to manage a state that we want them to be in, something that they will be able to continue until an appropriate time, and that will stand them in good stead for the future. Another way to explain engagement is as the link between a person and their action (Kemp et al., 2013).

The ability to engage is a key skill for everyone, although we can probably all also identify with frustrating times when we struggle to focus on our task, despite needing to concentrate on it. Engagement can determine a student's achievement and school behaviour; it is a prerequisite to learning and communicating. Maladaptive behaviours lead to poor engagement and can become an embedded aspect of a child, a pattern of behaviour, presenting a double disadvantage, i.e. not only failing to engage in the moment, but making good levels of engagement less likely in the future. Engagement is a protective factor against school absence and delinquency.

It is evident that engaged students will be easier to teach, and more successful, whereas disengaged students will attract more frequent negative attention. The need to frequently reprimand and redirect students who are not engaging often leads to poor relationships between students and educators and can escalate into a negative classroom environment that then impacts all students. As educators we may well be fearful for disengaged students, knowing that they are likely to face a range of negative outcomes in the future. What is clear is that educators can impact engagement with how they foster teacher–student interaction, how they deliver the curriculum and their active support for student engagement. Despite this, more emphasis is sometimes placed on testing students and schools than examining quality of relationship. The more rigid and authoritarian a classroom is, and the more student choice, decision-making and self-management is limited, the worse engagement is likely to be. Despite this, there is often emphasis on ensuring children look as if they are engaging, with teachers putting effort into having everyone sitting still and looking at them. For some pupils this will form a helpful basis for them to start engaging, but for others this might be counter-productive. Thinking long-term, we want pupils to develop independent skills to be able to work without external control, and teachers need to allow for this.

> To facilitate reflection on these issues, educators can ask themselves:
>
> 1. How do the students I am working with appear in terms of their engagement currently?
> 2. What am I seeking to bring to my classroom in terms of authority and building independence?
> 3. What opportunities do they have to find their own way to engagement?

Types of engagement

Engagement has been divided into types, including academic, intellectual, institutional, social and psychological. However, the most discussed and researched are the interrelated sub-types of behavioural, emotional and cognitive engagement (Fredricks et al., 2016). Aspects of behavioural engagement, such as attention, effort, participation and persistence, are visible to an observer, although someone may appear to be engaged but with thoughts elsewhere. Truly behaviourally engaged students will show appropriate behaviour for learning, comprising effort, attention, agency, action and participation. They will take part in extracurricular activities and complete their homework. They might enjoy being given roles of responsibility in school and show confidence in carrying them out, as well as seeking out their own opportunities. They are likely to have positive and supportive relationships with peers and interaction with educators. When students are behaviourally engaged, they are more likely to participate in class discussion and ask questions for clarification or seek help. These students can be seen to be active in the life of the school; they are those who appear confident, ready to answer questions and show enthusiasm. Every class will have those who arrive with these traits, then those who show them with a little encouragement, along with pupils who appear to be pulling themselves with great effort through the school day. When we consider this last group, we need to believe that as educators we can find ways to bring them also to a more comfortable engagement. For example, a highly anxious child can be supported to grow in confidence when being given a 'special' job, something that is helpful to everyone in the class but that they are in charge of for the term. This job can come with a title, such as Register Monitor, which the teacher can use to offer praise without necessarily bringing too much attention to the child.

Emotional engagement refers to our enthusiasm for school, sense of belonging, interest and willingness to participate in learning activities. With emotional, also called affective, engagement come curiosity and critical thinking, satisfaction and a sense of well-being. Students will show determination to do well, enjoyment and pride in their work. It is influenced by feelings of warmth, connectedness, attachment, bonding, and involvement. The extent to which students feel accepted by peers and educators will impact levels of emotional engagement. Emotionally engaged students will typically have positive reactions to educators, peers and the environment, being more willing to attend school and perform work, with the converse of negative aspects of alienation also apparent in some students. Children are likely to engage to greater extents with a teacher they respect and want to please. Teachers make connections with pupils by expressing warmth, through content and work assigned and through their pedagogical approaches. These interactions help students gain insight into themselves and what they need to do in order to function well in that classroom. The need for teachers to show warmth is a stark contrast to advice given to new teachers to not smile until Christmas! Children who appear uncomfortable in school might be helped by being given a role of helping other children, rather than what can often happen when we select those who already demonstrate emotional connectedness to support others.

Cognitive engagement is the process of investing in learning, wanting to succeed, and therefore putting in effort to learn or practise a skill. Cognitively engaged students work with purpose, and show understanding, self-regulation and deep learning strategies. They can set their own learning goals, integrate ideas, and show reasoning and reflection. They might do extra work in order to learn more, be diligent and thorough in their work, and prefer challenging tasks. Their general outlook will be positive and children who are strongly cognitively engaged will be motivated to work towards mastery of their area of interest. This is another example of where allowing children some freedom within the curriculum can encourage engagement in a topic of their particular interest regardless of what that might be!

A culture of engagement

As we have seen, engagement is related to school climate. Researchers have shown that people look at their environments for situational cues to understand the climate and values (Rudasill et al., 2018). Cues might be verbal, for example the sorts of messages that are given in assemblies by school leaders. They can also be communicated non-verbally through what is seen on the walls, or in school policies and practices. These clues will tell us about key values, i.e. top performance versus engagement; and who is valued in the classroom, i.e. those who learn easily or those who keep trying. They are communicated most strongly by the most powerful person in the class, i.e. the teacher. Once perceived, these cues influence people's psychological, cognitive and physiological experiences, being able to provoke emotions such as pleasure in learning or anxiety about the school day. Psychological safety results from trust in a place or person, and once this safety is established it allows students to take risks by, for example, asking questions. The opposite state, psychological vulnerability, leads to less feeling of belonging even to the point of imposter syndrome, feelings of anxiety and worrying that we will be negatively evaluated by others. The impact of psychological vulnerability is lowered motivation and self-belief. Students will therefore be aware of the school climate, and the beliefs and expectations of the leaders of the school, and their levels of engagement will be enhanced or diminished by what they see and feel. As discussed in Chapter 2, the way in which we, as educators, view our students will communicate messages about what we think of them, what we hope for them and what we expect. When we communicate positive views of our students, we can promote engagement. These communications will convey to students whether we hold a growth mindset for and about them, or whether we harbour less positive pictures, such as seeing them as less able within a particular school subject. Many adults will be able to relate something a teacher said to them many years previously that either helped them start to engage in learning or gave them a negative and hurtful picture of themselves. The 'you'll never amount to anything ...' speech frequently stays with people for their whole lives, sometimes as something to spur them on in an effort to defy the teacher, but just as often as an explanation for not attempting to achieve and lack of confidence.

Educators who are emotionally supportive, warm, available, and sensitive to student need and interest will foster engagement in their pupils. Students who experience their educators as caring for them as people and as learners will have higher levels of emotional engagement. As educators, we need to plan our classrooms to include measures that promote engagement, rather than waiting to react to non-engagement with punitive measures. Proactive planning leads to better classroom management where engagement is promoted throughout the day, avoiding disengaged behaviours. Students are more likely to feel cared for when placed in well-organised classrooms where they can see that teachers have planned the lesson, have high expectations and are clear and fair in what they want from pupils. We need to provide interesting activities and establish clear routines to build emotional safety. Educator monitoring within the classroom will focus more on levels of engagement than outcomes. Educators who monitor student understanding and address any concepts that need further explanation, as in mastery learning, prompt students to work harder and put more energy into their studies.

Despite evidence supporting the efficacy of mastery learning (Davis and Sorrell, 1995), with its ethos of everyone being able to succeed, many of our classrooms have a culture of performativity that serves to increase student anxiety and reduce engagement. School belonging and engagement increase with the numbers of positive relationships students have with teachers, and the opposite also applies.

In typical learners, engagement can be increased by presenting a challenge just outside the zone of proximal development of a child. Work that is too easy is unlikely to be highly engaging, whereas presenting something more challenging can lead to deeper levels of engagement in order to feel the pleasure of success. Children who engage when challenged show the ability to cope with failure and to persist despite setbacks, i.e. those who Duckworth (2017) describes as having 'grit'. Educators need not only to provide challenging work, but also to provide social support, which helps the child to feel confident in tackling something difficult, so that engaging with something challenging is seen as fun and exciting, not stressful and demanding. As discussed in Chapter 2, Dweck suggests that we praise students' attempts at engagement to ensure continued effort. In a typical child we will perceive certain behaviours as indicative of engagement, such as eye gaze to the speaker or relevant materials. Engaged students will often be quiet and still, will respond to instructions and continue tasks until completion. You may have experienced children who resist having to stop their activity if it has not been completed to their satisfaction. The ultimate form of engagement has been referred to by Csikszentmihalyi (2020) as 'flow'. This is engagement at such a deep level that awareness of anything outside our immediate activity is reduced. Flow was studied initially by Csikszentmihalyi in creative people. They described a sense of ecstasy, literally being outside everyday reality, finding inner clarity about what they were doing and why, and believing in their capabilities. This engenders a sense of serenity, timelessness and intrinsic motivation. This was broadened to encompass people engaging in any occupation or leisure activity. To feel flow a child needs to have a higher-than-average challenge matched with a higher than average belief in their skill to be successful. Despite the benefits of flow, there appear to be few opportunities to experience this at school, with the day broken up into short sections and limited time available for any particular activity, reducing the potential for mastery. Additionally, what prevents flow are feelings of anxiety and boredom.

To support you in reflecting on your responses to individuals and groups, you can consider the following:

1. How do you respond when a student does not give the right answer to a verbal question in class?
2. What does this say about your values and priorities?
3. How do you talk to a child who appears not to be engaged? Do you approach them with a warm smile and ask what they need to feel more positive about their work, give them a gentle reminder that they have limited time to complete the task, or remind them of a school requirement to finish the work or have to do finish it in breaktime?

Engagement and neurodivergence

Neurodivergence is not necessarily, or intrinsically, a barrier to engagement; however, some aspects of neurodivergence may make engagement more challenging within a school environment. Some children with severe physical or learning disabilities may have few independent skills, but this does not preclude engagement. Many children, including those with some degree of apparent independence, will find it difficult to spontaneously engage themselves purposively and will need our support. Others may resist our attempts to engage them for a range of reasons. However, all students will have to engage in order to learn, although what that engagement behaviour looks like may differ. As educators we may expect to see all children engage in typical ways; however, some people have explained that engagement is supported for them when they are free to behave as they need, often by moving, rocking, fiddling with something or looking away. I worked with a young autistic boy who spent his time walking around the room; all attempts to encourage him to sit down were met with strong resistance. When I tried to engage him with visual items he barely looked or paused. I started to read him a simple story, pausing to hold the book where he could see the pictures. Each time I showed the book I stopped talking and held it until I had seen him glance towards it. I then commented that I had seen him look and would turn the page and continue. As I did this his walking slowed, he started to pause to look more directly and for longer. I had increased his engagement in the activity with no instruction but a clear expectation that he would be interested, and this gave us a base to build on.

When students resist our attempts to engage them, we need to avoid finding ourselves in confrontation with them. Children's fear, anxiety and discomfort can make them highly effective in building resistance and we do not want this to become entrenched behaviour. A girl with Down's syndrome (DS) who was included in a mainstream school had a strong aversion to physical education lessons. As with many people with DS, she struggled with coordination, and low muscle tone often makes physical exercise more demanding and tiring. She may also have felt embarrassed by not being able to do the same activities as her peers. She showed her resistance by sitting on the floor outside the gym and refusing to go in. One of the school leaders came upon her and her educators who were trying to reassure her and encourage her to go in. The senior leader intervened and told her that if she did not go into the hall immediately, she would be suspended. She would not move, so was excluded from school for three days, something that she relished. Educators frequently fear losing control over their pupils and being seen by colleagues to lack discipline. This can prompt them to be over-zealous in their response to children. Schools that promote positive relationships over forcing a child to follow the rules will build more positive climates where over time a child can gain confidence and trust in entering any lesson. It is not weak to show patience, persistence and determination while showing compassion for a child's feelings and need to go slowly.

There are specific areas of challenge to engagement that many pupils encounter that are either physical, emotional in their origin, or both. As we have been seeing, success in school facilitates a sense of belonging and self-efficacy, which promotes further engagement. To build self-efficacy students should have the opportunity to not only succeed in academic subjects but also on non-academic tasks. School pets frequently have an important role in soothing children who have experienced loss or trauma. Self-efficacy can be built through opportunities for mastery and clear feedback on progress. As educators we need to carefully observe and reflect on our pupils to best understand their strengths and barriers they face with engagement. Some of these are intrinsic, aspects of themselves that they bring with them into school, but which we can make provision for and effectively plan to reduce sufficiently to improve engagement.

Sensory differences

A major obstacle to engagement in school for autistic learners, and others, including those with DS, is their level of sensory awareness and comfort. Schools are always places with a great number of sensations to become aware of or try to ignore. We might want our classes to be quiet, peaceful places that provide an ideal workspace for everyone; however, even when we manage to do this in our own class, we can still encounter distracting noises from corridors or activity outside. We need to understand that the way in which we typically process the sensations arising from the environment will present less challenge than for many of our students. Think of the difference between how on some days you might be able to focus in a noisy environment quite well, but when very tired, or stressed, you may be determined to find quiet. The experience of approaching sensory overwhelm will be familiar to many children. For example, students with DS may struggle to process sensory information, impacting other aspects including, motor development, leading to frustration and inappropriate behaviour.

We know that large numbers of autistic students in our schools have high levels of anxiety, and one contributor to this is the sensory environment. Autistic people can be hyposensitive, meaning that they feel less than would typically be the case, and this can lead to them feeling disorientated or missing cues. More typically autistic pupils have hypersensitivity, which makes the school environment with its smells, noise, bright lights, movement and proximity to other people very uncomfortable, or even painful. Someone who is hypersensitive to sound can spend much of the day guarding themselves against a sudden shout or unexpected noise. I took an autistic child on a history visit and he immediately spotted a cannon, put his hands over his ears and wanted to leave. We went to check whether it would be fired and were told what time this would happen. He was reassured and we continued our visit, although unbeknownst to me there was another cannon which was fired while we were there, ending our visit.

In research conducted with colleagues (Costley et al., 2021), we talked to autistic secondary school students about their school experiences. Many of the difficulties they expressed could be seen through the conceptual lens of 'intolerance of uncertainty'. Students focused on the anxiety caused by the transition from smaller primary schools to dealing with the unknown. They worried about not being able to find their lessons and being late, being adversely judged by other people and getting into trouble inadvertently. They talked about being very disturbed by the behaviour of other students, particularly in terms of the noise they made, and the uncertainty of when someone (child or staff) would get angry and shout. Interviewees described a variety of physical symptoms of their anxiety such as feelings of suffocation and sickness. For some pupils, spending the day trying to manage their anxiety made any engagement in learning unlikely.

We have to anticipate, in our planning, what might cause a sensory reaction in a pupil and ensure that they will be prepared for what might happen. A student who started at a mainstream secondary school, with support, was unprepared for the chemical reaction in a science lesson, which led to him being terrified and leaving the room without permission. This was seen as serious misconduct and he was reprimanded, leaving him highly distressed and unwilling to attend school. This could have been avoided had he been warned of what might happen and allowed to view from a distance or even leave the room for the duration of the experiment, at least as a newcomer to the school. Learning can be accomplished through video, which will be less threatening and afford pupil control.

Although in neurotypical children engagement might involve all senses at once, autistic people can be what has been described as 'mono' (Murray et al., 2005) and will engage best with listening if they do not look, or can take in visual information better in silence. Autistic people describe not being able to take notes if they are listening, or process speech if they look at the face of the person speaking. Our schools are typically not conducive to this difference. For example, an autistic child at home, with their own choice of activity, may engage, perhaps even reaching a state of flow, for long periods of time on a regular basis – similarly with a student with Down's syndrome who enjoys a creative activity such as drama or painting. Overall, however, neurodivergent children may find engaging in academic work and the life of a school more difficult than typical learners, mainly because our school systems are not usually designed to be conducive to learners with differences. Of neurodivergent students, those who are autistic or who have attention deficit hyperactivity disorder (ADHD) may find engagement particularly challenging, and anyone with an identified difference, impacting their communication and learning, will struggle with engagement. As educators we often worry the most about how to engage groups of children who have intrinsically poor attention or behaviour for learning.

Helping children to engage

What is key is that we ask ourselves questions about any child who does not appear to be engaging as follows:

1. Are they actually engaging but not showing in the way we expect?
2. If not engaging, what might be preventing this, e.g. sensory issues, motor disturbance, emotional challenges, low motivation linked to level of activity?
3. What can I do to prompt and support their engagement? Ask them for ideas, change the task, increase or decrease the level, allow a break or allow their own choice of activity with similar learning outcomes.
4. Remember to check how you are feeling in the moment; it is likely that if you find the environment uncomfortable or overwhelming, this will be even more difficult for many students.

Our aim is to help children gain insight into their difficulties in order to develop independent strategies to help them manage engagement in the best way for them. We can facilitate this through open conversation and careful questioning within a caring and supportive environment.

Motor impairments

We all utilise our ability to control and coordinate our movements as part of social interaction. Many of our education practices, and the way in which we assess understanding, involve coordination of movements. We will understand and anticipate the need for pedagogical adjustments when working with students with known physical impairments such as cerebral palsy. Through a mix of low-tech materials and high-tech equipment, we can foster engagement with most physically disabled students, allowing them to ask and answer questions, and complete work. Their pace will typically be slower; for example, we might give them multiple choice instead of open questions to measure their understanding.

What is less well understood and anticipated for in our schools are the sorts of motor impairments, and motor coordination difficulties, that are not immediately evident. These can range from poorly coordinated children who develop anxiety about any activity that includes physical activity so that they resist the practice that might ultimately help them. Some of my most assertive and creative thinking at secondary school was coming up with excuses not to engage in PE! Boys who are not good at football, which can often be the most prestigious activity in school, may find themselves with fewer friends and feel less emotional engagement with school. Conversely, the child who struggles with academia but excels at table tennis can preserve their confidence.

I was observing a young boy with Down's syndrome in the dining hall at school. Before him was his packed lunch of sandwiches. His lunch helper had opened the box and the tinfoil inside and said, 'eat your lunch'. The boy lifted his arms level with his neck, moving his fingers rapidly in a grabbing motion, but did not pick up his sandwich. The helper repeated her instruction with the same response from the child. She turned to me and said, 'he's like this every day, he won't start eating'. She then gave the boy the instruction to eat for the third time, simultaneously touching his elbow. His hand immediately went down to the sandwich, picked it up and he started eating. This series of steps was then repeated with the second sandwich. The lunch helper's understanding of the situation was that he was reluctant to eat. What I saw was a boy who was hungry and keen for his lunch, but who was struggling to initiate the movement he needed to make. When people cannot start a movement, a really helpful prompt for them is touch, which the helper offered in an unconscious way.

We understand that a difficulty with movement, including poor balance, hyperflexibility, low muscle tone and coordination difficulties, is frequently found in children with DS. Children may not develop their muscles to the same extent or at the same pace as their typical peers, leading to a lack of comparative strength and endurance. These physical symptoms lead to delayed milestones and higher levels of fatigue. If educators do not understand that many of the challenges a person with DS experiences come from their physical characteristics, they may interpret a lack of response, for example, as lack of intellectual ability. There is also an unhappy irony here, since in order to improve muscle tone and coordination they need to exercise; however, their difficulties are likely to make this very difficult, meaning that a programme of gradually increasing physical activity may be beneficial.

In 1996 Leary and Hill proposed movement disturbance as a facet of autism. For many years, to the current day, this has not been recognised as a characteristic of autism, and their suggestions have been mostly disregarded, although this is now starting to change. There is an irony in this, as when Hans Asperger first wrote about the form of autism that he put his name to, he included lack of coordination as part of the spectrum. However, there has been a gradual increase in focus on the sorts of movement disturbances found in the autistic population, and greater numbers of people now suggesting that challenges with some motor skills should be included in the diagnostic criteria for autism. A movement disturbance might impact abilities such as to start, continue, stop and combine a movement. All movements have to be executed with appropriate speed, control, direction and coordination; when we make an error with even one of these, we may miss our target or knock something over. People need to be able to switch easily from one movement to another. People who have a recognised movement disturbance can experience both a reduction in some typical movements and additional unusual movements, such as in the typically portrayed image of an autistic child engaging in repetitive hand or body movements. Any movement disturbance will have a serious impact on social skills since, in addition to speech and language, it usually involves facial expression, gesture, and head and body movements. In fact, social interaction can be seen as a complex 'dance' of movements. Our thoughts typically have movement, and the difficulty with switching from one thought to another could explain some aspects of autism. Whereas we are able to see difference in movements that occur externally, people with movement disturbance describe inner differences as well. These affect their perception, attention, motivation and emotion. What is crucial to understand about this is that what we see people do may not be what they are choosing to do. Autistic people frequently talk about their bodies dictating movements to them. This complicates our desire to use observation and conjecture to understand someone. For example, in a typical person, pacing around a room is likely to be a sign of anxiety, but this is often not the case for an autistic person.

An adult who was identified as autistic with a mild physical disability typically walked with a limp, was slow and cumbersome. At times he would go towards staff with a better gait and appear animated and excited. They assumed that this meant that he was happy, whereas in fact it was a sign of great agitation.

Pace and timing

Another aspect that impacts engagement for many pupils is time. The pace of many classrooms involves fast responses to teacher questions and set times to complete work. This is a highly challenging aspect for the majority of neurodivergent pupils, many of whom experience processing difficulties. When we ask a question, typical children will understand it immediately, and can come up with an answer, while neurodivergent children may still be working on understanding the meaning of what has been asked. When we see a child struggling to respond we will often think that they have not understood, and we might repeat the question. Our tendency, in situations where we were not understood, is to slightly alter our wording to see if that helps. However, this can actually do the reverse, by interrupting the processing of the first question and providing a different model to try to understand. Educators will tend to do this very rapidly and unconsciously, contributing to the perception that a child has poor understanding, or is not engaged in careful listening. This can contribute not only to a student's negative self-perception, seeing an educator who does not believe in them, but also denies them the opportunity to demonstrate capability that would change the educator's perception. When giving a verbal instruction, best practice with neurodivergent students is to give a long wait time, say around 15 seconds, then repeat using the same words, ensuring that our tone does not signal irritation. We can then wait again, perhaps for even longer, to see if a response will be given which can help us gain insight into the student. We need to encourage students to ask for a further repetition, or to request us to reword. This helps build independence in our pupils and maximises their potential to correctly respond. We need to aid understanding by writing our questions and providing visual cues to meaning; however, we also need to allow for processing time as we plan the lesson. Many children with processing disorders are at risk of stopping trying to understand, instead waiting and using their observations to work out what was said and what they need to do. This helps them to hide their difficulties to avoid shame.

Self-perception

How we see ourselves, particularly in comparison to others, will contribute to our self-perception. This is part of the 'self-fulfilling prophecy' where someone who expects to succeed at something is more likely to persist until they have. This is encapsulated in the notion of the 'locus of control'. Students with an internal locus of control will believe that they can influence outcomes by their actions, whereas those whose 'locus of control' is external attribute outcomes to luck or random factors. Neurodivergent children are highly susceptible to negative self-image built up through unsuccessful attempts at participating and succeeding in learning. I believe that children will have a clear perception of where they sit within the class in terms of their ability and may decide to 'settle' without trying harder. A child who has never had effective communication skills will see themselves as 'a non-speaker', become used to this state and find comfort in the familiar. For some children, even when provided with a means of communication, they may resist using it or appear disinterested. This can be seen as a form of learned helplessness, which educators have to work hard to counteract. Giving students new experiences, where they get to feel what it is like to be seen as more capable, are important small steps that can be built on. As a student who never felt successful at school, and always compared herself negatively with others, starting a new activity when I reached the penultimate year of schooling gave me this kind of boost. We were taken kayaking, and I not only loved it but seemed to have a natural propensity. Seeing that I had a chance of being the 'best in class' after a lifetime of being the last to be picked in sports teams gave me determination and I started going to practise at weekends to secure that position. I love to kayak to this day!

A child with speech that was extremely difficult to understand became increasingly reluctant to say anything outside of his family. He appeared to be highly anxious when any attempt to engage him was made. When I had one-to-one time with him over many months, he would attempt speech, but would often get out of his chair, open the door and check whether anyone outside might hear him. However positive I was at the efforts he made, his early experiences of failing in a mainstream school, and his parents' misguided efforts to force him to speak clearly, had a profound effect on him and his self-perception. It appeared that he was willing to treat his future life as a non-speaker rather than risk not being understood. The degree of resilience a child will have will vary enormously, but once a pattern of behaviour has become a firm part of identity, it is harder to alter it.

Mona: Teaching pointing

Children like Mona are rarely included in mainstream schools given their multiple challenges. She is non-verbal, with no effective alternative method of communication, and appears resistant to being engaged. She attends a special school and is identified as autistic with severe learning disabilities.

Our work with Mona was part of a research project with the aim of trying to teach her to point as a means of communication. Mona did not like to be approached by adults and would not let anyone other than people she knew very well come into her personal space. She liked playing alone with blocks or colouring, holding several wax crayons in her hands and making wide circles on the page. Any intervention in her solo play was met with screams and biting of the ball of her thumb, which was covered with callouses, and she kicked or hit any adult who came near her. Our approach was underpinned by the belief that if we could identify something that would create a desire to engage in Mona, her intrinsic motivation would be activated and her behaviour would change. We started with close observation, saying aloud what we could see her doing when it indicated any interest in what we had brought to show her, including looking towards anything we presented. All resistant behaviours were ignored, and to protect our shins we placed a hard board under the table in front of our legs so we could sit at the same table. We talked quietly to Mona about what we were showing her, even when she wasn't looking and was making loud, blocking vocalisations. We intended to convey the message that engagement would be her choice when she was ready. We modelled pointing and showed interest and curiosity about the material we shared with her. We commented on and showed calm pleasure in any glance in our direction. We did not give her instructions.

At the start of the work with Mona we saw her behaviours as either accepting or rejecting of our attention. Initially we could observe her glancing towards our materials, gradually starting to look more directly over the course of many months. Prior to our work Mona was thought to like certain books, but she would interact with these by rapidly turning all the pages and then banging the book down on the table. We discovered that it was difficult for Mona to resist looking if we presented something that was initially hidden and then revealed. We used 'lift the flap' books, showing intrigue about what was hidden ourselves and seeing it echoed in her. Mona gradually began to initiate taking our hand to get us to lift the flaps, and gradually we moved to taking her hand to support her to do a range of engagement actions such as slowly turning one page of a book at a time, looking and pointing to pictures in it, and matching words to pictures. During sessions Mona became increasingly quiet and still and stopped kicking; in fact she even began to show signs of pleasure when adults approached her. Her pace of engagement, as well as the length of interactions, gradually increased, and this was generalised into other school activities. Before our work the only way Mona had of indicating what she wanted was waving her hand towards something, particularly at mealtimes. She developed the ability to point, both supported and unprompted, throughout the day. She reduced her resistance considerably and her educators reported that they could try new things and encourage her to interact in ways that had not previously been possible. Mona demonstrated greater levels of understanding of spoken language than previously anticipated.

What was key in our work with Mona was that we adopted a person-centred and respectful agenda, rather than attempting to impose the curriculum on her. We accepted that she was not yet ready for that form of learning but believed that she could be if we first built a relationship with her that honoured her interests and timing. It was important that our verbal responses were focused on positives, and we drew as little attention as possible onto her resisting behaviours. If she appeared to be very upset, we would respond with reassurance and give her more space. It was slow work that required persistence but was an approach that offered something different than requiring additional time, making it possible for her school educators to continue. Schools need to be willing to make space for relationship building, which can be difficult given the pressures they are under.

Teaching Mona to point gave her an additional and more specific mode of communication. The importance of pointing can be seen in many examples of people who have become competent communicators through their use of communication boards or technological devices. Now that tablets are more affordable and can be used with free voice output software, many young people have a means of communication they did not have before. There is considerable controversy around some ways in which pointing is taught, specifically Facilitated Communication (FC) and the Rapid Prompt Method (RPM). When we use physical support to help someone to point, we can teach the skill, but alongside this there is a risk of teaching dependence. Many people who have learned to type with physical assistance find becoming fully independent difficult, either due to a learned dependence or more likely because of the neurological challenges that led them to need support for pointing in the first place. The majority of the people I know who use FC require life-long care since they have limited independent skills. In some ways there is less need for them to develop independent pointing since they will always have someone available to support them. The controversy arises when they cannot prove that they are directing their movements, and the suspicion falls on the facilitator as the origin of any message. There is research evidence both for and against the efficacy of FC, although the arguments of those against its use are often louder (see Nicoli et al., 2023). My experience is that many people who have spent their lives, including into adulthood, with no means of communicating anything, and with no one around them perceiving them as potential communicators, can benefit enormously when they start to engage in a communicative interaction, even if this requires support. Those who decry FC and RPM argue that it is unethical to present someone as communicating when the message may not be authored by them and see this as a form of manipulation and putting words in someone's mouth. In my view there are ways of using FC, and RPM, ethically. Both these approaches aim to teach independent communication. Independence is partly in terms of movement, but also in being able to assert their own ideas, even where physical support from a facilitator is involved. As a facilitator I sometimes had the experience of asking a young person not to type a swear word at the same time as I gave them the physical support to do so! In places where FC is used, guidelines need to be in place to ensure that something people communicate when facilitated is not immediately acted on, but is repeated with an independent person who is not informed of the content of the message. Ideally, people who might point to type a whole message with support are also taught to point independently to select from a small number of options. Anything that is requested through FC can then be checked through independent movement. These issues are not simple; for me communication generated with physical support is often a co-construction (see Nicoli et al., 2023), but that is still highly valuable for someone who may otherwise be without any voice. Additional benefits for some FC users are increased speech, practised through reading out what they have typed. People often also report greater levels of engagement, concentration and motor control, including eye–hand coordination.

Emotional responses

Schools need to work hard to foster positive relationships and sense of belonging, but currently many children still find school a highly disturbing environment. As we have seen, this can be from their reactivity to the environment, leading to anxiety and discomfort. Other children will bring their emotional distress with them, due to family issues, bullying or past trauma. Children arriving in a hypervigilant state, being in 'fight or flight', need a gentle and accepting environment. A child who arrives late, is surly and fights with peers and rude to educators needs to know that they are 'having a bad day' and that tomorrow can be more comfortable and successful, rather than being reprimanded and threatened. What makes offering a warm environment particularly challenging in schools is that even where educators can offer this, other pupils may act in unhelpful ways even before the child arrives in class. Tolerance and understanding are key values for schools to uphold and apply to every pupil. This not only fosters a supportive environment for every member of the school, but also models the sorts of behaviour that we would like to develop in all our learners.

Many schools make special provision for particular groups of learners, with separate parts of the school, and different staff, providing special needs support or nurture. This approach can help pupils, especially where smaller groups provide some respite from the noise and movement of a typical classroom. It allows them protection and support and hopefully makes school a place that they can look forward to going to. However, in order for them to develop into people who can take their place in society, they ideally also need to gradually learn to assimilate into the main part of the school. Two main provisions will do this, firstly a whole school climate that is welcoming and supportive, where difference is accepted and not just tolerated; and secondly, a phased approach where children can have a say in how often and for how long they spend in a mainstream classroom.

It may be helpful to consider the following:

1. Do you have a sense of how your pupils are feeling; is there a space for them to let you know?
2. Is there space for you to monitor how you feel yourself, an opportunity to vent frustrations and reset before going to support a pupil who is resisting engagement?
3. Do you take the opportunity to comment on who students are as people, what you see as their positive traits and likeable features?

Motivation

When considering how to promote and develop engagement in our pupils, we are generally instructed to use extrinsic rewards. The majority of schools include behaviour policies that utilise a range of points-based systems to encourage appropriate behaviour and engagement with learning. UK government (Department for Education, 2024, p. 5) advice is for schools to 'create environments in which behaviour is good and pupils can learn and feel safe', with an emphasis on teaching good behaviour. Teachers report finding reward systems invaluable in encouraging improved behaviour for learning. In the short term, children may work hard to gain stars or stickers, to complete charts in order to win time on a favourite activity. At my son's school, children with a certain number of points were invited for tea with the headteacher. As children progress through school the effectiveness of these measures tends to diminish – older children might not want to appear to value tea with the head! Research tells us that extrinsic rewards can have short-term positive impact, but longer term can be negative and limit the development of more beneficial intrinsic motivation (Deci et al., 2001). These authors apply Cognitive Evaluation Theory to understand intrinsic motivation, suggesting it is founded in 'the innate psychological needs for competence and self-determination' (Deci et al., 2001, p. 3). When children perceive themselves as having little competence or lack of opportunity to decide for themselves, their intrinsic motivation decreases. Rewards are seen as having two aspects: informational (i.e. letting someone know how they are doing) and controlling (i.e. when the intention is to get someone to do something we want them to do). Whereas success within a reward scheme might enhance feelings of competence, the feeling of lack of control within the scheme, such as when students feel that they or others were unfairly judged, will undermine intrinsic motivation. Within this model, all forms of reward, including verbal praise, can be experienced negatively as controlling, depending on the context. When we offer systematic rewards, we are suggesting to students that these are necessary to encourage them to do something they otherwise would not want to do. This gives the message that engagement in learning, and attentive behaviour, are not expected, but will only happen if the reward is sufficient. Deci et al. (2001) found that any form of reward that was offered spontaneously, i.e. not within a routine system, did not undermine intrinsic motivation, so classrooms where educators will praise a child at random times can be positive.

I experienced this when I lived with a family as their in-house speech and language therapist for their 5-year-old daughter. She was following a highly intensive developmental exercise programme with therapists outside the family. To gain her cooperation, they would constantly reward her with toys and by doing things to make her laugh. As someone who was working with her to improve her eating and communication, I found that she was completely unmotivated. She had learned that if she remained passive the adults present would perform all kinds of antics to make her happy and gain her cooperation, something that was exhausting to try to keep up throughout the day. This was an extreme situation; however, it illustrates for me what I have seen to lesser extents in many other children. The daughters of a working mother would go to her place of work after school where she would try to supervise their homework while also attending to customers. I observed that they would only do their work while she was there, to ensure that she gave them more of her attention for longer.

I have tried (although with little success!) to promote the replacement of 'behaviour policies' in schools with 'relationship policies' in recognition that positive connections between staff and pupils are more likely to build intrinsic motivation which has longer duration and greater effectiveness than extrinsic. Additionally, I believe that behaviour policies that apply strict criteria for every pupil are inequitable. As an example, a pupil with ADHD left the classroom without permission, and for a while no one could find him. This led to great concern and anxiety in educators in case he had left the school premises. Staff went looking for him and a teacher found him in a corridor. The teacher stood in front of the boy, blocking his escape, and asked why he had left class. I was not there to witness how the teacher spoke, but the result was that the boy pushed him in trying to get away. Within the school rules this was classed as 'assault' against a teacher, a very serious offence, and the pupil was expelled from the school. Staff need to feel safe in their school, as do pupils, and in these terms the decision to expel the pupil was understandable. The incident occurred shortly before the boy's national exams; a move to another school at that point would have severely impacted his success in these. Ideally I would like to see different approaches to tackling this sort of incident. The boy could have been deliberately challenging, or could have felt 'cornered' and panicked; he knew that leaving the classroom was wrong, but was in a highly agitated state and unable to inhibit his reactions at that moment. My preferred response would have been to show care for the boy; perhaps the educator could have said that everyone was concerned for him and was really pleased to find that he was safe. The boy could then have been asked if he was ready to go to a safe place to spend time recovering, or whether he needed to stay where he was for a few minutes. Giving control in this instance could be highly effective in starting the de-escalation process. Once the boy was feeling safe, and more emotionally regulated, any conversation about the inappropriateness of his actions, and consequences, may have led to a more positive outcome for everyone.

This book is looking at the multiple ways in which students can face barriers to learning, some of which are intrinsic, others environmental and/or derive from trauma or emotional distress. This puts a great number of students in every class into a situation where self-regulating and controlling their behaviour will be highly challenging. They come into our classrooms already disadvantaged, but we then apply the same rules to them as we do to children who learn easily, and have positive experiences of learning and socialising and secure and happy home lives. I am not suggesting that we form behaviour policies that we apply only to children we perceive as without disadvantage. That would also be inequitable. What I would ideally like to see happen is that all children are treated the same, i.e. with understanding, compassion and a belief that when provided with a supportive environment, which promotes flourishing, and does not impose punishment, they will come over time to behave in ways that are more acceptable to society. In my worldview children who are liked, treated warmly and allowed to learn from their mistakes are placed in a better frame to self-regulate. I want to listen to the views of children. Dean Cotton, in his training for positive behaviour management, gives the example of a child walking into a room and deliberately knocking over a chair (Cotton, 2017). He asks his audience what they think the teacher would say. People usually respond with 'why did you do that, pick it up, sit down'. He then places the same scenario in the context of a staff room where a teacher knocks over a chair. We then suggest that the teacher's peers will say 'what happened, are you OK?' If we apply our second response, which acknowledges the communication of the action, the autonomy, and shows concern and inquiry, to children, we are more likely to allow them to join our class in a better frame of mind. The confrontation response of 'why did you do that?' or an irritated or angry 'pick that up' pushes the child into a more defended and immovable position where their behaviour is likely to escalate. Instead, if we see the act as communicative, we can ask Dean's three questions: 'what happened; how did you feel; what could you do differently next time?'

We need to be aware of the degree of activation the child is likely to be experiencing when they are in this state, and give them a period of quiet and low demand, before gently approaching and asking our questions. This will maximise the possibility of them being able to reflect and arrive at a positive response.

In my papers on this issue published in the journal *Pastoral Care in Education*, I argue that typical behaviour policies disadvantage students with special educational needs and disabilities (SEND), suggesting that they are contrary to schools' efforts to promote equality, diversity and inclusion. School rules are predicated on children understanding what is required and being capable of controlling their behaviour; as we are considering in this book this assumption cannot be applied to large numbers of our pupils. To follow a rule, we need to utilise memory, planning and self-regulation, some or all of which the majority of SEND children will find difficult. Children who have experience of not succeeding are likely to feel anxiety about getting it wrong, making rule following even more difficult. Forcing children to publicly face the consequences of not being able to follow expected patterns of behaviour can be seen as one of the ways in which schools maybe 'trauma-producing' (Petrone and Stanton, 2021). Much of the behaviour found to be unacceptable in the school context is likely to stem from attempts to reduce stress or anxiety and to self-regulate, such as when children move around the classroom without permission. We could see this as an expression of need, even a way in which children are self-advocating and attempting to self-regulate, something we could build on to have the same emotions manifested more directly. Instead, we often view this behaviour as challenging and respond by reminders to follow the rules. This means not only do we risk shaming children through seeing their behaviour negatively, which was not their intention, but also missing an opportunity to encourage pupil insight and the making of accommodations to neurologically based needs. Our policies can stigmatise SEND pupils when their behaviour does not attract praise, or leads them to be punished. We utilise reward systems as they appear to have a positive impact, yet our rates of school suspension and exclusion, which could be seen as the marker of whether our systems work, continue to rise (Gov.uk, n.d.). We see from statistics that certain groups are more prone to school exclusion than others, with those from economically disadvantaged, ethnic minorities and those with SEND disproportionately represented (Gov.uk, n.d.).

> Consider these questions to help you reflect on your own practice:
>
> 1. Are all the classroom rules essential? Could some be altered to be positive guides for collaboration and care, i.e. avoid 'don'ts' and implement codes of conduct with explanations of how they benefit everyone?
> 2. To what extent do you rely on giving points or tokens to foster engagement?
> 3. Could you implement more instances of genuine spontaneous praise for what you see happening, ensuring over time that you find something positive to comment on for all pupils? This would allow acknowledgement of the effort of every pupil, without having to compare to each other.
> 4. To what extent do you encourage students to reflect on their own behaviour and support them to see what they are communicating, and how might they more positively have their needs met?

Building engagement

Educators successful at developing engagement in their classrooms will understand that their classroom management and pedagogy are inextricably linked. Seeing behaviour management as separate from instruction can lead to low educator self-efficacy and overwhelm. Effective planning needs to be combined with flexibility of decision-making to promote engagement and student development. This makes particular sense when we consider that ineffective instruction contributes to problem behaviour, which is then associated with poor academic outcomes (Nagro et al., 2019). The same authors suggest that effective classroom management comprises predictability, clear expectations, engagement and strategies to deal with both appropriate and inappropriate behaviours. The next section considers what educators need to consider to make their classrooms the most engaging and effective possible for every child.

Attitudes and beliefs

As already discussed, engagement is established through and within relationship, and so the attitudes and beliefs of both students and staff will be important and contribute to the climate of the school. A key factor in promoting engagement is educator self-efficacy, i.e. our beliefs in our own skill and competency with all children. Teachers with higher levels of self-efficacy tend to have more effective lesson plans as part of their classroom management, and since they believe that it is possible to teach everyone, they promote greater levels of student engagement. When teachers believe that they can influence the engagement of their pupils, and their progress, they are more likely to do so. We cannot help but communicate our view of a child to them. Students will be aware of whether they are liked by a teacher, which is not to say that all students are equally easy to like. This is where gaining insight and understanding into the reasons behind student behaviour, even where we do not like it, can help us to show compassion, understanding and fairness, which will be appreciated by our pupils. This will help us to separate the behaviour from the child. As we demonstrate our commitment to them, we afford them the opportunity to become people who might be easier to like.

When working with neurodivergent pupils we need to adopt a belief that everyone is eager for social connection, when that can be provided in a way that is comfortable for them. For some pupils this might be a very quiet approach with minimal interaction to build trust. Others will respond to a highly active and stimulating interaction. Phoebe Caldwell and those associated with Intensive Interaction (https://www.intensiveinteraction.org/) promote joining in with the child in their world, copying their behaviours in the way that a mother does when interacting with their baby. Adopting a belief that everyone will learn if we offer support in the optimum way for the individual will help our own motivation and persistence. Schools that lack a fully inclusive culture will usually hold a belief that some students are not able to benefit from what they can offer and so would be best educated elsewhere. This view can lead to a dismissal of a child's ability when we have tried hard to engage them, but they make only very limited progress. This might prompt feelings of doubt and discomfort in our own skills, which are eased by telling ourselves that it is not us who are lacking, but the child who is impossible to teach. I adopt what might be a very unpopular view that when a child is not making any progress we need to keep going and examine what else we might do to make a difference. We then need to watch for the smallest of changes, to help us to stay motivated.

I like to encourage children to 'write' stories by selecting images. I took this approach with a non-verbal autistic boy, asking him to create a story about things that he likes. He selected pictures from a series of categories that told me that he would like to live in a motorhome, prefer to wear only a hat and no clothes, have a dragon for a pet and work as a chef. The teaching assistant (TA) observing, who knew the child well, thought that he was making random selections. For me, this did not matter; it was a 'no fail' activity and what was most important was his engagement with the task. He pointed actively to pictures, sometimes making a few selections before settling on one, watching while the TA cut it out, applying glue with help and sticking it where he wanted on a sheet. This showed engagement and enjoyment at a level that was different from his usual behaviour, and when I 'read' his story to him he squealed with delight. Interestingly, the TA repeated the same activity with the same images, wanting to reaffirm her belief that he was pointing randomly, but she later told me that he had selected all the same items, much to her amazement. In this example I would argue that my belief, that when the boy was engaging with something meaningful to him, he would show competence, was in contrast to the view of the TA, who was working in a climate that frequently saw the children in terms of what they were not able to do. This is not to criticise the TA, or the other educators in the school, who were following 'best practice' in trying to respect the needs of their pupils by not placing too much demand on them.

I have met with criticism that holding high expectations for the ability of pupils could place them under harmful levels of pressure, and negatively impact parents by giving them inappropriate hope for their children's development. In the field of disability, much of the culture is negative. As previously discussed, our assessments are designed to highlight deficits and gaps so that we can aim our interventions at plugging them. When children are first identified as disabled, parents are frequently given the 'worst case scenario' by medical professionals. This is seen as less potentially damaging than false hope. The argument is that if parents are expecting the worst they will be highly relieved with a better-than-expected outcome. While this is sometimes the case, it is also true that parents can be so impacted by what they are told that they experience trauma, which stays with them and can impact future relationships with professionals. I believe it is possible to be honest with parents, tell them a range of possibilities and encourage them to celebrate instances of progress.

Child-centred approaches

Schools are not typically places where children get to make choices about what they do, for how long or where. There are myriad constraints on what is possible within any institution. However, within our classrooms we can plan to include a good level of child-led activities, knowing that children are more likely to engage with a topic that interests them. Any topic can be designed to promote learning in any curriculum area. Environments with low stress and high challenge are best to promote intrinsic motivation and engagement, whereas tasks that are seen as irrelevant or are too easy, or too hard, diminish motivation. By offering a range of activities, children can make independent decisions, with guidance where appropriate, and feel a sense of control over their own learning. Self-determination theory (Deci and Ryan, 2008) suggests that an environment where they feel included, but which does not promote too much control, allows the flourishing of autonomy, competence and relatedness, the three basic psychological needs of every child. Some children will immediately benefit from this opportunity, while others might find the freedom difficult to manage. Educators need, therefore, to be ready to provide scaffolding around choice-making for some students.

Making choices is a skill that many children acquire pre-school but others continue to struggle with. Effective choice-making, i.e. the critical evaluation skill of selecting an option and then staying with it, is a key life skill. Educators will see these difficulties manifest across all years and can probably think of adults who find being asked to make a choice, even about what drink to buy in a café, challenging and even overwhelming. Students will need to be making choices throughout their school career and beyond, so learning the skill, with support in the classroom, is crucial and evidence suggests that those who are good choice makers have more positive life opportunities and outcomes. This skill might be fostered through making 'low-stakes' choices on a regular basis; students get to experience the outcome of their choice in a situation where if they are not happy with it they can change, or at least learn for the next time. In the short term, having choices in relation to classwork increases engagement and academic success (see Nagro et al., 2019). In recognition of sensory differences, we need to adapt our pedagogy to also give choice of use of visual materials, schedules, etc., and these authors include movement in learning, e.g. mime, to give instructions, making shapes with walking in maths, sand letters and action rhymes.

An example of a choice we can offer children of any age is where to sit in the classroom. This does not mean that we would never assign seats. In my university classes people quickly establish a favoured place in the class with certain peers. Understanding that this brings comfort, I warn them when I am going to allocate them into different groups, but remind them that they will benefit from this by hearing different opinions and getting to know other classmates better. Some student feedback values this, acknowledging that it helps them not to be 'stuck' in rigid behaviours that they may want to change but don't do without support. In our classrooms children could choose what medium they write in, which assignment to do first, what materials to use, level of difficulty of task and what they might do after completing their work.

The risk of offering choice is that children may not want to stray from what is familiar, leading to a lack of learning opportunity. They need to be encouraged, with the support of a more knowledgeable other whom they trust, either an educator or peer, to try something new. There is always a balance to be struck between the safety of providing routine and the engaging affordance of novel materials. I see much of my practice as offering enticement to a child, based on observations of what draws their interest and attention. I frequently use materials where something can be hidden and then revealed. It is possible to play 'what's missing' with non-verbal children by preparing two sets of items that match. Depending on the stage of the child I might just place very few, or a greater number, of items on the table in front of the child and talk about what is there. I then place a cloth on top and without the child seeing remove one. When I lift the cloth and ask what is missing, I can then offer a choice of two items, one which is the one missing, the other that either matches something still on the table or is an additional object with no match. Many variants of this game can be offered, depending on the age and level of the child, to include verbal and literacy skills if appropriate. It is also something that can be played with groups and peers.

When working in a special school with predominantly non-verbal children I ran a communication group with a teacher and some TAs, allowing us a high staff ratio. We found that even though the children would not always appear to be aware of each other, an element of competition would seem to set in and children's response time and overall engagement improved. My colleague devised ingenious games based on popular TV quiz shows adapted for accessibility, incorporating the theme tune and other cues for the children to relate to. I tried this approach in a different special school for autistic children with just myself and the teacher, with similar results. We did a quiz based on pictures projected onto the wall, which helped to generate engagement, with students needing to point to matching images or words placed in front of them.

Children who are viewed as having low levels of understanding and performance are often given tasks that would be more suitable for a much younger child. Even when they appear to choose these tasks, educators need to consider the impact on the child and how this feeds the perception of those around them. I have seen a child with Down's syndrome in a mainstream secondary school being given colouring of a map in a geography lesson. This seems a very lazy and unhelpful adaptation of a lesson, which enforces the difference between the child and their peers and is very likely to demotivate. Children who are seen as having special educational needs often miss lessons in order to make space in the curriculum for additional support with the core curriculum. In my experience the decision about which lessons they might miss is frequently made without consultation with the child or their parents, and based on staff perception. For example, a child with DS was prevented from attending French classes, despite having family members whom she frequently visited in France and with existing knowledge of the language. It is likely that she would have felt greater confidence and higher levels of motivation in a French class than other topics that she found more challenging. This might have also been the only opportunity for her to be seen by her peers to have knowledge and capability that they were still gaining.

A UK charity called Achievement for All recommended termly conversations between parents and educators, to discuss the child and their preferences. When educators came to see the child as a whole person, including, for example, their interest in speaking another language, relationships between educator and child altered and children's performance started to improve. Just this simple action, which had the effect of altering perceptions, was found to have an impact on achievement. We can assume that the child feeling seen and known by the educator facilitated a greater sense of connection and school-belonging, that fed into engagement and intrinsic motivation. Another aspect is likely to be the impact on the educator, of being helped to see the child as a person, on their determination to support them with learning.

Autistic students are at risk for reduced engagement in terms of both frequency and duration. They also tend to engage more with objects than people, which can limit their learning opportunities. They need to experience success with a particular educator to build up trust and confidence. Repeated failure will do the opposite and establish a negative cycle. It is therefore important when starting to work with an autistic pupil, as with all students, that we find areas that interest them, allowing them to experience the enjoyment of sharing, and that stimulate and engage them. It is worth spending time on these sorts of relationship-building activities before attempting direct teaching. Much of the advice for teachers about engaging autistic students arises from behaviourist approaches, which work principally on rewarding desired behaviours. A suggested way of teaching autistic children as part of a behaviourist approach is to set up 'errorless' learning. In this the instructor ensures the student succeeds in the task by providing strong guidance. Providing the answer before allowing the student thinking time allows for positive reinforcement. This can then be followed by offering a repeat of the same task, to be done independently. An alternative to this is the 'no fail' approach described in Chapter 6, where activities are designed without right or wrong answers so any engagement from the pupil can be seen as positive and part of positive relationship building.

Fisal: The importance of routine

Like many autistic children Fisal needs strict routines to help him feel safe. He walks to school every day with his mother and brother, but the journey is punctuated with hesitations as Fisal checks for cars about to move or anything unexpected. His extreme sensory sensitivity means he is on constant alert for anything that might startle him. He wears ear defenders in the street, playground and sometimes in lessons when there is a lot of noise. He has a strict order to what he needs to do to be ready for school and his family know not to interrupt him or try to alter anything. He eats the same daily breakfast of plain white bread and water.

At school he finds waiting in the playground difficult, so will hang back at the entrance if he arrives before his classroom is open. Every morning, he hangs his coat neatly in the cloakroom, goes to his table in class, takes the same items out of his bag and places them in front of him in the same order. As other children arrive, he looks down, avoiding their gaze and does not greet them. His teaching assistant sits next to him, and he answers her when she says hello. His speech is clear but sounds a little robotic with an unusual intonation pattern. He is comfortable in his class; his teacher likes order and routine, too, and always remembers to warn him if something out of the ordinary is going to happen. She has talked to Fisal about the best length of warning of impending change or transition, and they have agreed that around 30 minutes works well for Fisal; any longer and his anxiety will start to build, any shorter and he may not feel ready and refuse to move.

He engages with his schoolwork and is meticulous in what he does but works very slowly and gets distressed if he is doing the same activity as his peers, but they finish long before him. His teacher and TA scaffold the activities to make them slightly shorter, while maintaining the learning objectives. He has difficulty structuring a task, remembering where to start and the sequence to follow. He is therefore provided with a written guide, which the TA talks through with Fisal at the beginning of any new task. A label of 'first' is set next to pictures of the materials he needs. Once he has these the second part of the instruction is revealed, showing him how to begin, and so on until the task is completed. Other children in the class, who like Fisal struggle with working memory, use the same guide to help them structure and remember. On every table is an emotion temperature gauge, which the children can use to indicate feeling anxious or upset. Fisal does not tend to use this spontaneously, but the staff, and sometimes his peers, will point to it and ask him how he is. He generally indicates the 'green' suggesting he is fine. When his TA sees that his anxiety is rising, she will model showing the amber section of the emotion gauge to help him learn to notice and understand his emotions.

Fisal smiles readily and looks approachable. He wants to interact with the other children but struggles to follow or remember the rules of some of their games. When invited to join them in playing football in the playground, he will sometimes play for a little while but then tends to wander around on his own. Sometimes he stands near the staff on duty and will answer when they ask him questions. His language development is fairly typical for his age and there are some topics that he feels very confident in, such as space, which he has extensive knowledge of. When talking about planets and his dream of becoming an astronaut he becomes animated and speaks more quickly. He does not take account of whether the person he is talking to is showing interest, and if gently told that he is talking for too long, he will resist having to stop.

Fisal does not read very fluently but loves stories and so listens to audiobooks at home. When asked to retell a story that he knows, he recites it perfectly verbatim, including instructions such as 'turn the page'. He has learned that people like jokes and will tell the same ones repetitively, particularly to adults, laughing himself each time. He is popular with his classmates, who are protective of him. He socialises with a small group of them outside of school, although he tends to spend more time with the adults in their houses than the children.

Fisal received a formal identification as autistic when he was 4 years old. As a second child his parents could see that his development was slower and different to his brother. Even as a toddler he would become highly distressed for no apparent reason. He would frequently take off his clothes and his parents gradually realised that certain fabrics made him uncomfortable. He watched the same video repeatedly and showed delight and excitement by flapping his hands. His parents learned as much as they could about autism and observed Fisal carefully. They recognised his need for consistency and routine and provided this. They also understood that he would need to gradually build on his flexibility, so they work on this at weekends by giving him new experiences that he has been well prepared for. This also allows them to build activities around Fisal's brother to give him appropriate attention. They write 'Social Stories' (https://carolgraysocialstories.com/) to let Fisal know exactly what to expect in new situations or when he has to attend an appointment at the doctor or dentist. Fisal has always hated having his hair cut: he doesn't like the noises or smells in the barber shop. His parents arrange for him to have his hair cut at the end of the day, always by the same barber, when the shop is quiet. The barber tells him what he will do at each stage of the cut and ensures that he is ready. This helps Fisal to feel in control and manage his anxiety.

His parents' in-depth knowledge and understanding of Fisal meant that they could work with his school to ensure that he would flourish there. The school had already included other autistic children and those with other SEND and were willing to be flexible with their practice. They provided a quiet room which any child who was feeling overwhelmed could ask to go to for a period away from other children. They recognised the need for calm acceptance, for a quiet and gentle approach and to not force anything on Fisal. They required him to complete tasks, as they did of all pupils, but without undue pressure and allowing the children to feel as if they had some level of choice.

Overall Fisal's experience of primary school was positive. He had TA support for 75% of his time there, and with structure and support from staff and peers he continued to feel safe when she wasn't with him. He increased his social skills, although these remained unsophisticated, and he was more comfortable with adults who made more allowances for him than with some peers. He made academic progress, too, and by his final year he had literacy and mathematical skills that would allow him to manage the curriculum at secondary school.

The situation at secondary was very different. Although the school gave his parents many assurances about their preparation for Fisal, his experience was negative from day one. He was accompanied to lessons by a number of different TAs, and he was not always told who he would be with. They had individual approaches to how they supported Fisal, the degree of independence they gave him and how much of his work they would actually do themselves. The school was big and noisy. He was allowed to move lessons before everyone else but felt that singled him out and he felt awkward and embarrassed. The school had a base for SEND students, which meant that he spent breaktimes with children he had not previously met and away from peers from his primary school. Naturally, he had many different teachers every day, the pace of classes was too fast for him and varying degrees of work differentiation was made for him. The school had received training in making provision for autistic students, but this was not embedded in their practice. Rather than looking at individual needs, they made blanket adjustments, which did not always work for Fisal. They had a strict code of behaviour that they regularly reiterated. Despite this Fisal remained unsure of what was, or was not, allowed, and this led him into a constant state of uncertainty. He was very frightened of getting something wrong and ending up in trouble, and this meant that he did as little as possible in order not to make errors.

His anxiety grew every day and his parents saw the impact of his distress at home. He stopped eating, didn't sleep and within the first months was showing signs of physical illness. His parents reluctantly removed him from the school at the end of the first term and entered him into a small private school that catered for SEND children. In this environment, which was flexible and protective, he was more able to flourish and make friends. He enjoyed his schooling, gained a few GCSEs and when he left school learned to drive and got a job in construction.

While our primary schools are generally able to provide some flexibility, the secondary school system is typically rigid and the environment generally hostile to anyone autistic with sensory sensitivity. Rates of inclusion are therefore greater in the early years when children's differences and support needs are not so great. Many children with DS, for example, are well supported in primary school but struggle with the pace and sensory overload of secondary. However, there are steps that schools can take, even within the system, to support learners. Firstly, it is imperative that we gain individual understanding of pupils, preferably by collecting information from the students themselves and their carers. Seeing someone as an individual rather than a grade on a spreadsheet promotes humanistic understanding and compassion. This gives us space to consider reasons behind someone's social and learning behaviour. As outlined throughout this book, when taking space to reflect, we can draw on our knowledge of how children learn and what skills the particular individual has to support them to overcome obstacles. Our focus can then be on helpful strategies. Ideally the support in primary could prevent students from developing a negative self-image as a learner, but this needs to continue into secondary. The effort they put into learning should be the focus of our feedback to students, alongside aspects of success and what areas they need to address to increase levels of achievement. Students need to understand themselves as learners, knowing what strategies they need to apply in situations they find challenging. I see this in university students who have been identified as dyslexic in their early years and given support to see this as a part of, but not defining, their identity. They will confidently tell me what they need to do in order to study successfully. Once they know this and can advocate for themselves, they can have positive self-image, greater levels of confidence and resilience. As educators our role becomes more straightforward when our students can tell us what accommodations they need in order to be successful.

An important concept to consider in relation to autism is 'intolerance of uncertainty' (IU). This was originally identified as impacting people within the general population with high levels of anxiety and subsequently applied specifically to autistic people (see Boulter et al., 2014). I have also become aware of research within the field of cognitive neuroscience that suggests that some autistic people may have a difficulty with prediction (see Sinha et al., 2014). In a paper I published in 2023 with Debra Costley, we make the argument that not being able to predict, in the sense of anticipating what may happen in any given situation, leads autistic students to develop high anxiety and IU. Without prediction, which calls on memory from previous, similar situations and interpretation of sensory information, the world is constantly unfamiliar and potentially alarming. Imagine going for a medical procedure where you have not been told exactly what to expect. You will have the anxiety about whether it will be painful, you don't know how long you will be there or what the outcome can be. Our understanding of how this would make an already difficult situation almost unbearable is why medical professionals give us preparatory information for any procedure, in the form of leaflets and appointments where we can ask questions. Autistic people often have permanently elevated levels of anxiety due to sensory discomfort.

They learn that even in familiar situations things can occur unexpectedly, so they have to be on their guard. Without the ability to predict, no situation can feel fully safe. In our paper we suggest that schools already have at their disposal ways of making the environment more predictable by utilising visual timetables and structuring work. We propose in addition that we examine students' ability to predict, and where we find difficulties, we set out to teach this as a skill. This could start by helping students identify the most relevant environmental stimuli to pay attention to in given situations.

Conclusion

Schools which recognise students' need for a level of autonomy will help their pupils flourish. I have long argued (Emerson, 2016, 2022) against rigid and draconian behaviour management systems, such as those recommended by the UK government and enforced in the majority of secondary schools. These are effective in making life more stressful and increasing the likelihood of failure for neurodivergent students in particular. In my view, exclusions, whether internal, temporary or permanent, should only be enacted when considered in the best interests of the child, which is likely to be on very rare occasions only – the vast majority of exclusions are for the benefit of the staff. Many schools use placing students in corridors to do their work as a way of managing those who persistently disrupt. At times this may help both the excluded pupil and those remaining in the classroom, but at a cost to the individual in terms of their internalised toxic shame. When schools are permitted and encouraged to offer flexibility, to assist students to weigh up the consequences for individual actions and decide on the best outcome for students and staff, they will foster cultures where everyone can flourish.

In summary, there is much that educators can do to foster engagement, which ultimately will bring greater enjoyment and satisfaction with their role. When we are allowed to be free of the curriculum pressure, to have time to build relationships with our pupils, more positive engagement will often ensue. The 'how to foster engagement' considered in this chapter can be summarised as the following points:

1. Start engagement support from a belief that children will engage if we can remove any obstacles to them doing so.

2. Plan for student engagement through activities they will perceive as giving them choice and independent decision-making, including regarding pacing of work and when they might complete it.
3. Teach children to consider their own engagement and what they need to do to help themselves within clear boundaries – this might involve drawing up a set of strategies that can be offered to students, along with the opportunity for them to add their own. Be willing to consider ideas we may not see as being suitable by asking how they feel that would help them, and look together for more feasible alternatives.
4. Take time to consider an unengaged pupil in terms of their current experience and what they bring to the learning context. How are they experiencing the task in terms of their sensory comfort, physical abilities and emotional response.
5. Adopt the use of intermittent and authentic praise to build positive self-image in our pupils.

References

Bilson, A. and Martin, K. E. C. (2016). Referrals and child protection in England: One in five children referred to children's services and one in nineteen investigated before the age of five. *British Journal of Social Work*, 47(3). doi:10.1093/bjsw/bcw054.

Boulter, C., Freeston, M., South, M. and Rodgers, J. (2014). Intolerance of uncertainty as a framework for understanding anxiety in children and adolescents with autism spectrum disorders. *Journal of Autism and Developmental Disorders*, 44, 1391–1402.

Costley, D., Emerson, A., Ropar, D. and Sheppard, E. (2021). The anxiety caused by secondary schools for autistic adolescents: In their own words. *Education Sciences*, 11, 726. https://doi.org/10.3390/educsci11110726

Cotton, D. (2017). *How to Teach Behaviour and How Not to*. CreateSpace Independent Publishing Platform.

Csikszentmihalyi, M. (2020). *Finding Flow: The Psychology of Engagement with Everyday Life*. London: Hachette.

Davis, D. and Sorrell, J. (1995). Mastery learning in public schools. *Educational Psychology Interactive*. Valdosta, GA: Valdosta State University. http://www.edpsycinteractive.org/files/mastlear.html

Deci, E. L., Koestner, R. and Ryan, R. M. (2001). Extrinsic rewards and intrinsic motivation in education: Reconsidered once again. *Review of Educational Research*, 71(1), 1–27. https://doi.org/10.3102/00346543071001001

Deci, E. L. and Ryan, R. M. (2008). Self-determination theory: A macrotheory of human motivation, development, and health. *Canadian Psychology*, 49(3), 182–185.

Department for Education. (2024). *Behaviour in Schools: Advice for Headteachers and School Staff*. Department for Education. https://assets.publishing.service.gov.uk/media/65ce3721e1bdec001a3221fe/Behaviour_in_schools_-_advice_for_headteachers_and_school_staff_Feb_2024.pdf

Duckworth, A. (2017). *Grit: Why Passion and Resilience Are the Secrets to Success*. London: Vermilion.

Dweck, C. S. (2002). The development of ability conceptions. In Wigfield, A. and Eccles, J. S. (Eds) *Development of Achievement Motivation*. Hoboken, NJ: John Wiley & Sons.

Emerson, A. (2016). Applying the 'least dangerous assumption' in regard to behaviour policies and children with special needs. *Pastoral Care in Education*, 34(2), 104–109. https://doi.org/10.1080/02643944.2016.1154095.

Emerson, A. (2022). The case for trauma-informed behaviour policies. *Pastoral Care in Education*, 40(3), 352–359. doi:10.1080/02643944.2022.2093956.

Emerson, A. and Costley, D. (2023). A scoping review of school-based strategies for addressing anxiety, intolerance of uncertainty and prediction in autistic pupils. *Education Sciences*, 13(6), 575. https://doi.org/10.3390/educsci13060575

Fredricks, J. A., Filsecker, M. and Lawson, M. A. (2016). Student engagement, context, and adjustment: Addressing definitional, measurement, and methodological issues. *Learn. Instruct*, 43, 1–4. doi:10.1016/j.learninstruc.2016.02.002.

Gov.uk. (n.d.). Suspensions and permanent exclusions in England. Accessed 18 September 2024. https://explore-education-statistics.service.gov.uk/find-statistics/suspensions-and-permanent-exclusions-in-england

Jensen, E. (2005). *Teaching with the Brain in Mind* (2nd edition). Alexandria, VA: Association for Supervision and Curriculum Development (ASCD).

Kemp, C., Kishida, Y., Carter, M. and Sweller, N. (2013). The effect of activity type on the engagement and interaction of young children with disabilities in inclusive childcare settings. *Early Childhood Research Quarterly*, 28, 134–143.

Leary, M. R. and Hill, D. A. (1996). Moving on: Autism and movement disturbance. *Mental Retardation*, 34(1), 39–53.

Murray, D., Lesser, M. and Lawson, W. (2005). Attention, monotropism and the diagnostic criteria for autism. *Autism*, 9(2), 139–156. doi:10.1177/1362361305051398.

Nagro, S. A., Fraser, D. W. and Hooks, S. D. (2019). Lesson planning with engagement in mind: Proactive classroom management strategies for curriculum instruction. *Intervention in School and Clinic*, 54(3), 131–140.

Nicoli, G., Pavon, G., Grayson, A., Emerson, A. Cortelazzo, M. and Mitra, S. (2023). Individuals with developmental disabilities make their own stylistic contributions to text written with physical facilitation. *Frontiers in Child and Adolescent Psychiatry*, 2. doi:10.3389/frcha.2023.1182884.

Petrone, R. and Stanton, C. R. (2021). From producing to reducing trauma: A call for 'traumainformed' research(ers) to interrogate how schools harm students. *Educational Researcher*, 50(8), 537–545. https://doi.org/10.3102/0013189X211014850

Rudasill, K. M., Snyder, K. E., Levinson, H. and Adelson, J. (2018). Systems view of school climate: A theoretical framework for research. *Educational Psychology Review*, 30(1), 35–60. https://doi.org/10.1007/s10648-017-9401-y

Sinha, P., Kjelgaard, M. M., Gandhi, T. K., Tsourides, K., Cardinaux, A. L., Pantazis, D., Diamond, S. P. and Held, R. M. (2014). Autism as a disorder of prediction. *Proceedings of the National Academy of Science*, 111, 15220–15225.

Wirthwein, L., Sparfeldt, J. R., Heyder, A. et al. (2020). Sex differences in achievement goals: Do school subjects matter? *European Journal of Psychology of Education*, 35, 403–427. https://doi.org/10.1007/s10212-019-00427-7

6
Supporting communication in the classroom

Introduction

In the previous chapters we considered fundamental attributes that lead to learning, i.e. attending, engaging and executive functions, all parts of every child's development. In this chapter we look at another key skill that determines learning and behaviour. Communication development interacts with our ability to attend, engage and utilise executive function (EF) skills. The direction of the relationship between EF and communication is not clear; however, it is theorised that development of both sets of skills go in tandem and interact with each other. Working memory and inhibitory control are thought to be essential for vocabulary development. When we hear language, we need to be able to focus on the relevant aspects and inhibit focus on less relevant aspects. Children with better inhibition ability are able to attend well enough to retain vocabulary and learn the rules of language. A child's 'inner speech' is utilised to support them in following an instruction or completing a task. Development and coordination of EF and communication skills mostly take place in pre-school years in typically developing students, meaning that they arrive in our classrooms with the requisite skills to learn. However, as discussed below, there are also many students who lack development in some or many aspects of communication, and their progress in these fields continues throughout their school career.

All pupils need strong communication skills, no matter what they decide to do after school. The World Economic Forum (2016) states that verbal skills are seen by employers as the top entry level skill graduates need in the workplace. This is in contrast to educator estimations, where teachers rate confidence as the most important life skill, with communication being less important (Cullinane and Montacute, 2017). Our schools frequently place insufficient emphasis on communication skills, unaware that they may be placing pupils at future disadvantage and limiting social mobility. We would better serve all pupils if they were supported with a strong foundation to enhance communication, ensuring they can effectively listen to others and work in teams, seek clarifications, make suggestions, offer and receive constructive criticism, negotiate and know how to use persuasive language.

Language is acquired by most of us without our awareness, and we probably can't remember much about the process. When we listen to a language that we don't know, it is often difficult to figure out where word and sentence boundaries are, yet we started this gradual seven-year process as babies. Researchers who have been trying to understand how humans manage this feat propose a number of theories. Firstly, Chomsky (in Palmer, 2000) suggested babies are born with an innate predisposition to acquire language, also referred to as the nativist approach. He theorised that our 'language acquisition device' is located within our brain and allows us to identify parts of speech, such as nouns or verbs, irrespective of what language we are brought up hearing, given that these elements are present in every language. This theory, unlike the 'behavioural' or 'learning theory', accounts for how children learn to use words they have never directly had experience of. Alternatively, learning theorists, such as Skinner (1986), believed that children are not born with any intrinsic 'language device' but only learn from experience. According to this theory, the baby will make random sounds, and the adult will respond to those that resemble words. The reinforcement of the response received to the sounds leads to turning these into words; however, this is generally considered to be inadequate as an explanation for all aspects of language acquisition. Vygotsky's (2012) explanation of language acquisition is that humans are born with a strong desire to communicate with others and that they develop language through the intrinsic motivation to interact and learn from 'more knowledgeable others', in other words, those who have already formed language and can act as a model and guide. Children's learning is active and cannot happen in isolation. Carers use particular ways of speaking to infants, termed 'motherese', that offer a simplified version adapted to the level of the child.

Although all theories have their critics, and Piaget (2002) proposed some differences in language acquisition to Vygotsky, we can see that a social process is part of language development and know that how we act and respond to our pupils will have emotional and cognitive impacts. Many factors are likely to influence the language acquisition of our pupils, including genetics, environment, neurological systems and emotional state.

Anyone with a communication difficulty or difference is at a disadvantage in our societies. Research has demonstrated that young children from economically disadvantaged families start school with less developed communication skills (Law et al., 2011), and that without additional support these differences carry on over the years. Statistics suggest that our classrooms include seven times the number of children with language disorders than other, arguably more recognised, developmental conditions such as autism (ICAN, n.d.). Despite this, in my experience and presumably due to the pressure on an already very full training curriculum, educators have had little instruction in the development of communication or how to identify anyone who is having difficulty in this respect. A national charity, Speech and Language UK, disseminates research and offers training to teachers about the communication of their pupils. Their work has highlighted rates of children in our schools who will have speech, language and communication needs (SLCN) as a primary difficulty, i.e. not one associated with another characteristic such as autism or Down's syndrome (DS). Research conducted in the UK indicated that over 50% of school starters in areas of social deprivation will have SLCN impacting their learning (Locke et al., 2002). Some of these pupils will gradually catch up with their peers, although probably missing out on learning as they do so, but 10% of children have persistent difficulties through secondary education and into adult life. Even where children's actual communication delay has resolved, earlier experiences can leave a lasting impact. This is a serious situation given that we know poor communication skills in adult life lead to a range of unwanted outcomes, including poor employment rates, increased mental ill-health and criminality. We also understand that, in the short term, there is a direct connection between lower levels of communication skills leading to poorer peer relationships, social rejection and unacceptable behaviour. Providing support as early in life as possible is therefore imperative; however, since teachers do not usually receive training in developmental language disorder children may not be identified and provided with special educational needs and disabilities (SEND) support.

Communication is the means for education to happen, primarily through children listening to speech or reading information. Knowledge is also acquired through visual stimuli and interaction, which also supports the understanding of other forms of input. Children also learn through talking and sharing their ideas, but attending to their educators will still take up much of their day, and as we have seen in previous chapters, giving full attention can be challenging for multiple reasons. Educators who maximise attention and engagement through enhancing their speech with visual input will significantly support their pupils. As a governor of a school, I sometimes go on 'learning walks' in empty classrooms to look at what I can understand about the experience of the pupils from what is in the room. Use of the space, the placement of furniture, and what is on the walls and available to interact with will be part of the meaning making process. The multiple modes of providing information offer a rich learning experience for the pupils. Educators frequently place emphasis on these aspects of their provision. However, perhaps less attention is given to how they use their spoken language to enhance meaning. Educators, understandably, might adapt their language to the age of their pupils by simplifying vocabulary, for example, but there is much more that could be done to assist those with speech, language and communication needs to enhance their inclusion. This chapter offers information about these needs and considers ways to provide support.

Communication as the foundation of learning

Our education systems are founded in the expectation that children can, and will, communicate. From their first day in school, children will be spoken to, given instructions, asked questions, and expected to remember their learning and carry it forward. In the early years, provision is made for children who do not immediately evidence these skills; a child who does not answer the teacher may be understood to be shy and given time to grow in confidence. However, it is imperative that these early signs of what might be an SLCN are identified. Early language is the most important factor in levels of literacy at age 11, and children's language skills at 5 years of age predict their reading and mathematics levels at age 7. There is evidence that language intervention at many different ages can support children in overcoming SLCN and making improved academic progress (Law et al., 2012). Despite the UK government inspection of schools service, OFSTED, placing priority on communication skills, a direct curriculum focus on these is only included in the early years. Therefore, in the UK, education policy is not effectively supporting educators to focus on communication development, and therefore doing a disservice to children and their teachers.

When students struggle with any aspect of communication, they can still learn, but the foundation of this learning may be unstable and untypical, i.e. they may find their way around a gap in ability and mask their difficulties. For example, children who have not fully understood may show a misconception. When this leads their peers to laugh at them, some children adopt this as a deliberate way of being funny, to deflect attention from their difficulty. Although in the short term this can allow a child to be successful in fitting in and meeting targets for their learning, in the long term their inherent areas of difficulty go unaddressed, and they don't get the support they need for a strong foundation for future learning. It can also shape their personality and self-perception. Sometimes, difficulties only start to become manifest in the later stages of education, where the coping strategies the child developed are not adequate to support them in more complex levels of learning. I see this at university level where students who have achieved good grades at school may seek learning support and be identified as being dyslexic or having attention deficit hyperactivity disorder (ADHD), for example. They often comment that they always thought they were different, had always struggled, but since they were also achieving academically, they had not sought help, or it had been denied. In an even more concerning example, research identifies two-thirds of young offenders in the criminal justice system as having SLCN, but only 5% of these had been identified before their offending began (Coles et al., 2017). Identifying children with communication difficulties as early as possible is therefore imperative to ensure that they are supported to learn in the most helpful way possible for them as an individual, and not left coping alone. Although parents obviously have a role to play, educators, with their broader experience of child development, are arguably in a better position to identify children who struggle with learning due to SLCN. Given that SLCN occur as one of the highest groups of occurrences in our schools, the knowledge and skills of educators in identifying need is crucial. What follows is a brief description of the sorts of needs that occur. Educators may choose to learn more about these through, for example, the online course offered by Speech and Language UK.

> Before continuing you may want to consider these questions:
>
> 1. Are you aware of the range of communication skills shown by the children you work with?
> 2. Do you notice communication difficulties, such as a child not following instructions, waiting so they can follow others, not being able to retell a simple story or telling a story from pictures? In older children, can you spot techniques students may use to cover up their difficulties?
> 3. What might you notice in your students that would suggest a difficulty with understanding or expressing themselves?

Aspects of communication

Speech

I start this section with speech, as it is the most immediately evident aspect of communication. For clarity, 'speech' in this context refers to the way in which words are said, or articulation, rather than the broader term referring to someone's ability to express themselves, which will incorporate additional elements. Articulation is the ability to make the sounds of speech clearly and distinctly. These sounds need to be combined within a system to make meaning. The sounds that comprise each language are not the only sounds that we can make as humans. Babies experiment with sound production and gradually reduce those they make to match those heard in the speech around them. Sounds vary across accents and dialects, but words are usually comprehensible to those who share the same language. As speech develops, sound production goes through a series of stages. Children's first words are often simplified, so a child might, for example, reduce a cluster of consonants to a single one, for example calling a swing 'wing'. Articulation is determined by neurological maturation, and we do not expect a child to have mastered all speech sounds, within connected speech, until the age of 7 years, although most children will have clear speech by the age of 5. There are differences that can occur in speech which are more individual. These can be minor changes to the way in which an 'r' or 's' is pronounced, as in what may be termed a lisp. Generally, people live with these differences without them significantly impacting their lives. At the other end of the spectrum are people whose speech is so unclear that others may struggle to understand them. This is mostly seen in young children, and can be part of typical development as a child matures neurologically and gains more control over their muscles and coordination. Children mature at different rates, so you might meet a 2-year-old who can articulate clearly, and a peer of the same age who can only be understood by close family.

When difficulties with articulation extend beyond the early years, and particularly as children start school, this can begin to affect their willingness to talk. When children meet multiple people who cannot understand what they are saying, they might start to refuse to repeat themselves, become shy or introverted, and lose confidence. It is at this point that they may receive some support from the speech and language therapy service, although where resources are scarce their impediments may not be categorised as severe, leading parents and educators to support their children as best they can.

Most children with unclear speech in their early years will improve, but the impact can still be long-lasting. Even where they do not remember the specifics, carrying the embarrassment or different treatment their difficulty caused them at the time can leave a shadow, particularly in terms of confidence in speaking in public. In addition, children who do not articulate clearly are disadvantaged when learning to read, potentially leading to a delay or protracted literacy difficulties.

Another aspect of speech, which will be immediately apparent to educators, is a child with dysfluency, such as a stammer. As with speech difficulties, stammering can occur as part of typical development, but if it endures it can become part of a child's identity and lead to negative self-perceptions. This is particularly the case if children are constantly made aware of their dysfluency, or are communicating with people who won't wait for them to complete their sentences. Current thinking about young children who stammer is that an indirect approach from parents may be effective, based on an understanding that stammering occurs when children's existing language ability does not enable them to express themselves the way they feel they need to. This pressure to communicate can come from the child's own desire, but often comes from the environment; therefore parents, and educators, may be able to offer a more supportive approach. This would include ensuring a relaxed and calm environment for talking, with adults modelling speaking slowly, taking turns and careful listening. Adults need to offer children opportunities to practise fluent talking during activities when they are relaxed and confident. It is really important that children are not criticised for the way they speak or made fun of.

Educators who wish to support a dysfluent pupil need to listen patiently, allow the child to complete what they are saying without rushing them and not comment on the stammer, or try to improve it. Show that you are interested in what they are saying and maintain eye contact. Although it can feel helpful to finish someone's sentences in the thought that it will reduce their frustration, this action can inadvertently lead to further irritation. Children with persistent dysfluency can be referred for assessment by a speech and language therapist (SALT) who may advise different actions for the child since the longer a stammer continues the more difficult it can be to treat it. Older children who stammer are at increasing risk of not wanting to speak, fearing that they will stammer and feel embarrassed. Educators can focus on building up general communication skills and the child's confidence in speaking.

Expressive language

Our use of the term 'language' can be ambiguous given that we use it both to refer to the language spoken by a particular group of people usually related to their country, but also the universal systems of words that convey meaning. In this chapter, the term 'language' refers to the system of vocabulary and grammar which people from a particular group share. What I say about language would be applicable to students speaking English, Hindi, Mandarin or any other mother tongue. Although languages can vary in grammatical structures, such as where a verb is placed in a sentence, the learning to acquire the established code in order to communicate is universal. Expressive language is therefore the term for the words, phrases and sentences that someone speaks in order to convey meaning. This can further be divided into terms from the study of linguistics, such as phonology and phonetics (speech sounds), morphology (word structure), semantics (words and meaning), syntax (structure) and pragmatics (context). Typically developing children go through a series of stages as they learn language. First words are generally nouns, with a few verbs. By the age of two we expect children to put two-word phrases together such as 'Mummy shoe', where the context might provide the actual meaning, e.g. 'this is Mummy's shoe', or 'Mummy put on your shoe so we can go out' or 'I want to put on Mummy's shoe'. At age 2 children are expected to use 150–300 words, although some of these may not be clearly articulated.

Parts of grammar such as plurals, past tenses, pronouns and prepositions start to be included and longer phrases constructed by age 3. Four-year-old children often practise their language skills through self-talk and show gradually increasing complexity until by the age of 5 we would expect them to incorporate adjectives and adverbs as parts of complex and grammatically correct sentences. Social functions of language become increasingly evident: 6-year-olds should be able to tell us stories that we can follow, and by 8 we expect conversation at adult level. Although children can communicate their feelings and needs from a very early age, pre-speech, the process of developing adult-level language is slow, meaning that children who encounter delays and difficulties in their early years may take time to catch up. It is generally accepted that there is a critical period for language development, and for children to develop they need to be hearing and absorbing language from before they are born. When children do not develop language during the typical stages, therefore, they are at risk of not developing in typical ways. However, progress in expressive skills can continue as children mature.

What educators need to look for is a child's ability to clearly explain themselves in the way that would be typical for their age. A word of caution: in areas of economic deprivation, such high numbers of students had SLCN that teachers' view of what might be expected at a particular age became inaccurate (The Communication Trust, 2017). They incorrectly assessed the most proficient as being above average, and those who were in fact falling behind as developing typically. Signs of an expressive language disorder, usually termed 'developmental language disorder', that educators can observe include children who have ideas that they want to express but who have difficulty saying what they want; appear to talk in sentences but are difficult for the adult to understand; use very limited vocabulary, perhaps repeatedly, and find it hard to remember the words they need; and are excluded by their peers in the playground as they struggle to join in play. Educators can watch out for children using words incorrectly or in the wrong order, missing verb endings or missing out words. More specifically, we may notice difficulties with verb use in young children, such as not using tense indicators and asking questions without 'be' or 'do' verbs, such as 'why he hit me?'

Selective mutism

Another communication difference that educators may encounter, occurring at a ratio of around 1:140 children (NHS, 2023), is what is termed selective mutism (SM). Children who speak confidently and fluently at home are not able to speak in outside settings, which can include school. This is generally considered to be an anxiety-based issue, and the term 'selective' is inaccurate since children are not choosing to not speak, or refusing, but rather are unable when pressured to do so. A more accurate term, as suggested by the charity SMiRA, which exists to inform parents and educators of the condition, is 'situational mutism'. Children's anxiety triggers a 'freeze' response, making speech impossible, and over time children may try to avoid situations that prompt this response. Children with SM may have other fears and social anxieties, including worrying about making errors, and will avoid drawing attention to themselves. Anxiety can present as children avoiding eating or drinking at school, as they cannot ask to go to the toilet, which sometimes leads to urinary infections. They may struggle with academic work, as they are unable to ask questions for clarification. Older children may not develop independence, as they don't want to enter situations alone where they may need to speak.

There is no known cause for SM. It affects girls more frequently than boys and can be seen at higher rates in children who are being educated outside their country of birth, or who have other forms of communication difficulty. It is usually first seen between the ages of 2 and 4 as children start to encounter social situations. An early sign, which separates SM from shyness, is seeing the child become very still with a frozen expression on their face. They are likely to appear nervous but also might be taken as being rude or disinterested. They might cling to familiar adults or become upset and aggressive, particularly on return from school having experienced fear and anxiety throughout their day. Some children with SM may be confident enough to use gestures or signs, or whisper, in school for communication, but others might avoid this and even refuse to write. It is imperative the SM is identified early; the longer it continues unsupported, the higher the risk that it will continue into adulthood or become a social anxiety disorder. In my university teaching experience, I have had two women in my classes who were still selectively mute and would never participate in class. A further student, when taught about SM, realised for the first time that this was what she had had as a child.

Schools and families need to work together and not assume that this is a shy child who will grow out of it if we wait. Educators need to remove all pressure from the person to speak to increase their feelings of safety at school. A supportive educational environment for a child with SM is one that avoids adults expressing anxiety, focuses on relaxed interactions and fun, ensures the child they will speak when they are ready and rewards them for any interaction. If a child does interact, respond in a gentle way, as you would for any child, avoiding too much praise or excitement. You might also have a quiet word with them afterwards to say how well they did. Educators will also need to seek support from a SALT or educational psychologist to ensure that children receive the support they need at the appropriate time.

Bilingualism

I want to add a note here on bilingualism as, despite clarity from research studies (Fibla et al., 2022), understanding of how best to support children who come into contact with multiple languages, beliefs and practices differs widely. Children who learn to speak more than one language in infancy have multiple advantages as they get older, yet many parents are still concerned about using more than one language, for fear of confusing or delaying the child. These concerns are highlighted when they know children growing up bilingual whose language development appears initially to be behind that of their monolingual peers. When this delay occurs, it is generally temporary and appears to signal a time when the child is making sense of multiple languages. Progress then develops well, and children who are bi- or multilingual learn other languages with greater alacrity than their monolingual peers. Children who speak more than one language are in a majority across the world; and they are thought to have advantages in executive functions, including attention span and flexible thinking, although the evidence for this is unclear (Gunnerud et al., 2020). The theory about this advantage is that the practice gained from needing to inhibit one language while communicating in another strengthens executive function skills. In early years, children may muddle their languages, using words from more than one language in a sentence, referred to as code switching. This is a normal part of development and not a cause for concern; in fact, it is usual practice with multilingual people.

Chomsky's theory of language development, mentioned in the introduction, suggests that the critical period for learning language lasts up to around the age of 8 years. More recent research suggests the aptitude for learning languages may last longer but still decline as we age (Hartshorne et al., 2018). Therefore, learning multiple languages simultaneously may be better than waiting until the first is fully developed and then trying to acquire another. Although, obviously, this is still possible, it is a harder task and likely to involve learning in a different way, with a different representation within the brain.

Bi- or multilingual children can still have communication impairments, which means that educators need to be careful with assumptions they might make about a child who is not speaking English well, ascribing this as due to a language acquisition difficulty. Educators can look out for children who have difficulty learning new words and talk to parents about how the child functions in their home language. Children learning more than one language may need support with acquisition of vocabulary for the curriculum since they are learning a greater number of words than their monolingual peers. Multilingual children may go through a period of adjustment where they do not talk in school; however, they would be expected to partake in activities. Only if the silence goes on for a long time, and impacts their anxiety, should concerns be indicated.

Understanding

In order for effective communication to take place, one person must express themselves and their communication partner needs to 'receive' the message, to understand. Understanding is referred to as receptive language or comprehension, not to be confused with reading comprehension. In parallel with the development of expressive language, children gradually acquire understanding through their early years, although typically comprehension will be in advance of expression. Children need to understand the meaning of words before they can go on to use them with appropriate meaning.

The developmental progression of comprehension can be seen from very early in the child's life. At around 6 months of age children will respond to their name and their parents' emotional tone of voice. Using 'no' firmly with a very young child can reduce them to tears. Initially what we can observe about a child's understanding may be limited by their motor skills, but they may turn their eyes or head to look at something we indicate. We expect that by the age of 1 year they will show understanding of the social value of speech, enjoying interacting with others even without words. Between 18 months and 2 years children will usually start to follow simple instructions, such as 'clap hands' or 'show me your eyes', especially when these have been practised or are part of a routine. We can expect children to answer questions or tell us something they have been doing around the age of 3, and this ability gradually increases with following more complex language, so that by the time they enter school they can follow instructions with up to three parts.

Whereas expressive difficulties in terms of speech or language may be relatively easy to identify, comprehension difficulties among many children go undetected for many years. Children are frequently adept at covering up lack of understanding. In a classroom they can wait and watch what their peers do. They may be quiet or withdrawn, avoiding interaction, or they may act as the class clown, making people laugh to hide their embarrassment. Signs of a receptive language difficulty will include children who are poor listeners, seem forgetful or slow to respond, who cannot settle to do their work, those who provide an answer that does not fully match the question asked or fail to follow instructions. Educators may observe children who struggle to play with their peers, or have difficulty following the rules of a game or negotiating with their friends. Children who are finding it hard to understand may avoid doing their work, stare into space or fail to complete tasks. One of the biggest tactics that children will use is to watch what others are doing and copy actions and the work of others. Children may also become distressed, going very quiet or getting angry due to their frustrations at not understanding. Teachers might experience explaining something to a child, who appears to listen and understand, but the work they produce does not match what was requested.

Prosody

The way in which people speak also has a code that is typical to each language spoken, involving intonation, stress or emphasis, pauses and rhythm. Prosody also includes speed of speech, pitch and volume. These are used to clarify the meaning of the words and sentences, with stress usually being placed on the words that are key to our message. One example of where stress is placed would be the sentence 'many people are unhappy', with the stress on 'many' suggesting a comment about number, while the stress on 'unhappy' emphasises the emotion. Stress within a word is also important to signal meaning, such as in the word 'object'. When said with the first syllable stressed, it would refer to an item, while stress on the second syllable would mean an objection. These differences can pose challenges when we try to acquire a new language.

A rising intonation pattern usually indicates a question in English, but is a more common pattern when Australians speak. Our understanding of what someone is saying is impacted by stress and intonation; if you listen to someone with a foreign accent reading English, errors of stress and intonation may make the text difficult to follow. Think of how many ways there are to say the word 'no' to indicate a negative, surprise, disbelief, anger, as an instruction or a question. The intonation someone uses will often tell us something about their mood or their attitude to the topic being discussed. The prosody we use can help our learners to understand meaning. For example, when teaching opposites, such as 'loud' and 'quiet', we are likely to match the way we say each word to its meaning. There is research evidence that suggests that prosody can support memory (Mandel et al., 1994). As with every other aspect of language, children will acquire what is typical for their linguistic code from being immersed in a language-rich environment. Adults will typically model and teach children to use the appropriate intonation and how to 'listen' for the hidden meanings in what someone says. Educators may highlight meaning in what they say by asking children to reflect on their tone, asking, for example, 'do I sound happy?' This offers crucial learning to children to understand others and regulate their own speech.

Further support to meaning comes from what are called 'paralinguistic features' of speech, or 'non-verbal' behaviour. The posture of the talker or listener will convey enthusiasm or boredom. Use of gestures can show excitement or dismissal and facial expressions give additional meaning. All of these features can agree with, or contradict, the essence of the words we are speaking.

Some children can articulate clearly, and form and understand grammatical sentences, yet have unusual use of prosodic features. Deaf children may struggle, as they do not have auditory feedback to help them mirror and match what they hear around them. Autistic children may show differences in how they speak, which can contribute to a perception of them being odd or unusual or even make their meaning difficult to follow. They may speak in a monotone, appearing lacking in interest or animation.

Pragmatics

Pragmatic language includes a set of skills that allow us to adapt the way we speak according to the situation and needs of the listener, use language for varying purposes, follow rules for conversations, including turn-taking, and understand language holistically, such as beyond the literal meaning. Understanding what someone intends to communicate when they speak generally requires familiarity with or knowledge of the context. Pragmatics is the study of what is intended, even if not specifically explained; the ability to use language effectively in interactions. The earlier example of a young child saying 'Mummy shoe' is one where knowledge of the child and the context would allow the listener to guess and clarify the meaning. Even where people use full speech there is frequently a sub-text which may be missed by people unfamiliar with context. We understand that we need to be more precise with our use of words, and provide more detail in some settings than in others. With a close friend, just a short phrase could indicate what would require several sentences with someone we don't know. Ambiguity can occur in communication, which is reduced by context. Some words have multiple meanings. For instance, they can be used to good effect in jokes such as 'what jam can't you put on toast? A traffic jam'. Factors that help to resolve ambiguity are contextual, e.g. knowing who the speakers are and the place and time of what is said. The words 'I love you' might be spoken within a committed relationship, but also by someone to a stranger who has just given them valuable information, or sarcastically by someone unhappy with a friend who has let them down. Playwrights and screenwriters need to provide the contextual information for actors to understand the intention behind the words.

Social acceptability might make us speak in a way that does not directly convey our meaning. An educator saying to a student 'I wonder when you will sit down?' is not looking for an answer but rather a behavioural response. Saying to a class 'I think it's time for quiet now' is actually an instruction rather than sharing of an idea. The relative directness of language will vary across social groups, ages, settings and nationalities. Gaining understanding of anything that someone says is rarely as simple as comprehending the words. Educators in early years classes are likely to use more simple and direct language, clearly indicating something as an instruction, perhaps even warning the class to attend because they are about to be given one, in recognition of the more basic pragmatic awareness of their pupils. Good practice when supporting people with SLCN, or who are additional language learners, or even in helping older learners to focus, is to continue this regardless of pupil age. Rather than expecting our audience to be able to utilise context to reduce ambiguity and decipher unexpressed meaning, we can ensure that our communication is specific. Working with students from across the world, I have adopted a practice of explaining the sorts of utterances they will come across, such as culturally specific idioms and metaphors, as I use them. This helps to build meaning and would be good practice for younger learners, too. Educators don't necessarily need to change their customary way of expressing themselves, although avoiding sarcasm or too many obscure phrases is always helpful, but they do need to check the understanding of their pupils rather than assuming it has been conveyed. This practice is particularly helpful for all neurodivergent pupils and especially autistic students.

Another aspect of what is usual in communication are the cultural norms around, for example, holding eye gaze as we speak, the force or intensity of our speech, and appropriate volume and tone for a given situation. These are aspects that children typically learn throughout their early school years, particularly since school may have different expectations of them than their home; hence children being reminded to 'use their inside voice' (meaning not to shout).

Children with communication difficulties, including those who are autistic or who have cognitive impairments, may have particular difficulties with pragmatic features, even where they use other aspects of language well. We saw, in Chapter 3, how the sort of pointing that autistic infants engage in can be different to typically developing peers, and this is related to pragmatics. The profile of an autistic child is very likely to include difficulty with understanding non-literal language and making inferences from what someone has said. This sort of difficulty tends to become more apparent as children get older and the nuance of social language uses increase. I was very surprised to see an autistic child I knew well dribbling in a way I hadn't seen before. I asked him why he was dribbling and with a mouth full of saliva he said he wasn't. I asked if he could swallow, and he said 'smoking kills'. As we were standing near an open fire at the time I realised that he was afraid to take in the smoke, so had stopped swallowing, in accordance with his literal interpretation of the phrase.

Whereas most of us learn and adapt to rules of conversation through experience, autistic children often have a particular difficulty picking up this learning. Culturally specific 'hidden' rules and social expectations can therefore be confusing to autistic children, resulting in challenges across the lifespan. In addition, autistic children may struggle with turn-taking, knowing what an appropriate topic is to discuss or how long to talk for. Together with another aspect of autism for some people, a difficulty with 'theory of mind', i.e. knowing that people can see the world differently to ourselves, children may not understand other people's perspectives or be able to structure narratives. They may make errors with knowing what needs to be explained or left out. It is often these difficulties that make an autistic person stand out and negatively impact their peer relationships. I witnessed a boy of 10 years walk into his classroom where he saw an unfamiliar teacher. He loudly exclaimed, 'my teacher has gone and been replaced by an old lady'. His classmates gasped, fearing that he would be told off, and knowing this would be devastating for him. The teacher started to turn around as if to admonish such a rude pupil, and then presumably remembered having been told about the boy and instead introduced herself. The boy was not intending to be rude; he was just stating what he saw, and unaware that what he said could be offensive.

Before moving to the next section, you may find it helpful to reflect on the following:

1. How do you tend to respond when a child shows difficulty communicating?
2. To what extent are communication skills emphasised in the setting you work in?
3. Are there situations where children are pressurised to communicate?
4. To what extent do you accommodate for communication difficulties by enabling children to show their ideas in alternative ways to speech or writing?
5. Can you think of ways of supporting students to gain self-insight into their own communication strengths?

Language and literacy

Typical development

In typical development, people gain their language skills before learning to read and spell. Literacy skills include recognising words, decoding unfamiliar words, speed of processing, accuracy and taking in meaning. These facets need to work together seamlessly within a system to be an effective reader, and a difficulty with any one of them can impact others, and ultimately impact not only literacy acquisition but classroom learning. The time at which children are expected to learn to read varies greatly across nations. In the UK we have one of the earliest starts, with children as young as 3 being given basic reading instruction, with the expectation they will start formal literacy when they start school. This can disadvantage children who naturally mature more slowly in terms of the processing of sound, meaning they may start to fall behind their peers as soon as they start school. Other countries focus on play-based learning for longer, with literacy not being introduced until the age of 6. In Finland, children start at 7 and score higher than UK students at age 15. Our systems for teaching reading rely on giving children a way of representing the language they have already acquired. We expect that they know the sounds of a word (phonemic awareness) in order to make the link between this and the written representation.

For children with speech difficulties, as outlined above, identifying sounds in words can be difficult, which impacts their ability to relate them to letters. This 'auditory processing difficulty' is one reason for literacy difficulties children encounter and is sometimes considered an aspect of dyslexia. Young children with good phonemic awareness will be able to recognise, analyse and interpret what they hear, being able to separate connected speech into words and syllables (phonological awareness). For children having to focus much of their cognitive processing on deciphering individual sounds within words this can detract from meaning making. By the time a child has gone through the process of decoding a written word into sounds, they may have lost the sense of what they previously processed. This makes gaining meaning from text a considerable challenge.

Emergent literacy

The view that literacy is acquired after language is seen as disadvantaging non-typical learners with communication impairments. An alternative school of thought is that children who have not developed speech, or language, may still be able to access literacy, and in fact this may support the development of communication skills. Although 'literacy' frequently refers to the practice of reading, writing and spelling, the skills associated with it are much wider. Early literacy teaching involves the use of visual images, since 'reading' these, i.e. making sense of them and starting to create stories about what they see, is a support for typical literacy development. The ability to interpret what is happening in an image is not automatic; it has to be learned, as we know from studies of autistic children who sometimes process images differently. We can look at any image either as a whole, which contributes to meaning or a story, or we can look at individual components and perhaps not 'read' or interpret the entire image as intended. Emergent literacy suggests that there are many pre-stages to reading that we can focus on to support learning. With some pupils we may need to specifically address how to take in all the relevant information in an image in order to gain its meaning. There has been little focus in research on whether children with learning disabilities learn to read, or how best to teach them. There is a view that they have been denied 'literacy citizenship' (Kliewer et al., 2006), whereas our schools should support 'literacy for all'. Keefe and Copeland (2012) suggested that the way we define literacy affects what we teach; it can be seen as a relatively narrow traditional skill or through an expanded view to include pictures and symbols. Contemporary society incorporates multiple literacies accessed through a range of media.

Teachers will have the power to decide on the access to literacy that their children with severe learning difficulties get.

> Understanding how teachers think about curriculum, and literacy in particular, is important because teachers' conceptualizations about disability, the nature of learning, and the purpose of teaching reading, writing, and communication result in teaching practices that can expand or contract the future quality of life of students.
>
> (Ruppar et al., 2015, p. 209).

Teachers are likely to be influenced in their practice by both their personal beliefs and the workplace culture. Even if, in our estimation, a student does not have the potential to acquire literacy skills, it is important that we allow them to start on this journey. This is their right, and something that could allow them some functional skill, along with raised status from their learning. Being able to read is prized in society, and those who are unable to do so face discrimination and exclusion, as well as feelings of shame. Historically, there has been an attitude that a focus on literacy for students with the most challenging learning differences would be an incorrect approach, denying them the opportunity to learn self-help skills that would have a greater impact on their lives. Happily, this attitude has been replaced with greater awareness that the possibility of some level of literacy would make enough of a difference to quality of life to be worth the investment of time.

We also need to consider symbolic representation here. Real objects, and images, have almost unlimited styles of representation. For example, a chair will vary in size, shape, colour, material and functionality. We have to learn that all of these different four-legged (usually) items come within the same category. The word 'chair' can also be written in many different ways, print may be different sizes and styles, handwriting individual and characteristic. However, 'chair' is always spelt the same way, and representations of this that are in a plain printed font will all look more similar to each other than images. We might make the assumption that children learn better from images, but this may not always be the case. The stability of the written word can offer a greater opportunity for learning to pupils with visual processing challenges. We will only find this out through assessment or experimentation, and we will only offer this opportunity if we think of it as a possibility. As a general approach, providing a printed word alongside an image is good classroom practice. It may help recognition and sight word learning simultaneously.

Letters are a form of symbol, as are images. They represent something in the real world. In an attempt to support the literacy development of groups of children who find the alphabet too difficult, symbol systems were developed to be more systematic and representative than our random alphabet shapes. To support accessibility, symbols should have high iconicity, i.e. they should look as much as possible like the meaning they represent. Many children with SEND will be given access to symbol systems to support them with their communication barriers. As before, good practice is to accompany symbols with the written word. Not only does this help other people who have not learned the symbols to understand what a child might be indicating, but also gives the child a chance to learn the written representation. One of the limitations with learning through symbols, or through sign language, is that these are not universally understood, and all children are more likely to experience general inclusion if they can take in written information in the same way as their peers.

Symbols are present in most environments, often as logos advertising companies, or as instructions for drivers or warnings of potential hazards. Many children, regardless of their ability to read, will recognise the symbol for their favourite eateries from an early age. This gives us a clue as to how to teach, i.e. frequent exposure and motivation. A child who is looking out of the bus window on their way to eat their favourite food may feel animated and excited, which feeds their motivation and stimulates them to process and recognise. Our classrooms may not always be able to replicate this level of excitement, but there is much to do to mirror these learning opportunities.

Acquiring literacy skills, or finding them challenging, will impact learners' self-concept. Dyslexic people are particularly disadvantaged in a society that relies heavily on the written word. For many years dyslexia was not accepted as an actual disorder and people were negatively perceived, and took on board the message that their literacy difficulties arose from their lack of intelligence, or laziness in learning. How a dyslexic person sees themselves can impact their self-concept. We want to avoid children thinking that they have a deficit that cannot be fixed. Learners who view dyslexia as a learning difference recognise the positive and negative aspects of their skills, which enables them to take positive steps towards managing their literacy difficulties.

The shame resulting from dyslexia, particularly when it was not recognised by educators, can be lifelong, impacting how comfortable people feel in school and in society. People who struggle with literacy may be constantly anticipating a situation where they will be required to read or write and experience the associated anxiety. Dyslexia can also affect other areas of functioning, meaning that planning and organising skills are more challenging. A long-distance lorry driver had many difficulties at work because of his struggle to follow directions, due to dyslexia. His frustration with his challenges, and the effort of constantly covering up his difficulties, led to him being volatile and aggressive and eventually he lost his job. Not being able to earn a living enforced his feelings of shame and embarrassment and he became depressed, with high levels of anxiety. He dwelt on the treatment of his primary school teacher who called him 'thick' and told him he would amount to nothing. He had frequently run away from school, missing crucial learning. The lack of understanding of the nature of his difficulties led to lifelong shame and humiliation.

A former student of mine, who had been more successful at school and became an English teacher, wrote about her experience under the title 'I can't read like a grown up'. She explained that she had not been able to read a complete book independently until she was 25 years old. However, she had filled her shelves with books to hide her reading difficulty and make her look intelligent. She encounters a great deal of surprise from colleagues that she is both an English teacher and dyslexic, with a slow reading pace, which she finds hurtful. Their responses bring up feelings of embarrassment and shame. She has strategies to support her with her literacy difficulties, but not to support her with people who make her feel worthless for something outside her control. She then doubts her right to be a teacher. Her perspective is that parents of dyslexic pupils tend to blame themselves or poor teaching. Teachers are pressured by the poor grades of a pupil and blame the system for lack of support. Pupils are then taught to blame, but if they blame dyslexia for their difficulties they can be seen as using it as an excuse, or a crutch. Parents sometimes resist diagnosis of a learning difference in their child for fear that it will prevent the child from making effort in their learning.

Areas of difficulty with communication

Unfortunately, all the aspects of communication outlined above can pose difficulties for children and their educators. In terms of 'primary' communication difficulties, children can have speech, expressive language, comprehension, and pragmatic skill delay or disorder, or a combination of any of these. Delay refers to children who are typically developing in terms of the order of their acquisition but are behind their peers. Very often these children will ultimately catch up, but the initial delay frequently causes long-term difficulties. Our education systems move so fast and initial skills are taught early and then built upon. Children who miss out on gaining a basic skill such as meaning making from an image will be impacted on all subsequent learning. Even where skill development is subsequently supported and successful, emotional difficulties may follow into adulthood. What we experience as children, particularly when negative, can stay with us, even if we are not always conscious of this or what the origin is.

The term 'disorder' refers to someone who is not developing typically; their profile may show areas of ability alongside gaps. A disorder does not generally disappear with time and may require specialist support and teaching. What is imperative is that we identify our students as having intrinsic, or extrinsic, barriers to learning as early as possible, in order to put support in place and protect them from the negative emotional consequences of issues that are not of their choosing or making.

Impact of communication difficulties

As already noted, the impact of a communication difficulty can be all-pervasive and life-lasting. You may know someone you think would make an excellent presentation, but when you approach them they are horrified at the thought and tell you that there is no way they would put themselves into the position of public exposure. This frequently stems from a time when they made an error in class and were laughed at or made to read out loud in class when they were not confident or fluent. Very sadly our prisons and young offender institutions include very high numbers of people who struggled with

Supporting communication in the classroom

communication and/or literacy in school, many of whom were not identified with these difficulties at the time. The shame, lack of confidence, negative self-image and missed learning can all lead to someone leaving school with no or few qualifications, leading to reduced opportunities to make a living. The feelings of failure and of public shaming often lead children to be angry and defiant, which further impacts their opportunities. Another sector where I have encountered large groups of people with a history of learning disabilities, and particularly late-recognised dyslexia, is within social care staff. Many residential social workers went into care work as something they could do without many qualifications. They frequently offer fantastic support to those they care for, but in my experience also express a lack of self-confidence, which does not match their skills.

It is imperative that schools identify children who are not proficient with communication and literacy as early as possible in order to limit the long-term damage that can occur. In the UK few children receive an assessment for dyslexia before the age of 7, yet there is much that schools could do to support emergent literacy prior to this time. Special schools who provide education to many children who may never develop proficient reading still do much in terms of symbol recognition and meaning making. Our education systems need to continue to encourage children in their efforts, measuring progress in small steps and celebrating the effort they put into learning.

To help you consider the children you support, reflect on these questions:

1. Are you aware of any children who are reluctant communicators, and do you think this could be in order to cover up difficulties?
2. Do you work with a pupil you think routinely avoids interaction with you or who appears to struggle with peer relationships?
3. What support is given to struggling readers in your setting, and to what extent does this seek to build confidence and self-belief?

Ben: Acquired difficulties

Ben's childhood was proceeding happily; he was the older of two boys, lived with both parents and loved playing outside with friends in his village. He enjoyed school and was showing above-average abilities in science in particular. His father was an engineer who liked to make things in his workshop at weekends and Ben would join him, learning to use a range of tools. He was confident, sociable and outgoing. When he was 9 years old, he contracted meningitis and was seriously ill. He was hospitalized for many weeks and missed half a year of schooling while he recovered. Immediately after the illness, he showed difficulties with physical coordination, his speech was unclear and he found it difficult to understand and retain what people told him. His parents were severely shocked, having thought at one point that they might lose him, and now experiencing a different child to before the illness.

Over the months following his hospitalisation Ben gradually improved his physical skills to some extent, although he could no longer run or use his dad's tools safely. His speech and language became more comprehensible, but Ben remained reluctant to talk in front of anyone outside his immediate family. Once he was deemed ready to return to school his teachers and classmates welcomed him with excitement. At first, he could not manage a full day, so he had a phased re-entry and over the weeks gradually increased his length of attendance. However, fatigue remained a huge difficulty for Ben: as the week went on, he would be increasingly lethargic and had no energy for the playground. He stopped wanting to go out after school to join his friends, feeling too tired and preferring to be at home watching TV.

Ben had missed a lot of content while he was away from school, and this was compounded on his return, as he found concentration difficult for more than a few minutes at a time. This was particularly the case if there was a lot of noise or movement in the classroom. When he returned to school, he was given full-time support from a teaching assistant (TA). Ben's teacher adapted his work, structuring it to avoid having to use working memory or attempt multiple aspects of a task at the same time. Ben would appear to have understood a topic, but would not retain what he had learned, leading to frustration. Whereas Ben had learned to read smoothly and had grasped many mathematical concepts before his illness, he now had reduced spatial awareness, not always remembering to read from left to right, and often confused letters or numbers.

As Ben struggled to re-adapt to school, he became increasingly withdrawn. He felt anxious about his abilities and increasingly reluctant to try in case he failed. He found it hard to express what he was feeling, his language skills were more basic than they had been and he found sustained attention difficult. When people around him conversed at normal speed he couldn't follow, became lost and distressed. Although his peers were kind to him, and sympathetic, he was no longer an active playmate, and he couldn't keep up with their pace.

The whole family were affected by Ben's illness and subsequent disability. His brother had reduced attention from their parents who needed to devote more time to Ben. They were enormously concerned about his mood, seeing him experience loss of confidence, listlessness and anxiety. They had to try to compensate for the loss of his friends and social life, always looking for ways to support his recovery and seeking useful occupation. In their frustration and grief, they placed pressure on his school to do as much as possible for Ben, knowing that he had little time left in primary education and fearful about his secondary school placement. Ben's school, which was already doing as much as they felt able to support Ben's learning, found the parental demands unrealistic and unreasonable.

By the time that Ben was in his final year at school his recovery had continued but it was also fairly certain that he would have long-lasting disabilities. Efforts then turned to developing strategies to help him with his areas of difficulty. Time management was an area he needed support with to help him monitor his tiredness levels and plan to do the work that required the greatest levels of concentration early in the day and towards the start of the week. Ben was taught to monitor and communicate his energy level and allowed control over when he might tackle a task. His teacher and TA had to plan his work in advance in order to give him extra time to complete it. They also instituted daily routines and gave visual support to all instructions. They ensured that Ben was able to give his full attention before any instruction was provided. They allowed Ben to work at a slower pace and removed any unnecessary aspects to what he needed to do, such as copying from the board. His TA supported him throughout every day with organisation. Their understanding of his memory problems meant they were willing to repeat information as much as possible. They recorded short videos containing key concepts that he would watch at the start of activities to help cue him into prior learning. They provided Ben with a workstation that removed many of the distractions in the class and encouraged the other pupils to work quietly. Ben was encouraged to take regular short breaks between activities, including getting up and moving around the classroom. They encouraged Ben to take an active role in group activities, often assigning roles to each member of the group to ensure children could work to their strengths.

At the school's suggestion Ben's parents practised memory games, along with his brother. From joining an acquired brain injury (ABI) support group, they learned about the need for increased amounts of practice, but managed this through games, fun activities and regular family tasks. Understanding that meningitis can lead to sensory impairment, particularly hearing and visual difficulties, with a risk of muscle weakness or even limb loss, they were relieved that Ben did not experience these outcomes. However, they were anxious to know that some children experience epilepsy following ABI, and ideally monitoring of their progress and difficulties would be ongoing throughout their schooling. They helped him with homework at the weekends but also ensured that he had fun and time for rest. Ben's parents understood that although he needed a lot of support with organisation, and it was much easier to do things for him than to wait for him to think through a task, that he also needed to develop independent skills with strategies to manage all situations. They gave him a checklist to complete his morning routine on a laminated board and encouraged him to follow it every day. They monitored his energy levels and saw that on a good day Ben would tend to overdo things, leading to 'bad days' where he could hardly function and would become irritable and distressed. They made regular time for relaxation and encouraged Ben to join his mother in her yoga routine.

Ben's parents sourced an adapted game controller to enable him to play computer games. He practised with his brother and then started to invite some of his peers home to play with him after school. He found that he could cope fairly well with having just one friend with him at a time, and the shared focus on the game meant that he did not need to talk much. He began to relax in the company of a small number of friends and family, gradually building his confidence. His father also engaged him in using software for design, taking the place of the physical making of objects, although he also found ways to include Ben in the workshop, despite his reduced coordination.

Ben's difficulties were such that they were easily apparent to his parents and educators, as well as to himself. However, large numbers of pupils who experience acquired brain injury have difficulties that are subtle and remain unidentified, i.e. a 'hidden disability'. They may return to school appearing to be much as they did before. Research estimates that around 1 child in every class in UK classrooms will have experienced an ABI, through accident, injury or illness, by the time they leave school (The Children's Trust, n.d.). Although many of these pupils will not experience long-term issues, educators need to be aware of the potential for impact. Affected children are likely to experience impact in all four areas of special need, i.e. communication and interaction; cognition and learning; social, emotional and mental health difficulties; and sensory and/or physical needs. Some difficulties will only emerge over time as the brain develops. A frequent experience is that different parts of the brain have greater difficulty coordinating meaning, that messages are passed less successfully across the brain and that processing meaning takes longer. Since children's brains do not mature for 20 years or more, having a head injury or illness that causes damage also disrupts development. There is no clear pattern of difficulty that we can look for and signs of the damage may not become apparent until months or years after the injury. Difficulties can be slight and specific, meaning that they only become apparent as cognitive demands increase with level of schooling. Educators can look out for difficulties with memory, concentration and planning.

Rather than becoming withdrawn like Ben, students with ABI may become impulsive and aggressive, showing disconcerting changes in behaviour and personality. If schools are unaware of a head injury, they may put this down to disobedience, and the typical fatigue that is experienced to laziness. It is imperative that schools identify areas of difficulty a child is having, both in order to put appropriate strategies in place and to provide emotional support. Since children's behaviour can appear as unusual, or unfriendly, they can also become the victim of bullying. Children with ABI are at higher risk for mental health disorders, including depression as they get older, perhaps due to frustration at unacknowledged challenges. Many educators know little about ABI; however, a focus on understanding the EF skills of all students would promote the provision of effective support to pupils such as Ben, even where ABI goes unidentified.

How to support communication – the MORE model

In 2013 Jackie Dearden and I published a paper outlining our approach to supporting students with communication impairments. We built this mainly from work with non- or minimally verbal autistic individuals, but the principles apply to anyone, including those who may already communicate quite well. Based on the work of Money and Thurman (1994), the MORE model divides communication into four aspects to help us locate where and how we can best intervene and support, further elaborated below. For effective communication everyone must first have a 'means', a way in which they get their message across. Second, they need to have opportunities to practise their communication skills, whether these are self-sought or offered by another person. Motivation is then a key factor; people may not push themselves to communicate, where it is a challenge, without a good reason. These three factors were part of the original model, but when we worked with these it occurred to us that another element was needed. Our work with very hard-to-reach children led us to add the 'E' in MORE: expectations. This aspect, encompassing our perceptions and assumptions of people, influences what we see as means; how we offer opportunities and help people find reasons.

Means

Effective communicators typically speak, or write, in clear and comprehensive language, following the norms for their culture. However, there are many other ways to communicate. Think of good friends who spend a lot of time together. All they may need to establish mutual understanding is a glance or gesture. Much of what is vocal is actually sounds rather than words; we 'hold space' in a conversation by using 'umm', for example. Our intonation patterns convey meaning, while much of the emotion of an utterance is shown by the prosodic features, such as speed, intensity, volume. There is an engaging children's television programme called Pingu, about a penguin who communicates through sounds, which, along with the context, we can interpret as having meaning.

We use lots of gesture, both when listening and when talking. We can dismiss ideas with a flick of the eyes or hand, show that we are joking with our eyebrows or a wink. To be seen as a highly effective communicator we need to be flexible to incorporate the appropriate movements, sounds and words for every specific situation. Many educators will talk differently to their class than their friends and adapt according to the age of their pupils. We need to hold in mind the possible impact of anything we say, both for ourselves and our listeners. As we are communicating, we are making endless subconscious and subtle interventions, most of which add to a holistic meaning. On occasion, all of us 'slip up', use an inappropriate tone or speak more harshly than we intend, which requires another form of communication – the apology. This poses both challenges and barriers to people with SLCN. If they struggle to combine all these multiple elements, it may lead to perceptions of their ability in other areas. For example, someone who speaks in a monotone may appear miserable, depressed or lacking in interest or ability. An autistic person who has mastered language may still be misunderstood if their intonation or rate of speech seems strange to the listener. People with Down's syndrome who struggle with making clear speech sounds may tend to speak less, conserving energy and improving clarity but then appearing language-impaired and not always demonstrating their ability. On the other hand, since meaning can be conveyed by many aspects of communication some people can make themselves understood despite difficulties in one area. An experience most of us will have had is an exchange with someone speaking a language we are not familiar with. Using a mix of pointing, facial expressions, sounds of agreement or denial, we might grasp that they are asking us for directions, the time or wanting to know where they can buy something. We are generally good at making interpretations and checking our understanding and reinterpreting if we have guessed incorrectly.

Young children are almost always keen to communicate, but, as already discussed, those who are not easily understood may be prone to negative outcomes. We need to remain responsive to all aspects of someone's behaviour, seeing this as communication and responding positively to it. In my view, it is better to offer a comment such as 'I can see that you are trying to tell me something, but I haven't understood it yet', than to pretend you have understood in order to complete the interaction. Ideally this would be followed by efforts to find alternative means to establish their message.

The field of Augmentative and Alternative Communication (AAC) offers ways to support those who may not speak or form sentences well. I have already mentioned symbols, and sign language, which are both facets of AAC. When we augment communication, we might still be using the spoken word but adding support for us or the person to understand, such as captioning on a screen when someone has a heavy accent we may not be familiar with. You may be familiar with someone with hearing impairment who speaks; their words have variable degrees of clarity, as they do not have the auditory feedback loop to support their precision, so they may also use sign or informal gesture. Alternative communication is aimed at people with minimal or no spoken language. It may comprise basic picture boards, or books of symbols that a child can point to, usually organised by theme, but can also be complex systems utilising technology. Communication aids are usually organised into a sort of system with teaching stages to support learning.

Whatever system someone is using to communicate, the role of their communication partner is vital. In all communication the person receiving the message needs to be active, as a listener, observer, interpreter, checker and repairer. We need to use our eyes and body to show attention and interest, to give space to the other person but also to signal when we would like to join in. We might need to repair, either because we have failed to attend closely enough to grasp meaning or because our partner hasn't been clear enough. Just as expressing ourselves is complex, so is receiving meaning. At any moment our behaviour can jeopardise someone's attempts to join with us in a communicative exchange. Of course, if we do this, we risk appearing rude, unsupportive or hostile, which can lead to us running late for an appointment, as we did not feel able to stop someone talking to us.

Opportunities

As educators we have a lot of control over the opportunities we provide for our students to communicate. Traditional education, which still predominates in some parts of the world, expects students to be passive receptors of the teacher's words. However, in other systems, we give children multiple opportunities to learn through talking each day. Again, this offers both positives and negatives to children with SLCN who may benefit from the opportunity to practise, as all children do, but repeating errors or ways of covering up difficulties entrenches patterns of behaviour that may not be helpful in the long run. Even when practice may be beneficial to them, they might not feel competent or confident enough to keep trying in a busy classroom where there is much competition for space to talk. People with fragile communication systems tend to fare less well under pressure, meaning that a teacher may avoid asking the AAC user, for example, knowing that they will take a long time to answer and worrying that this might make them uncomfortable and annoy their peers. However, there are ways for educators to ensure that all children have the opportunity to develop through practice that is both appropriate and helpful to them. In fact, this approach is imperative if we are to build children's positive self-image as a communicator. Much of current good practice involves thinking of ways to encourage all children to have time to answer a question. This might be through prepared worksheets where children consider their answers and mark them on the sheet to either hand in or indicate in the classroom. Some educators use individual laminated boards for children so that they can write their answer in 'real time' and hold it up when the teacher tells them. Children who would struggle to write can be given cards to select from and hold up instead. Asking children for a response that will only be given some minutes later, and giving the whole group thinking and preparation time, will put a slow communicator on a more equal footing and ensure parity of opportunity.

Our education systems measure children's ability through their verbal and written answers. This will inevitably disadvantage those with communication and literacy impairment, meaning we find it hard to ascertain their learning and they lose out on the opportunity to check and develop deeper understanding. With adaptations there are many more ways that we can seek to understand what a child has learned. We need to allow for multiple and flexible means of expression, including creative approaches. Many tasks set by educators can offer flexible means of engagement or response. It can be difficult to find images that represent everything that a child might need to learn or express, which is why having an ongoing focus on the development of literacy skills is important. Being literate offers opportunities to everyone that may not otherwise be possible.

Reasons

Most of us are social beings who communicate for a wide variety of reasons, with multiple people, across the course of the day. Making these social connections is important for our well-being, and our feelings of being seen, heard and valued. An age-old action of punishment or disapproval is to stop talking to someone and encourage others to do the same so that the accused person is isolated and alone (being 'sent to Coventry'). During the Covid-19 pandemic, when people were locked in their homes and not allowed to socialise, concerns were expressed of increasing mental ill-health due to isolation. There is ongoing concern that the lack of social opportunities has led to poor outcomes in children, such as reduced immunity and poorer skill development, suggesting multiple benefits from social connection.

Analysis of what we communicate indicates high levels of requesting and giving information, asking for something we want, telling people about ourselves and complaining. We greet people, offer positive comments, ask questions and prompt for further information. Despite the ostensible reasons for our communication, much of the underlying purpose is to make connections with other people. Any communication, no matter how brief, can help us to feel included, part of a community, noticed and accepted. Interactions that go well are usually sources of great pleasure, and with this as the priority the actual content of much that is said is of far less importance. We tend to enjoy easy communication exchanges where both people understand each other without effort. We may avoid people who retain us for too long when we are in a rush.

When I was a teenager, I had a Saturday job in a greengrocer's shop. Most weeks a deaf customer would come in, and when my colleagues saw her approaching, they would find a reason to leave the shop floor. They were not cruel or unkind people, but they worried that they would not understand her speech, to know what she wanted, and they felt awkward. Communication with people with SLCN can be effortful and perhaps embarrassing for them and their communication partners, who have to work to make the interaction successful. This often makes people with SLCN prone to being and feeling excluded, unwelcome and ignored. This happens even where they have been included in school, and appear to get on well with peers; they still generally get fewer invitations to birthday parties and social gatherings, particularly as they get older. Once people with SLCN leave school, they often live a life of increased isolation and dependence on parents and carers, with fewer friends and social opportunities than their peers. While children are in the education system, they have the opportunity to build, and reinforce, their self-concept as communicators, showing them that it is worth persisting and building skills. For this there must be strong motivation from the young people themselves and their peers, since becoming a competent communicator will require persistence and determination. So having said that the ultimate reason for communication for most people is social connection, we need to consider how to develop and use this motivation, through a focus on skill building.

When we seek to support students with SLCN with reasons to communicate, a good starting point is to look at what would make a difference to their social connectedness. In my experience this is not the usual approach; rather, we think that the biggest motivation will be to teach them to ask for something they want. It is undeniable that children are frequently motivated by a favourite toy, activity or food, and so we might focus on teaching them words or symbols for these. For some students this can make a considerable difference and is the basis of the way that symbol systems are typically taught. This follows the typical developmental progression of expression, where children's first words might be requests for a drink, for example. However, very early communication also offers comment on something, which brings them into a social world, such as saying 'mummy', 'daddy' or the name of the dog. In these examples, saying the word can be an expression of happiness at the

Supporting communication in the classroom

appearance of the person or animal, or a request for them to come closer, depending on the accompanying gesture and intonation. In my view, a focus on only teaching children to ask for what they want limits them, and following a developmental route where learning another communicative purpose only after they have mastered requesting potentially limits their opportunities. While some children are going to be highly motivated to ask for food, for example, others know that they will get the food anyway, and they may be much more motivated when given the opportunity to greet someone they like.

When I worked in a large institution for disabled people of all ages, I thought a lot about the man who waited in the car park for the arrival of the staff every morning. He would greet us with 'one lady' or 'one man', not our names, but we all knew his name and would say 'hello Roger, how are you today?' This made me think about how greetings are an essential part of our day, ritual forms of acknowledgement of others and drawing of attention to ourselves. They form a part of the day in many classrooms, too, from name rhymes in nursery to the formal calling of the register with older pupils. However, in my experience little focus is given on teaching children with SLCN to greet people, which they might be able to do in multiple ways. Think of walking into a classroom of 12 children with limited communication skills. Most of us would be attracted to, and interact with, the child who smiled or waved at as when we walk in, but less so with the children who ignore us. A lack of greeting looks like a lack of interest, but this may not be the case. Even if a child is avoiding attention, it does not mean this is the best outcome for them, in terms of ongoing social connection.

Our main current ways of teaching children with SLCN to communicate is through extrinsic motivation, i.e. when we see them make an attempt, we offer praise or tangible reward. The Picture Exchange Communication System (PECS) is one example of this approach. There are six stages that are taught systematically. In the first stage two adults support the child. One helps them to make the required response, which is to offer a picture or symbol card to the other adult in order to gain what that person has, usually a favourite toy of the child or something they like to eat. When the child is helped to offer the card, perhaps with hand over hand support, the second adult takes the card and offers the requested item. This procedure is intended to teach the child how to effectively request, acknowledging that initiating this in a systematic way, which can be clearly understood by the receiver, has not so far been mastered. Children may have existing ways to request, but these may happen only when in their home kitchen, for example, and are not systematic and generalised. Through PECS, support is gradually reduced, choice introduced and independent requesting skills built, and the programme moves on to learn commenting such as 'I like book'. Children who find this approach helpful can go on to become proficient communication book or technological device users, being able to utilise these for a range of communicative functions. PECS is popular partly due to the amount of research data that supports its effectiveness; it is widely promoted and there is a paucity of other approaches that can relatively easily be adopted in schools. However, PECS can be criticised because it is based on rewards and compliance. Rather than seeking to value and enhance a child's own methods of communicating, they are taken through what can be an arduous training programme to adopt an unnatural means of communication. Children are motivated to exchange a symbol by being frustrated at seeing a desired item but not being given it. Food is frequently used due to being highly motivating. PECS is limited in what it teaches, and in fact many schools who claim to use it are really operating symbol systems but not following the rigid six stages of PECS.

Symbols can be used to encourage and support children's communication, through modelling by teachers and peers. However, noticing and responding to the way a child naturally communicates and interacts will enable intrinsic motivation to support engagement with others.

Other children who do not respond to the motivation of requesting may develop communication skills in different ways. Ideally, children will respond to their own intrinsic motivation, i.e. finding a way to express the motivation that comes from within them, linked to their preferences and desires. This does not depend on external motivators, although it does usually need to be recognised and encouraged in order to flourish. For any of us, however much we might want to achieve something, constant knockbacks and lack of success will erode our desire and motivation will reduce. When this happens, a child may be helped through offering extrinsic rewards to help them get started, or through praise and the rewards of social connection. As educators it is imperative that we hold in mind that children will have intrinsic motivators, and we need to be creative and imaginative to find them. Through observation we can often discover interests that a child may have. For some children their initial response to the environment may be habitual, meaning that they always interact with the same toys or books, and this blocks us, and them, from further discovery. We need therefore to be creative in offering opportunities in order that we discover more about their motivation.

A non-verbal autistic man, with severe epilepsy, was typically difficult to engage and appeared unmotivated for basic communication. When asked a question he would often sit passively or engage in repetitive behaviours. However, he demonstrated attention when read to from adult books about art or science. He would respond by pointing to answer questions about what had been read to him, particularly to show his opinion or answer a complex question. He was also motivated to show that he could spell challenging words.

One block to examining motivation that I have encountered in my practice is the fear that someone will want something that those around them are sure will not be possible. What do we do when the child with Down's syndrome says he wants to be a racing driver? Adults faced with this can feel awkward and embarrassed knowing that few adults with DS even get to hold a driving licence. My argument is that we all have dreams that will be unobtainable: when I was young, I wanted to be an actress, but I had stage fright and very low confidence, so that wasn't going to happen; however, now that I am an educator, I get to 'hold the floor' and talk to groups of attentive listeners, much like actresses do! So, although I can understand someone expressing fear of prompting children to say that they want something that will be impossible, my response is that they have a right, as we all do, to express these desires. So going back to the example of the child wanting to be a racing car driver, this is a highly unlikely ambition for any young person, but many children who express the dream will find other things they love, either connected to the sport or which provide something of the same excitement and continue to engage in racing driving as a spectator. When we know that someone loves fast cars and the thrill of the race, or whatever aspect it is that attracts them, we can use that as a motivation. To develop maths skills they can count cars, work out and sequence timings, and calculate distances. We can engage them in design of colours and patterns for the cars, encourage them to learn to spell the names of the tracks and their different turns. Any learning can be supported through this internal motivation. Our classrooms need to be places that are planned to allow engagement through the interests of the children, while still learning from our curriculum.

To illustrate further here is a story from my practice with an adult. My colleagues and I had been working for months with an autistic non-verbal man called Josh. His means of communication included some verbalisations and gestures, and he used these to request or make choices. We felt that he had potential to express himself more fully than he currently could, and were supporting him to use communication and letter boards but with only limited success. One day I was with him in the dining hall of the institution where he lived, and he appeared upset. He was starting to become highly agitated, although there was food available, and no one could understand what he wanted. I offered the spelling board and with my physical assistance he typed 'hot food'. It transpired that in place of the usual hot food choices that day there was only cold food being offered, much to his displeasure. The kitchen staff were able to come up with something to satisfy Josh's request that day, and this was instrumental in his subsequent development of communication skills. His huge motivation to get hot food had somehow given him the determination to overcome difficulties he had previously shown in using the letterboard. Once we, and he, knew it was possible when he had sufficient reason to communicate, we could find ways to continue to practise until spelling became easier.

Expectations

Research has long provided us with an understanding that the expectations our educators have of us are highly likely to influence our academic achievement (Gentrup et al., 2020). Expectations refers to the process by which educators make judgements about pupils as to how they are likely to behave and perform in school. There is a highly troubling study that was published by Rist in the *Harvard Educational Review* in 1970 and republished in 2000, as the journal's editors wanted to question whether there had been significant changes in society in the intervening 30 years. The observational study, in a school in New York, USA, examined the impact of teacher's perceptions of the social class of their students on their potential academic achievement. The researchers observed the children for two and a half years from when they entered kindergarten. At school entry the teacher was provided with demographic information about the pupils, including their parents' names, addresses and whether or not they received welfare support. Although all pupils and staff in the school were black, around 55% were on low income. Parents were also interviewed and asked to complete a form to indicate any concerns they had about their child. In addition, teachers in the school shared information about the families gathered through interactions with older siblings and the parents. The kindergarten teacher assigned permanent seats to the children on the eighth day of school, based on background information and her observations of the children since they arrived. There was no information collected about academic ability at this point; all judgements were based on social and environmental factors. The teacher divided her 30 pupils into three groups, which, when analysed, had particular characteristics. Those in group 1, characterized by the teacher as the 'fast learners', were better dressed and cared for than the others and came from more economically stable families. In group 3 were those who 'had no idea what was going on in the classroom'. From this point she gave more attention and spoke more with those in group 1, also giving them roles within the class and school. She was frequently disparaging of the 'less able' students, referring to those in group 1 as children to emulate. Group 1 children began to echo this behaviour towards their peers, and children in groups 2 and 3 were observed to frequently use abusive language to others in their own group. The author notes, 'Those children at Tables 2 and 3 who displayed cruelty appeared to have learned from the teacher that it was acceptable to act in an aggressive manner towards those from low-income and poorly educated backgrounds' (Rist, 2000, p. 430). Another key finding was that teachers utilised more control-oriented language with the perceived lower ability children, setting up a downward spiral, where the more the children were disciplined, the less interest they showed in academic work. This then reinforced the teacher's perception of them as being 'slow learners'. Further, the allocation of student groups remained stable across the three school years, and their academic ability matched the expectations originally generated by the kindergarten teacher.

More recent research, from many parts of the world, has shown that teachers' expectations of students were not accurate, according to more objective measures of ability, but that they did determine academic outcome, even in older pupils (Gentrup et al., 2020). Teachers are not setting out to have these deterministic views of their pupils. I would suggest that the competitive educational climate, however, forces teachers to make decisions about where to place their time and energy in order to maximise school outcomes. Children who need support to learn are perceived as needing greater amounts of educator time, but with potentially lower academic results. Schools in the UK measure 'value added' as a key metric of teacher success, i.e. if your lower achievers made a good rate of progress, even though remaining below average in academic results, you could be viewed as an effective educator. However, the focus on overall exam results still tends to predominate, and schools must decide where to place resources to maximise these. Teachers are required to teach all their pupils, but it is almost inevitable that those who easily demonstrate engagement in learning and success will be perceived more positively and have a different experience of school, and what is possible for them, than their peers.

We can tend to lack awareness of the assumptions we make about others, unless challenged in our views. Children at my son's secondary school were given the opportunity for a mock job interview with a volunteer member of the community. My son said that he was thinking about either studying to be a lawyer or a physiotherapist. The response of the 'interviewer' was to tell him to focus on physiotherapy as he might have a better chance at that. I saw this response as not only ignorant regarding physiotherapy training, but also demotivating and offensive, based on his view of the average level of achievement of pupils at the school, few of whom went on to university.

A key aspect of my psychotherapy training was to examine my beliefs about people to ensure that I can separate what I bring to an interaction from what my client brings. Unless we can do this, there is a risk that we will listen and interpret clients' meaning from our own perspectives and beliefs, not theirs. All educators are encouraged to focus on being reflective and reflexive practitioners, as a continuing process of skill development. Practising as both reflective of our lessons and reflexive of ourselves is a way of gaining personal insight and enhancing ourselves as educators. In our evaluations of pupils, we can have an orientation of looking for strengths and assets, or focusing on areas of deficit. Both views may have a level of accuracy, but the attitude of looking for strengths will be more likely to accord with assumptions of possibility in our students. An example of the deficit view in action comes from one of my students, who described a colleague saying, about a child, 'He's supposed to be dyslexic, but I think he's just lazy, and a bit thick'. This was followed by advice to just keep him occupied doing something he likes as he wasn't going to pass the course anyway. In this example the teacher is indicating their belief system that allows them to focus less on the hard work of supporting a child who is struggling with reading and writing. This has to do with their own needs and assumptions, to allow them to blame the child for their difficulties, rather than themselves as an educator. These differences are encapsulated in the contrast between 'universal', i.e. everyone can succeed, or the converse, where educators believe that only certain people can succeed. Even if this 'non-universal' belief were to be accurate, we cannot know who is in what camp, yet the beliefs we hold will have instrumental influence on students' future success. Therefore, the 'least dangerous assumption' is that everyone can succeed, and we need to work towards this.

Pupils with disabilities are frequently those who experience low expectations of them. In fact, parents may be told at the point of diagnosis that they should lower their expectations as an act of kindness to themselves and their child. An attitude I have encountered in many educators, when faced with particularly challenging children, along with all the other enormous demands on their time and resources, is that particular pupils are unreachable and unteachable. This belief allows educators to feel comfortable when they reflect on the progress of their pupils and where some have not done as well as hoped. This belief, even if attempts are made to hide it, will communicate itself to pupils and colleagues, contributing to a limiting class and school culture. All educators need to reflect that all of us, when we are struggling with something, respond positively to someone who shows understanding, tells us we can succeed, instils greater confidence in us and offers support of the kind we need.

Some high-profile people with DS who have achieved beyond expectations that would usually be applied have done so through the belief and hard work of their parents and/or educators. Dr Karen Gaffney, Olympic medal swimmer who has completed many wild water swimming challenges, including crossing the English Channel, had parents who had to fight hard for her to gain a mainstream education. Pablo Pineda, a prize-winning Spanish actor and the first person with DS in Europe to graduate with a degree, has experienced huge discrimination due to people's attitudes about DS. Sujeet Desai has mastered seven instruments and is the first person with DS to play at Carnegie Hall. Although these people's achievements are exceptional, many people with DS now have higher achievement levels than in the past. This has resulted from better understanding of both physical and health aspects of the syndrome, plus better teaching for their particular needs and higher expectations.

When parents are told that their child has DS, this is generally seen as devastating news. It can be very difficult for them to see the positives and trust that their child will be happy and fulfilled. However, the 'least dangerous assumption' is that we do not know how someone will develop, based only on their chromosomes, and we need therefore to keep an open mind about what they might achieve. In the early days it is imperative to keep looking for positives, noticing and recognizing every attempt the child makes to join with us in the social world, since this will be a key to future learning.

As seen in the Rist study, the attitudes and behaviour we present towards the less able learners in a class, or those who are perceived as different, will communicate to other learners. When a school community makes negative assumptions about a child, this frequently leads to them having a poor experience of inclusion and troubled social relationships, potentially including bullying. The quality of relationships between children with SEND and their peers is suggested as being different; children with SEND are generally less accepted and more rejected than their typically developing classmates. This is often based on perceived differences and teachers have a role in countering negative assumptions. The relevance of this is the overall experience that children with SEND tend to have and the impact of low social acceptance, which Frederickson (2010) suggests: increases the risk of peer rejection, victimisation and bullying, and higher levels of academic difficulties, discipline and truancy in secondary school. Children who have experienced this peer rejection are more likely to drop out of education early, participate in delinquent behaviour and have mental health problems in early adulthood.

Total communication

With every pupil we work with, regardless of their ability or challenges, we want to encourage them to communicate through every means they have at their disposal. As we have seen in this chapter, communication can take many forms, and to encourage confidence and persistence we need to pay attention to what children show and tell us. Much of this communication will be independent, i.e. the child does not need us to make it happen. However, thinking also of Vygotsky's concepts of zone of proximal development (ZPD) and more knowledgeable other (MKO), there will be times when children will need our support to maximise their communication with ourselves and their peers. Providing the right amount of support for the right length of time for each child and each context is highly skilled work. The demands on a communication partner can be almost as high as those placed on a communicator when the latter is struggling. It may tax our skills and our patience, but when we do this well the rewards in seeing a child explain something successfully, perhaps for the first time, are immense. It is key, always, to notice and be appreciative of the efforts the child makes.

Much of my career has been working with non-verbal people who use alternative communication methods. One of the challenges with this work is that the motor control difficulties that prevent a child from speaking may also make a communication board or device difficult to use accurately.

Some children with severe cerebral palsy that prevents them from accurate pointing can use their eyes to control a voice output device, allowing them to 'talk'. This innovation has allowed us to assess and support the language development of non-verbal children in a way that was previously very difficult. This area of AAC is highly specialised, and if you are educating a child who is using an alternative means of communication you are likely to also receive SALT support and training. What is important for educators to know is that with adaptations to how children communicate they can be full members of the class who interact with adults and peers. In the example provided in Chapter 2 about Nihal, who could turn his head to indicate 'yes' or 'no', his peers loved to be the person who would place their hands beside his cheeks and report which side he turned to. His friends loved to push his wheelchair in the playground and ensure that he could see what they were doing. These were enriching experiences for everyone.

Behaviour as communication

All children will be communicating all day every day, but not always in ways that are part of our usual code or that we can easily understand. Mothers come to know the emotions of their babies when they only have a very limited range of vocalisations to interpret. With our close friends we will understand the nature of the smile they give us from many previous experiences that we build on. We can follow the same process with children who are non- or minimally verbal, but with these children it can be difficult to check our perceptions with them. As an educator we spend a lot of time with our pupils and will come to have an understanding of them. We will know their likes and preferences, when they get tired and irritable, and what is important and motivating for them. However, since these are all interpretations rather than objective findings, we have to be careful that we don't assume understanding without continuing to examine our perceptions. Children change, and we can make errors about them. My teachers knew that I talked too much in class and did not complete my work to the best of my ability because I was more interested in interacting with classmates. They did not know how I would develop as a grew older. I did not know that I would pursue an academic career – in fact I am still amazed many years into it; I would never have thought I had the necessary skills, and only when I was highly motivated to learn more about autism and communication, prompted by work I was doing, did I learn how to study and write academically. My point is that we should attune to what our pupils are communicating through their words, interests, actions and behaviours, in their totality, but not allow what we see to lead our belief that this is all there is or will be. People frequently defy expectations, and we must continue to encourage growth rather than limit possibilities.

One key reason for the upholding of high expectations for everyone is the risk of children who fail too often developing behaviours that perpetuate poor impressions. These roughly fall into two categories, those who 'act out' and those who give up. The term 'learned helplessness' describes those who continually meet failure and ultimately withdraw and stop trying. This term was first used in relation to animal studies, where animals who were unable to escape from painful electric shocks stopped trying to avoid them, even when escape was possible. Researchers found that being helpless to avoid pain led to changes in the brain, which meant no future attempts at escape (Maier and Seligman, 2016). This was then applied to people explaining the inertia we might see in our pupils when we try to encourage them and are met with the attitude that there is no point trying because they know they will fail. Once this mindset has developed it is very challenging to change it, as explained by the brain changes that have already ensued. We will need to continue to challenge gently and persistently, using small gains to gradually instil more self-belief in our pupils and motivating them to continue trying.

Thinking about the following questions will encourage you to reflect on your students:

1. To what extent are you aware of your role as a communication partner in clarifying, modelling and checking meaning?
2. Are you able to give individual students the space to talk to you in a quiet and relatively stress-free setting?
3. What routine opportunities do children have to talk to each other and to adults about topics of their choice?
4. Do you have similar expectations for all students or do you differentiate, and if so on what basis?

Bo: Building alternative communication

I met Bo when he was 10 years old and had been attending the same special school since he was 3. Like Mona, described in Chapter 5, he was considered to be autistic, non-verbal with severe learning disabilities. He had a loving and supportive family, his mother attended school meetings and was keen to know of ways to support her son. He usually had a smile on his face and made a continuous vocalisation that could intensify when an adult tried to interact with him or persuade him to do something. At times he would show distress and the sound of his vocalisations would change. His hands were in constant action, tapping the table, tapping any object near him or pulling at his clothing. When I approached him, he started to giggle, for no apparent reason, and the sound he made threatened to drown out anything I said. I learned that when I decreased the volume of my speech, he also became quieter. When I placed objects on the table in front of him, he only tapped them and did not show any sign of interest in them or understanding of what they were. It was difficult to know how to start to engage him with anything, his vocalisations and tapping seemed like barriers to participation. Anything I placed in front of him he grabbed but as a random object, not anything of interest.

I wanted to see whether I could help Bo gain any functional use of his hands, and I needed to build a positive relationship with him. I started with a physical approach of holding his hands and encouraging him to straighten his arms and push against me. He showed very little strength or control of his arms but used his whole body to push so that we could engage in a see-saw action, with me either pushing him back in his seat or considerably reducing my resistance and encouraging him to lean forward to push me. As we did this, I made direct eye contact, and he did not resist. I also made vocalisations a little similar to his and found that we could move in synchrony and make similar sounds. I used 'ready' repeatedly and heard him make an approximation of the word. Bo showed enjoyment in this game. My aim was to increase the muscle tone in his arms and shoulders to see if this would increase his hand control, but it also set up our sessions as somewhere he could have fun and where demands were not too great. This was the start of work that went on regularly for a couple of years and progress within that time was very slow.

The aim of my work with Bo was to try to give him an alternative communication system, and for this he would need purposeful movement of his eyes and hands. I found that he could look at what I was showing him, but when trying to use looking to get him to select between two objects or pictures his response was unclear. In our sessions I combined a focus on purposeful movement, simple speech and written words. For example, I used the bridge from a wooden train set and wrote the words 'over' and 'under' on separate pieces of paper. I modelled the action, showed the word, and used hand-over-hand support to guide him in the action of pushing the train over the bridge, gradually fading my touch to see if he could continue alone. My motivation in incorporating written words was to find out whether he already had some word recognition, and to give him the opportunity to learn some words by sight. His school routinely used symbols and words with Bo when trying to engage him and letting him know what he would be doing. When Bo became active in a game and focused on using his hands, I found that he vocalised much less and his whole body became more still. Rather than paying much attention to the written word, he appeared more intent in trying to say the key words that I was stressing. In context I could tell that he was saying 'over', but his speech was not clear enough to be interpreted in a different setting. Before attempting to say a word, he became very still and quiet, appearing to have an inner focus. When I recognised his attempt at speech, he often turned to me and made eye contact and mirrored my facial expressions. His responses were often delayed, and I had to maintain silent expectation that he would act before giving a prompt.

Bo's unstructured responses to anything in front of him continued to seem only random touching. However, over time, within our sessions, he maintained greater stillness and began to be able, with prompting, to inhibit his repetitive movements. As the next step I worked on teaching him to point, with two main aspects of focus: moving in the direction of his eye gaze and pointing with a single finger rather than the whole hand. I held his hand with his index finger straight and other fingers folded back, but as soon as I let go he stretched all his fingers wide apart. With me holding his hand he appeared to be able to focus intently and would look at one of the objects, but not move his hand in the right direction. We slowly built up his ability to control his arm, and by persisting with this over many months he ultimately learned to point, independently, to something he was asked to indicate. This did not immediately translate into a communicative behaviour, although had the work continued I am hopeful that it could have.

Most sessions with Bo were video recorded, and it was only when watching these back and analysing them in detail did I realise how much speech he was attempting. Not noticing it in real time was because his efforts often came many seconds, or longer, after my model. He made approximations of many words; whether he was directly prompted to do so or not, it seemed that speech was a primary motivation for him. We started to increase the focus on speech in sessions, but I found that the more he tried the more difficult it appeared to be for him to make specific sounds. He showed frustration when he couldn't say something, but with support remained highly motivated to try. When I waited long enough, he would make a recognisable attempt at many words. Again, the progress we made over two years did not help him to develop functional speech, but awareness that this was something that he was motivated by was important for his school and family. Since his attempts at speech were typically very quiet, and delayed from the point of the stimulus, no one working with him, including his family, were aware that he was doing it. There was no expectation on Bo being able to speak, given the extent of his disabilities, so no one was looking for it or trying to engage him with this. In my view, many of Bo's challenges that were put down to learning difficulties and lack of connection with the world could be more accurately viewed as emanating from EF skills of initiation and coordination. Once aware that he wanted to say words, it was possible to see him working intently at this, with deep concentration. He appeared to have dyspraxic-like difficulties with controlling his muscles for speech. Had this been picked up at an earlier age he may have received help that could have made a difference. When children fail to develop in their early years, do not achieve milestones and have no way of demonstrating interest in the world, we consider them as 'globally developmentally delayed', and this is seen as indicating considerable cognitive impairment. Children who cannot control their bodies will have difficulties with learning, which in turn will impact their cognitive development, but unless we analyse where blocks to engagement are, we may see them simply as learning disabled, and lower our expectations of their future.

Conclusion

The situation in the UK, and many other countries, with teachers who are not trained to recognise communication and literacy difficulties, means that many children remain unidentified as communication impaired and unsupported to improve their skills. This directly impacts their ability to benefit from the curriculum and indirectly causes a range of other problems. Children who struggle to communicate clearly are disadvantaged in school, social relationships, further education and employment. There is likely to be an emotional impact, compounded when their difficulties go unrecognised and the perception of them is that they are poor at learning or not motivated to try. Many children will become shy or withdrawn, therefore not fulfilling their potential. Others will become defiant and often have conduct disorders, frequently so severe that they enter the criminal justice programme. Our schools are founded in good communication skills, yet we only serve those who acquire these easily and with little direct teaching. We need to improve this situation, by increasing our understanding of communication difficulties, screening children for areas of difficulty and knowing how to support them. Ideally this will be a whole class and whole school initiative as all children will benefit from high-level communication support and practice.

To summarise how to do this:

1. Always support what you say with an image or piece of writing to aid understanding and support those with poor working memory.
2. Avoid pressurising children to speak or read aloud.
3. Encourage children to self-audit their communication skills as a way of seeking support from you and peers.
4. Encourage a climate for learning that views progress as individual, acquired through focus and practice, reducing competition amongst peers and minimising embarrassment.
5. Rather than criticising pupils for inappropriate communication, focus on explaining and providing a model for what would have been a better form.
6. Provide children with opportunity to answer questions in their own time and to practise communicating with peers in any way they feel confident and about a topic of their own interest.
7. Hold beliefs that children can continue to learn and improve, no matter what their current level of ability and behaviour.

References

Coles, H., Gillett, K., Murray, G. and Turner, K. (2017). *Justice Evidence Base*. The Royal College of Speech and Language Therapists. https://www.rcslt.org/wp-content/uploads/media/Project/RCSLT/justice-evidence-base2017-1.pdf

The Communication Trust. (2017). Talking about a generation. https://www.bettercommunication.org.uk/tct_talkingaboutageneration_report_online_update.pdf

Cullinane, C. and Montacute, R. (2017). *Life Lessons: Improving Essential Life Skills for Young People*. London: The Sutton Trust.

Fibla, L., Kosie, J. E., Kircher, R., Lew-Williams, C. and Byers-Heinlein, K. (2022). Bilingual language development in infancy: What can we do to support bilingual families? *Policy Insights from the Behavioral and Brain Sciences*, 9(1), 35–43. https://doi.org/10.1177/23727322211069312

Frederickson, N. (2010). Bullying or befriending? Children's responses to classmates with special needs. *British Journal of Special Education*, 37(1), 4–12.

Gentrup, S., Lorenz, G., Kristen, C. and Kogan, I. (2020). Self-fulfilling prophecies in the classroom: Teacher expectations, teacher feedback and student achievement. *Learning and Instruction*, 66, 101296. https://doi.org/10.1016/j.learninstruc.2019.101296

Gunnerud, H. L., ten Braak, D., Reikerås, E. K. L., Donolato, E. and Melby-Lervåg, M. (2020). Is bilingualism related to a cognitive advantage in children? A systematic review and meta-analysis. *Psychological Bulletin*, 146(12), 1059–1083. https://doi.org/10.1037/bul0000301

Hartshorne, J. K., Tenenbaur, J. B. and Pinker S. (2018). A critical period for second language acquisition: Evidence from 2/3 million English speakers. *Cognition*, 177, 263–277. https://doi.org/10.1016/j.cognition.2018.04.007

ICAN. (n.d.). *Developmental Language Disorder: A guide for every teaching on supporting children and young people with Developmental Language Disorder (DLD) in mainstream schools*. Accessed 20 July 2024. https://speechandlanguage.org.uk/wp-content/uploads/2023/12/ican_dld_guide_final_aug4.pdf

Kliewer, C., Biklen, D. and Kasa-Hendrickson, C. (2006). Who may be literate? Disability and resistance to the cultural denial of competence. *American Educational Research Journal*, 43(2), 163–192.

Keefe, L. and Copeland, C. (2012). What is literacy? The power of a definition. *Journal of Intellectual Disability Research*, 56, 704.

Law, J., McBean, K. and Rush, R. (2011). Communication skills in a population of primary school-aged children raised in an area of pronounced social disadvantage. *International Journal of Language & Communication Disorders*, 46, 657–664. https://doi.org/10.1111/j.1460-6984.2011.00036.x

Law, J., Lee, W., Lindsay, G., Roulstone, S., Wren, Y. and Zeng, B. (2012). 'What Works': Interventions for children and young people with speech, language and communication needs. Department for Education, Research Report DFE_RR247-BCRP10. https://www.researchgate.net/publication/267409192_What_Works_Interventions_for_children_and_young_people_with_speech_language_and_communication_needs

Locke, A., Ginsborg, J. and Peers, I. (2002). Development and disadvantage: Implications for the early years and beyond. *International Journal of Language and Communication Disorders*, 37(1), 3–15. https://doi.org/10.1080/13682820110089911

Maier, S. F. and Seligman, M. E. P. (2016). Learned helplessness at fifty: Insights from Neuroscience. *Psychological Review*, 123(4), 349–367. https://doi.org/10.1037%2Frev0000033

Mandel, D. R., Jusczyk, P. W. and Kemler Nelson, D. G. (1994). Does sentential prosody help infants organise and remember speech information? *Cognition*, 53(2), 155–180. https://doi.org/10.1016/0010-0277(94)90069-8

Money, D. and Thurman, S. (1994). Talkabout communication. *College of Speech and Language Therapy Bulletin*, 504, 12–13.

NHS. (2023). Selective mutism. https://www.nhs.uk/mental-health/conditions/selective-mutism/

Palmer, D. C. (2000). Chomsky's nativism: A critical review. *The Analysis of Verbal Behaviour*, 17, 39–50.

Piaget, J. (2002). *The Language and Thought of the Child*. London: Routledge.

Rist, R. C. (2000). Student social class and teacher expectations: The self-fulfilling prophecy in ghetto education. *Harvard Educational Review*, 70(3), 257–301.

Ruppar, A. L., Gaffney, J. S. and Dymond, S. K. (2015). Influences on teachers' decisions about literacy for secondary students with severe disabilities. *Exceptional Children*, 81(2), 209–226.

Skinner, B. F. (1986). The evolution of verbal behaviour. *Journal of the Experimental Analysis of Behavior*, 45, 115–122.

The Children's Trust. (n.d.). Understanding acquired brain injury (ABI). Accessed 20 July 2024. https://www.thechildrenstrust.org.uk/brain-injury-information/info-and-advice/return-to-education/introduction-for-educational-professionals/teachers#:~:text=Every%20year%20over%2040%2C000%20children,misinterpreted%20or%20not%20even%20spotted

Vygotsky, L. S. (1978). *Mind in Society: The Development of Higher Psychological Processes*. Cambridge, MA: Harvard University Press.

Vygotsky, L. S. (2012). *Thought and Language*. Cambridge, MA: MIT Press.

World Economic Forum. (2016). This is the skill employers are looking for in new grads. https://www.weforum.org/agenda/2016/07/this-is-the-skill-employers-are-looking-for-in-new-grads/

7
Conclusion

Introduction

In the previous chapters we have considered how all of us are constantly engaged in a circular process by which our brains determine our actions, in conjunction with our emotions, and how we behave feeds information to our brains, serving to shape them in our individual ways as we mature. When faced with a pupil, who is a high academic achiever, or excellent sports person, someone who goes below the radar and is rarely noticed, or someone with a recognised disability, the person we encounter is a mix of genetics, health factors, experience and emotional regulation. There is little that we, as educators, can do about the child's inherited traits, but arguably much that we can do regarding the other factors. For example, a child who has experienced negative aspects in their upbringing, including neglect or abuse, can benefit enormously from the stable and trusting relationship they can form with their educators and peers. Children who have been brought up in poverty with poor diet, or who have been allowed to make food choices that lead to obesity and potential ill-health, can be helped to make better decisions for their future. Research that attempted to measure teacher impact in terms of economic value found that pupils who had a teacher who was able to raise their test scores had greater rates of higher education and higher income as adults (Chetty et al., 2014). Obviously, these sorts of tangible benefits are of great importance, but perhaps the ways in which teachers can make us feel about ourselves are even more important. Most people, if questioned, can recount stories about what teachers said, or did, that impacted their self-belief, for the good or to poor effect. We can give children positive, restorative, inspirational experiences that help them to manage their own emotional expression and develop intrinsic motivation and ultimate autonomy. Whether and to what extent educators provide these opportunities to all their pupils will depend on who the educator is, what they see as their role, and their ability to form positive relationships with children who may make considerable demands on them. As I have been writing this book, I have been considering the barriers to these outcomes and discuss some of them below.

Educator perceptions ...

... of children

We come to our work with a set of beliefs and assumptions about the children we encounter. We might express these in some of the following ways: 'my group are lovely, with just a few notable exceptions'; 'I love my job, every child has strengths and difficulties and I enjoy the challenge they bring'; 'I have a really troublesome group this year, they have no idea how to behave, I'm going to have my work cut out'; or 'this job has really changed, the children have got worse and I don't know how I'm going to cope this year'. There will be endless versions of these, all of which tell a story of educator stress, energy and engagement. All of us want to make a positive difference to the children we work with, but our own successes and challenges impact how we see the work and therefore what we bring to it. The external pressures of student results and school inspections can push us into a more negative view of the children than we might want to have. Overloaded curricula make finding the time and patience that some children need very difficult. How we respond to these pressures may be linked to our philosophical stance about education, what we think its purpose is, the degree of autonomy we have and the extent of our own agency to enhance learning.

Working in the field of inclusion I am often aware of the predominant view of students within a school. The most inclusive schools are often those with a firm shared belief that all children can learn when supported well, and children have a right to be educated with their peers. Proponents of special education may have a varying view, that most children can achieve but that some will require highly specialised teaching in order to make progress. There are schools who believe that all children can obey rules for the sake of community, will be responsive to and responsible for their impact on others, and hold high expectations. Other schools will have the view that they are only able to cater to certain types of pupil, such as those who have high ability, or those who naturally behave in desirable ways.

Conclusion

The philosophy that I promote in this book is that certainly all children have a right to education, that all children can learn when supported appropriately, that all can learn self-regulation with support over time and that undesirable behaviour is a child communicating a time when they experience lack of control, perhaps severe distress, and emotions that they may not be able to name. The messages that we give students when they do not reach desired standards of academic work or behaviour are fundamental in the adults they become.

... of themselves

I would imagine that the vast majority of educators have experienced a time when they lacked confidence in their ability to connect with a particular child or group and where they may have doubted their approach. Of course, a certain lack of confidence as an early career teacher is appropriate, which is why supportive mentoring is essential. Educators, as well as children, will thrive in settings where they feel accepted and a sense of belonging, which comes from positive relationships with peers who they feel they can turn to for help or advice. Teacher training is generally effective in equipping educators to know what to teach and how to manage the curriculum. There is less space given to how to build relationships with pupils that are founded on trust, particularly since this is likely to be a highly individualised pattern where a teacher needs to be true to their own personality. Some of us are more naturally expressive of warmth and affection, but children will also love and respect a teacher who is calm, if distant, consistent and maintains a well-run classroom. The need to adhere to rigid school policies can get in the way of teachers bringing their whole selves to the classroom and figuring out how to build positive relationships with pupils. Schools are generally very keen on consistent practice across classes and year groups. This ambition, even when reinforced by highly directive policies, tends to be implemented individually by teachers, leading to student complaint of inconsistent rules. I would argue that individual implementation is virtually inevitable; adults should not be made to follow a formula, particularly when children benefit from individual responses within a trusting relationship. Behaviour policies are generally adopted in an effort to ensure consistent treatment of pupils in the interest of ensuring equality. However, a more variable approach to achieving equity would be more desirable for everyone involved in education. The UK government guidance to schools on behaviour management issued in 2024, for example, states: 'Behaviour will often need to be considered in relation to a pupil's SEND' (Department for Education, 2024, p. 13). An improvement to strict enforcement of a rigid behaviour policy is an agreement about intended child outcomes, with educators being trusted to work towards those goals in accordance with their own style and the needs of their particular group of pupils or even individuals. Some children will benefit from an action that addresses a behaviour before it becomes entrenched, while another will need an approach that will gradually, over many years, support self-regulation. A compassionate approach will value all the individual styles and approaches that work towards pupil learning, self-regulation, emotional literacy, caring for others and autonomy.

As teachers train and gain experience they develop a teacher identity. They may describe themselves as someone who is strict but fair, someone who shows the children love or someone who can instil passion for their subject in their pupils. These identities guide teachers to place emphasis on certain codes of behaviour or aspects of learning. Children will be aware of teacher identities and will spread the word about who will follow through with threats or who is more lenient. They will also know the sorts of reactions that their behaviour is likely to elicit in a particular educator, which is almost as likely to prompt them to push for negative responses as it is to make them obey.

Teaching assistants (TAs) will come into the work for different reasons, and they too will form identities. Whereas TAs may be attracted by the work hours, fitting in with their own parenting, or the opportunity to work with children without the full responsibility that teachers have, their role has become increasingly professional, with training and responsibilities enabling them to develop specialist practice. How they perceive their role will also impact how they approach their work. The best TAs will be constantly aware of building the independence of the individuals they support. They will know not to over-protect or do the work for the child. They will be highly skilled in making learning accessible to children with a wide range of aptitudes and helping pupils keep their focus. Many of them will form close bonds with their pupils, spending much of the day with them and following them to lessons, which allows building of trust but also, unless they use their skills, risking over-dependence. They may feel protective of children who are vulnerable to bullying or academic failure and have a role in boosting children's self-belief.

Educators who adopt a growth mindset will find ways to support children to continue to develop skills and independence. They will hold constant the belief that children can and will make progress in both learning and behaviour. They will view lapses in concentration, lack of effort or non-conformity as signs that a child, despite trying their best, has a difficulty they cannot overcome at that moment and will increase their support. They will reassure the child that this is just a temporary difficulty, remind them of previous success and prepare them for a more positive outcome the next day. When it is appropriate to bring a child's errors to their attention, this will be done away from others, with kindness, encouraging the child to articulate their difficulty, helping them to gain insight and making a plan for a better way forward.

Student perceptions

As educators develop identities in their workplace, so do children in their class. A child will place themselves in terms of academic ability and behaviour. They will see themselves as quiet, chatty, cheeky, confident, assertive, naughty or even bad. Some of these perceptions will be echoed, or even derive from, what educators have said about them. We can agree that the 'ideal' pupil is someone who listens, has a thirst for learning, engages in the class, gets on well with peers and answers teacher questions when invited. There are probably children in every class who might be seen this way. For some of them this will be a natural state, while others are likely to be working hard beneath the surface to achieve this veneer. They may go home exhausted from having kept up this appearance all day, by having 'masked' their actual difficulties, motivated by staying out of trouble or not attracting attention to themselves. Alongside trying to please educators there will be peer pressure, with children sometimes pulled to be something other than they are in order to fit in. The competing pressures children are under, and their lack of neurological maturation, may make finding the identity they will eventually adopt as adults very challenging.

We know that children who feel safe in school, and have a sense of belonging to a group, will have the best outcomes in terms of academic achievement and are more likely to be able to regulate their emotions (Smith and Culbert, 2024). It is therefore imperative that educators know how to foster these feelings. When we show children that we care, when they know that the adults around them will look after and support them, and preferably when they feel liked by their educators, they are going to be in a better state to learn. This brings me to something that writing the book has led me to comment and reflect on – the extent to which our systems and practices can lead to children feeling shame. Frequently in previous chapters I have presented shame and humiliation as what we need to avoid at all costs. This is the antithesis of what the 'ideal' pupil feels, and something we must avoid for every child, as shame is an entirely damaging emotion that leads only to negative behaviour. A shameful pupil will either hide or defy, acting out in the rage that ensues from shame.

Shame as a barrier to belonging

When any of us do something inadvertently that harms another person, we usually feel guilt. This leads us to apologise or try to make amends, so guilt is an emotion that, although uncomfortable, can lead to a positive social outcome. If a child loses their temper in the playground and pushes their friend who was teasing them, adult intervention can help them to reflect on this action as something that hurt someone they care about, something to be avoided. Shame is different from guilt as it suggests that it is the person, rather than the act, that is undesirable. It leads us to feel that we are wrong, undeserving and even unlovable. It is therefore linked to psychological maladjustment, resentment, irritability and anger. Shame takes away our human dignity and is generally regarded as entrenching negative behaviour in a sort of self-fulfilling prophesy, i.e. 'I am a bad person, so I act badly'. For many pupils an atmosphere that promotes shame takes them on a process of, firstly, feeling that it is not worth trying to improve; and secondly, moving towards defiant behaviour – and ultimately blocks positive interactions. We have examined in earlier chapters the extent to which a child's behaviour may be governed by poor executive functions, so when we adopt policies that require them to have control that they do not possess, they cannot meet our expectations. This failure, and how we respond to it, risks taking them down the path of feeling shame.

If we look historically at how children in school have been controlled, we quickly encounter the use of violence. My father talked of beatings in school in the 1940s, while my contemporaries talk about the teachers who pulled their ears or hit them from behind, when they were in school in the 1970s. Corporal punishment was outlawed in state schools in the UK in 1986, followed by private schools, and I was surprised to discover that corporal punishment is still within the law in some states of the US, particularly in private schools, despite the evidence that black pupils and disabled pupils are more likely to be physically punished than white and non-disabled pupils (Beers, 2024). When educators were prevented by law from turning to physical punishment, we moved more into an era of shame. Shame was already present alongside corporal punishment, with pupils made to stand in corners, perhaps even wearing something to mark them out as 'bad'. My incessant talking in primary school led to me being moved to a different table, sometimes on my own. This may have been intended simply to stop me talking as there was no one to talk to. However, I remember blushing, feeling hot and highly self-conscious. Since I remember this happening multiple times it didn't seem to work as a deterrent!

Once the negative repercussions of shame became apparent with awareness of potential long-lasting harm there was an ostensible move away from overt shaming practices in schools. However, I would argue that the whole system of dividing and categorizing students leads to inadvertent shaming. We stopped the public posting of exam results in an effort to reduce the shame of those who did not do well, yet as I have described in earlier chapters much of what happens in schools, usually under the guise of rewarding something good to encourage others to aspire to it, still has the potential to humiliate pupils. I recently heard from a PhD candidate that they carried the shame of having had extra lessons at school, designed to support their learning but experienced as highlighting their inadequacy, but had never felt able to discuss this. Even this seemingly innocuous and helpful action inadvertently led to shame.

I am not claiming that educators set out to shame pupils consciously, although some may believe that this is the only 'weapon' they hold with a particularly difficult-to-reach pupil. Sometimes educators find that shaming a student appears to work, at least in the short term. However, even educators who try hard to avoid shaming pupils may struggle. For example, many school behaviour policies require a teacher to write pupil names on the board for all the class to see as a response to either desired or poor behaviour. I would argue that even where this has the desired effect of pupils trying harder, such as with those who are close to achieving, this is at a cost to those who either fail to follow rules or fail to excel. Where whole classes are threatened with punishment for one child failing to reach expectations this could be a deeply shameful experience. Detentions and exclusions are public and humiliating, even if teachers feel that the purpose is different.

Many would agree that it would not be appropriate to shame those who have difficulties learning, hence not overtly labelling groups as low achievers, but this does not stop the effect. When children repeatedly see others rewarded, but not them, they can internalise shame from not being seen positively. It is not only educators who provoke shame; this may also come from peers, particularly within an environment that appears to utilise and promote these practices. Just as we see how parents speak to their children echoed in their children's speech to others, so we can see how educators behave copied in the playground. Groups of students may use shaming to enforce hierarchies and exclude peers from their social network.

Teachers need to always separate a poor act, which may lead to guilt, from anything that suggests the pupils themselves are lacking, which in many cases will lead to shame. For example, we need to avoid comparing students (which often happens with siblings) or suggesting that someone has let themselves down. We have to ensure that a child who struggles to learn to read does not end up thinking that he or she is 'useless'. The least dangerous assumption will lead us to always protect children's self-esteem, resisting the urge to treat harshly those pupils who appear defiant and rejecting of our efforts. These children are communicating their shame in the form of defensiveness. Repeated kindness in response to their defiance is likely to have a positive effect over time. Unfortunately, within our systems, a lack of academic ability repeatedly leads to shame. Until we adopt the view that the natural variation of how our brains work, i.e. neurodiversity, leads to differences and not deficits, we will find avoiding shame impacting students' negative self-perception almost impossible.

The nature of discipline in schools

As I write this book the media and educators are reflecting on the legacy of the Covid-19 pandemic. It is common to hear educators who work with pupils across the age spectrum stating that behaviour has become worse since the pandemic. While there is lots of good advice for educators about the use of consistent routines, seeing pupil behaviour as suggestive of academic work needing adjustment and building positive relationships, there is what seems to be a growing emphasis on more rigid ways to control children in our schools. Some UK schools are adopting practices that were introduced in the US, such as SLANT (Sit up, Listen, Ask and answer questions, Nod your head, Track the speaker), which purport that adopting and enforcing this behaviour in all pupils means that you can see who is, and who is not, engaged. As discussed in Chapter 5, not only is this likely to be very difficult for some pupils, placing them at risk of feeling ashamed when they can't remember or perform what is expected, but it also puts the emphasis on children appearing to engage when this might take all their effort and actually block their learning.

What educators need to do

Given that we know that the optimum conditions for learning are feeling welcomed and appreciated, educators in potentially hostile systems will have to 'go the extra mile' to ensure that children feel a strong sense of belonging. We need to be able to practise care, to ensure that children feel safe at school and are in a fit state to learn. As far as possible we need to reduce the pressure that adults and students often feel in schools, to do what is expected and to be successful, focusing instead on fostering the 'growth mindset'. It is not possible for educators to have all the answers. We cannot know everything we might want to know, nor is that necessary. What is imperative is that we practise being the person we want our pupils to become – someone who is engaged, activated and well-regulated. Someone who can control their responses to others, take time to reflect, think about the needs of others and look after themselves. Educators need skills just as much as pedagogical or subject knowledge and, perhaps, in order to foster the sorts of environments that are most conducive to learning and well-being, the most important skill of all is to listen.

When we can practice active listening many positives arise. Firstly, the person being listened to feels heard, seen and supported. This does not mean that we will always be able to put into action what they request of us, but they will be better able to cope with that if they feel that their voice was heard and respected. Max Biddulph, colleague and friend, recently told me a story about an email that appeared out of the blue asking if he was the same person who had taught at a particular school 40 years previously. When he confirmed that he was, the email sender identified themselves as one of his former pupils, saying that they wanted to make contact to say that he was the only person who ever listened to them. This underlines not just the in-the-moment feeling of being heard, but its longevity and memorability.

Secondly, when we listen well, we give ourselves time and space to consider. We are less likely to lose patience and show irritation. The action of listening is demanding in itself – it takes focus and concentration, which leads us to put our own emotions aside. Many educators are already fantastic listeners, while others will have to practice.

The emphasis on avoiding shaming pupils in this chapter risks ending on a negative note. While shame undoubtedly has the power to negatively shape lives, so kindness and compassion can reap long-term benefits. As we have seen throughout this book, we need to feel compassion towards the children we work with, for their best long-term interests. The good news is that even when this can be a struggle, when we react to defiant and confrontational children by feeling we are being personally attacked, focusing on the idea that they are doing their best, feeling compassion for and kindness towards them will be beneficial for ourselves. Research suggests one of the most important factors in leading a happy life is to help others (Espinosa et al., 2022). A possible mechanism for how this happens is the understanding that learning to be compassionate towards others helps us to do the same for ourselves.

Compassionate cultures can be created from one person's actions slowly spreading, since compassion breeds compassion. When we exercise compassion by helping others, we feel a sense of purpose, and this in turn improves our own quality of life and has even been linked to living longer (Turner, 2019). In the words of the Dalai Lama, 'If you want others to be happy, practise compassion. If you want to be happy, practise compassion.' Feeling compassion towards others is good for us; it leads to an improved quality of life, it requires us to be aware and to express empathy towards others, and through this we learn to be more compassionate towards ourselves. Research in the field of self-compassion suggests that we can reduce rumination on our faults and inadequacies, the tendency to which reduces self-esteem and happiness (Odou and Brinker, 2015). We want our pupils to reduce feelings of anxiety and depression and improve their well-being and sense of belonging, so when we model self-compassion we are also helping them. And so, the cycle of a compassionate culture perpetuates. Children in compassionate classrooms are found to cooperate more and have gains in learning (Hart and Kindle Hodson, 2004).

Moving from compassionate classrooms to compassionate school systems provides another positive cycle. Educators who express compassion towards their colleagues raise their own and others' job satisfaction. I don't want to minimise what hard work it will be to change cultures in schools with inflexible and authoritarian climates, and teachers trying to maintain a different approach alone may be at risk of compassion fatigue. This is another place where self-compassion can help to reduce stress and minimise burnout and fatigue. The Dalai Lama addresses this when he talks about the energy needed to exercise compassion, which he says comes from:

> reason and patience. These are the most powerful antidotes to anger. Unfortunately, many people misjudge these qualities as signs of weakness. I believe the opposite to be true: that they are the true signs of inner strength. Compassion is by nature gentle, peaceful and soft, but it is very powerful. It is those who easily lose their patience who are insecure and unstable. Thus, to me, the arousal of anger is a direct sign of weakness.
> (Dalai Lama website, n.d.)

In summary and to answer 'how to be and remain a compassionate educator', my belief is that we need to continue to:

- Be a reflective practitioner in the sense of wondering about the actions of our students in the light of our understanding of their executive function skills, and communication abilities.
- Be a reflexive practitioner in the sense of asking ourselves, gently, and with compassion, why we were perhaps not quite as excellent today as we would like to be and figuring out a different response when the next opportunity arises.
- Adopt a mantra about our students that helps us to pause, take a breath and approach each interaction with a keen listening ear.
- Be a part of creating a culture where you can happily be yourself, act with integrity, find meaning in helping others and ensure you look after yourself.

References

Beers, N. (2024). Ending corporal punishment in schools: AAP policy explained. *American Academy of Pediatrics*. https://www.healthychildren.org/English/ages-stages/gradeschool/school/Pages/ending-corporal-punishment-in-schools-aap-policy-explained.aspx

Chetty, R., Friedman, J. N. and Rockoff J. E. (2014). Measuring the impacts of teachers II: Teacher value-added and student outcomes in adulthood. *American Economic Review*, 104(9), 2633–2679. http://dx.doi.org/10.1257/aer.104.9.2633

Dalai Lama website. (n.d.). Compassion and the individual. https://www.dalailama.com/messages/compassion-and-human-values/compassion

Department for Education. (2024). *Behaviour in Schools: Advice for headteachers and school staff*. https://assets.publishing.service.gov.uk/media/65ce3721e1bdec001a3221fe/Behaviour_in_schools_-_advice_for_headteachers_and_school_staff_Feb_2024.pdf

Espinosa, J. C., Anton, C. and Grueso Hinestroza, M. P. (2022). Helping others helps me: Prosocial behaviour and satisfaction with life during the COVID-19 pandemic. *Frontiers in Psychology*, 13. https://doi.org/10.3389/fpsyg.2022.762445

Hart, S. and Kindle Hodson, V. (2004). *The Compassionate Classroom: Relationship Based Teaching and Learning*. Encinitas: CA: PuddleDancer Press.

Odou, N. and Brinker, J. (2015). Self-compassion, a better alternative to rumination than distraction as a response to negative mood. *The Journal of Positive Psychology*, 10(5), 447–457. https://doi.org/10.1080/17439760.2014.967800

Smith, P. K. and Culbert, C. (2024). *School Belonging*. The National Children's Bureau. https://www.ncb.org.uk/sites/default/files/uploads/attachments/School%20Belonging%20-%20A%20Literature%20Review%202024_2.pdf

Turner, L. (2019). Why being kind could help you live longer. BBC. https://www.bbc.co.uk/news/world-us-canada-50266957

Index

abuse 35, 70, 100, 187
acceptance 3, 4, 7, 33, 34, 72, 84, 132, 178
accommodations 13, 23, 25, 27, 52, 69, 123, 134
acquired brain injury (ABI) 16, 161–165
aggression 32, 36, 50, 69, 92, 95, 148, 159, 165, 175
anger 50, 69, 91, 92, 152, 192, 197
anxiety 9, 23, 24, 27, 28, 31, 32, 35–37, 43, 51, 83, 86, 92, 94, 103–106, 108–111, 113, 115, 118, 121, 123, 130–134, 148, 150, 159, 162–164, 196
articulation 36, 144–146, 152, 191
assessment 3, 22, 28–31, 42, 43, 64, 126, 146, 158, 161
assumption(s) 2, 22, 24, 26, 27, 48, 50, 56, 57, 69, 72, 76, 80, 82, 97, 113, 123, 129, 148, 150, 154, 158, 166, 176, 178, 179, 188; *see also* least dangerous assumption
attention: attending 14, 46–72, 139, 142; difference 72; improving attention 15, 56, 57, 60–65, 67, 71, 72, 87, 142, 163, 173; joint/shared 53–55, 62; listening 58; poor/lack 12, 14, 15, 37, 48, 50, 53–61, 65–72, 76, 79, 86, 101, 110. 113, 120, 162; as skill 13, 27, 47–50, 55, 89, 101, 103, 135; stages of 55–56; working memory 86
attention deficit hyperactivity disorder (ADHD) 11, 12, 15, 26, 37, 50, 56, 59, 60, 66–72, 86, 101, 121, 143
auditory processing 25, 75, 76, 152, 156, 167
Augmentative and Alternative Communication (AAC) 167, 168, 179
autism 11, 17, 141, 156; with anxiety 9, 109, 134; and attention 56, 61; autistic adults 49, 81, 82, 173;

autistic children 12, 26, 50, 61, 63, 109, 130–135, 154; and cognitive flexibility 88; and communication 152, 154, 165, 167, 181–183; and engagement 107, 110, 129–130; and eye-contact 51–52; and eye-gaze 53; and intolerance of uncertainty 134; and movement 112–113; and neurodiversity 26; and pointing 54, 115–118, 154; positive attitudes to 23, 30; sensory processing in 15, 37, 41, 50, 109, 110, 133; support for 84, 125, 128–130, 154
autonomy 28, 33, 34, 38, 39, 71, 122, 127, 135, 187, 188, 190

barriers to learning 1, 4, 13–15, 23, 24, 39, 55, 80, 93, 97, 107, 108, 122, 160, 181, 188, 192; communication barriers 158, 166
behaviour: that challenges 3, 6, 10, 11, 14, 22–24, 31, 32, 36, 37, 44, 48, 59, 60, 66–72, 78–82, 88, 91–97, 109, 115–119, 122–124, 141, 178, 189, 194; as communication 13, 38, 54, 61, 80, 86, 91, 92, 124, 152, 167, 177, 179–180, 182, 194; and engagement 15, 48, 53, 56, 101–107; for learning 27, 71, 79, 110, 120, 134; policy 70, 79, 119, 121–123, 135, 189–190, 193; risky 70, 78; and shame 80, 192–194; social 52–54; support for 63, 71, 73, 77, 84, 98, 122, 128, 130
bilingualism 94, 149–150
bullying 7, 32, 35, 94, 118, 165, 178, 190

care (pastoral) 1–2, 8, 12, 27, 34, 35, 38, 39, 105, 117, 121, 124, 191, 192, 195
cerebral palsy 39, 82, 111, 179

199

Index

Chomsky, N. 140, 149
cognitive flexibility 15, 75, 88–89, 93, 98
communication difficulties 6, 11, 141, 143, 144, 147, 148, 154, 155, 160–161, 184
compassion 3, 4, 12, 34, 38, 44, 71, 80, 82, 92, 108, 122, 125, 134, 190, 196–197
competition 31, 33, 43, 84, 94, 95, 100, 128, 168, 175, 184
concentration 12, 13, 31, 38, 67, 76, 82, 101, 118, 162, 163, 165, 183, 191, 196
confidence 4, 8, 30–32, 43, 44, 47, 50, 52, 55, 63, 68, 69, 81, 83, 85–87, 95, 97, 98, 103, 105, 106, 108, 112, 129, 131, 134, 139, 142, 145, 146, 148, 160–164, 168, 173, 177, 178, 184, 189, 191
consistency 37, 42, 43, 54, 57, 61, 78, 132, 189, 194
coordination 26, 47, 67, 70, 108, 111–113, 118, 139, 145, 162, 164, 183
criminality 70, 75, 141, 143, 184

Dalai Lama 4, 196, 197
defiance 47, 79, 95, 161, 184, 192, 194, 196
deficits 12, 28, 126, 159, 176, 194
dependence 117, 170, 190
depression 50, 70, 159, 165, 167, 196
diagnosis 10, 21–22, 113, 160, 177
Diagnostical and Statistical Manual of Mental Disorders (DSM) 21
distraction 8, 12, 13, 48, 55–57, 59, 61, 65, 67, 76, 84–86, 109, 163
distress 5, 12, 23, 24, 32, 36, 41, 47, 50, 59, 67, 86, 88, 91, 95, 110, 118, 122, 131–133, 151, 163, 164, 181, 189
Dix, P. 37, 91
Down's syndrome 11, 25, 108–110, 112, 129, 133, 141, 167, 173, 177
dyslexia and dyscalculia 17, 25, 26, 86, 134, 143, 156, 158, 159, 161, 176

economy 93, 123, 139, 141, 147, 175, 187
educator attitude 2–4, 8, 14–16, 21, 23, 34, 38, 71, 90, 124–126, 157, 176, 177
embarrassment 44, 68, 79, 108, 133, 145, 146, 151, 159, 170, 173, 184
emotional difficulties 10, 12, 20, 36, 47, 50, 111, 118, 122, 160, 165

emotional regulation 37, 39, 60, 187
empathy 2, 34, 44, 196
emphasis 151, 182–183
energy 3, 70, 72, 77, 83, 86, 91, 98, 101, 105, 162–164, 167, 175, 188, 197
expectations 2, 15, 16, 22, 29, 32, 34, 39, 60, 81, 91, 105, 108, 124, 126, 142, 154, 155, 174–178, 180, 182, 183, 188, 192, 193
expression 50, 69, 97, 104, 123, 144, 145, 148, 150, 153, 161, 162, 168–170, 172, 173, 187–189, 196; facial 113, 148, 152, 167, 182; expressive language 146–147, 151, 160
eyes 15, 55, 58, 61, 101, 150, 166, 168, 179, 182; eye contact 50–52, 55, 71, 146, 181, 182; eye gaze 52–55, 106, 154, 182; eye-hand coordination 118

facilitated communication 117, 118
failure 30, 31, 36, 43, 44, 47, 54, 58, 59, 78, 80, 81, 85, 102, 106, 115, 129, 135, 151, 161, 168, 180, 183, 190, 192, 193; avoidance of 64, 162, 180; no-fail approach 62, 63, 126, 130
fatigue 27, 112, 162, 165, 197
flourishing 69, 132, 133, 135, 172
flow 106, 110
frustration: in adults 80, 82, 97, 101, 119, 163; in children 11, 20, 30, 67, 69, 79, 81, 92, 94, 95, 109, 146, 151, 159, 162, 165, 172, 183

Gardner, H. 29
genetics 70, 141, 187
gesture 54, 113, 148, 152, 166, 167, 171, 173
giftedness 12, 16, 84, 93–96
grammar 146, 147
grit 33, 106
growth 33, 44, 57, 82, 180; growth mindset 4, 11, 15, 30–33, 39, 47, 84, 105, 191, 195

identity 16–17, 26, 95, 115, 134, 145, 190, 191
impairments 22–23; cognitive 154, 183; communication 3, 11, 12, 59, 150, 156, 165, 167, 169, 183; hearing 23, 59, 76, 164, 167; physical/motor 22, 111–113; sensory 164; visual 17, 42, 51

Index

independence 5, 17, 38, 42, 57, 64, 72, 75, 82–84, 107, 111, 114, 117–118, 127, 130, 133, 136, 148, 159, 164, 172, 178, 182, 190, 191; living 25, 40
information technology (IT) 8, 15, 25, 40, 42, 56, 57, 71, 117, 167, 172
inhibition 49, 56, 75, 77–79, 82, 93, 95, 121, 139, 149, 182
initiation 49, 55, 60, 77, 91, 112, 116, 171, 183
intelligence 6, 28–32, 82, 85, 159
Intensive Interaction 125
interaction 6, 15, 16, 32, 41, 43, 54–57, 60, 61, 63, 75, 77, 92, 102–104, 111, 113, 116, 118, 125, 141, 148, 151, 152, 161, 165, 167, 169, 170, 174, 176, 192, 197
intolerance of uncertainty (IU) 109, 134
intonation 130, 151–152, 166, 167, 171
intrinsic 4, 12, 13, 15, 29, 34, 43, 79, 107, 108, 110, 140, 160; motivation *see* motivation

joint attention 53, 55

kindness 34, 49, 163, 177, 191, 194, 196; unkindness 69, 93, 170

language: acquisition 57, 140–141, 150; development 131, 140, 147, 149, 179; disorder 141, 147
learned helplessness 15, 115, 180
learning disabilities 3, 5, 6, 10, 11, 16, 17, 29, 30, 36, 48, 50, 59, 80, 81, 107, 115, 157, 159, 161, 181, 183; learning differences 12, 160
least dangerous assumption 4, 11, 14, 15, 39–43, 47, 61, 72, 78, 176, 177, 194
letters 62, 65, 86, 127, 156, 158, 162; letterboard 174
listening skill 56, 58, 59, 67, 68, 75, 76, 82, 110, 114, 140, 145, 151, 191, 195, 196
literacy skills 40–42, 128, 132, 142, 155–156, 161, 169; difficulties 145, 156, 158, 159; emergent literacy 156–160; impairment 169, 183

masking 30, 52, 95, 143, 191
mastery 25, 47, 64, 65, 104–106, 108, 144, 167, 171, 177

mathematics 1, 5, 12, 29, 68, 69, 85, 86, 88, 127, 132, 142, 162, 173
maturity 47, 69, 78, 79, 89, 96, 144, 145, 147, 156, 165, 187, 191; prematurity 78
means of communication 5, 10, 15, 16, 20, 115–118, 165–169, 172, 173, 178, 179
medical model 21–24
memory 13, 35, 123, 134, 152; difficulties 37, 163, 165, 184; games 164; working 15, 75, 76, 85–87, 89, 90, 93, 98, 131, 139, 162, 184
mental health 30, 100; difficulties 35, 52, 96, 141, 165, 169, 178; disorders 165; needs 36
mindfulness 34, 35, 92
modelling 33, 38, 47, 53, 54, 57, 62–64, 114, 116, 119, 131, 152, 172, 180, 182–184; role 1, 91, 92, 97, 140, 145, 196
mono 50, 110
Montessori, M. 20
more knowledgeable other (MKO) 4, 64, 92, 128, 140, 178
MORE model 15, 165–178
motivation 2, 8, 13, 15, 67, 69, 79, 83, 87, 91, 94, 96, 113, 119–123, 125, 129, 158, 166, 170, 172–174, 182, 183; extrinsic 171; intrinsic 16, 33, 106, 116, 119–123, 127, 129, 140, 172, 187; lack 68, 86, 105, 111, 127
motor skill 67, 109, 150; difficulties 40, 111, 178; impairments 111–113; independent movements *see* independence; movements 23, 24, 42, 49, 54, 56, 67, 68, 92, 109, 111–113, 117, 119, 127, 162, 166, 181, 182

neglect 27, 35, 54, 100, 187
neurodivergence 10, 11, 13, 15, 19, 20, 36, 48, 49, 51, 56, 59, 60, 71, 75, 79, 86, 93, 107, 110, 114, 125, 134, 135, 154; neurotypical 19, 27, 51, 110
neurodiversity 11, 13, 26–28, 194
neurology/neuroscience 4, 5, 11, 14, 30, 31, 35, 46, 69, 76–78, 80, 117, 123, 141, 144, 145, 191
neuroplasticity 15, 77
non-judgmental 11, 34, 38

Index

non-verbal 10, 41, 42, 50, 61, 63, 80, 81, 104, 115, 125, 128, 152, 165, 173, 178, 179, 181
nouns 140, 146

Oliver, M. 22
opportunity: for attention 49, 57; for communication 15, 16, 42, 50, 119, 136, 146, 158, 166, 168–169, 171, 180, 184; for learning 6, 25, 31, 44, 78, 79, 82, 86, 94, 97, 123, 128, 129, 157, 158, 182; for participation 40, 62, 125, 127, 161, 169, 170; providing 14, 16, 27, 40–42, 56, 62, 102, 103, 106, 172, 187; for success 73, 76, 85, 108, 114, 120, 129
organisation: educator support for 33, 105, 163, 164, 167; lack of 37, 59, 67, 70; skill of 33, 46, 89–91, 159
overwhelm 20, 26, 27, 41, 51, 53, 59, 68, 109, 111, 124, 127, 132

pace 76, 85, 94, 111–114, 116, 133, 159, 163
perceptions of educators 13, 21, 47–49, 51, 53, 56, 60, 90, 95, 114, 129, 152, 166, 174, 175, 179, 184, 188–189
performance 5, 29, 62, 94, 97, 104, 128, 129; performativity 37, 96, 106
person-centred approach 33–35, 117; child-centred 126
Piaget, J. 20, 140
Picture Exchange Communication System (PECS) 171–72
planning 10, 24, 27, 37, 72, 77, 89–91, 105, 108, 110, 114, 123–125, 127, 136, 159, 163, 165, 173, 191
pointing 53–55, 154; as communication 49, 61, 82, 126, 167, 173, 179; modelling 49, 62, 131; teaching 115–118, 128, 182
poverty/economic disadvantage 93, 100, 123, 141, 147, 175, 187
pragmatics 146, 152–155, 160
praise: parental 31; for students 32, 63, 67, 103, 106, 120, 123, 124, 136, 149, 171, 172; for teachers 96
predictability 69, 89, 124
prediction 134–135
pressure: on children 10, 31, 36, 43, 52, 55, 62, 65, 72, 91, 95, 126, 132, 145, 148, 155, 168, 184, 191; on educators 20, 48, 61, 93, 117, 135, 141, 159, 163, 188, 195

processing 12, 25, 29, 69, 75, 86, 87, 114, 155–156, 158, 165; see also auditory processing
prosody 151–152
punishment 14, 70, 78, 80, 92, 98, 122, 123, 169, 192–193

reading 20, 25, 49, 52, 53, 62, 75, 85, 86, 88, 94, 107, 118, 126, 131, 141, 142, 145, 150, 155–162, 173, 176, 184, 194
reasons 3, 5, 10, 13, 15, 16, 46, 51, 57, 79, 81, 95, 107, 125, 134, 142, 166, 169–174
receptive language difficulty 150–151
reflections 12, 13, 30, 37, 38, 42, 44, 57, 65, 80, 85, 87, 89, 96, 102, 104, 107, 108, 123, 124, 134, 152, 155, 161, 176–177, 180, 192, 194, 195, 197
reflex 47, 49, 53, 176, 197
regulation 36, 46, 60, 122, 152, 187, 191, 195; dysregulation 37, 41, 91; self-regulation 29, 37–39, 44, 69, 76, 80, 91, 93, 95, 104, 122, 123, 189, 190
rejection 55, 141, 178
relationships 13, 14, 19, 27, 33–36, 39–41, 53, 57, 65, 69, 70, 77, 80, 82, 92, 95, 97, 100–103, 106, 108, 117, 118, 124, 126, 129, 130, 135, 141, 154, 161, 178, 181, 184, 187–189, 194
relaxation 71, 89, 145, 148, 164
reprimands 76, 78, 79, 90, 92, 102, 110, 119
resilience: of educators 2, 3, 9; of students 19, 29, 59, 73, 82, 88, 96, 115, 134
resistance of students 49, 62, 88, 95, 107, 108, 115–117
respect 1, 3, 14, 33, 48, 50, 52, 66, 90, 104, 117, 126, 189, 195; disrespect 16
reward 48, 67, 79, 98, 119–121, 123, 130, 148, 171–172, 193, 194
Robinson, K. 43
routine 71, 86, 88, 89, 105, 120, 128, 130–135, 150, 163, 164, 180, 194
rules: adhering to 46, 48, 77, 92, 108, 121–124, 139, 152, 154, 188, 189; disobeying 70, 80, 81, 131, 151, 193

safety 34, 36, 38, 39, 49, 55, 64, 86, 100, 105, 120–122, 128, 130, 132, 135, 148, 162, 191, 195

Index

scaffolding 6, 27, 63–65, 73, 83, 89, 97, 98, 127, 131
school belonging 19, 41, 76, 90, 100, 101, 103, 105, 106, 108, 118, 129, 189, 191, 192, 195, 196
selective mutism 147–149
self-belief 31, 50, 92, 180
self-determination 103, 120, 127, 170, 174
self-efficacy 108, 124, 125
self-esteem 4, 67, 194, 196
self-image 47, 79, 114, 134, 136, 161, 168
self-monitoring 3, 71, 77, 91–92, 119, 163
self-perception 25, 60, 62, 114–115, 143, 145, 191–192, 194
self-regulation 37–39, 44, 60, 76, 80, 93, 95, 104, 123, 187, 189, 190
sensory: experience 15, 51, 75, 109–110, 127, 134, 136, 164; sensitivity 23, 24, 41, 93, 111, 130, 133, 165
Shakespeare, T. 23
shame 28, 31, 44, 47, 71, 79, 80, 114, 135, 157, 159, 161, 192–196
shy 55, 142, 145, 148, 184
sign language 148, 158, 167
Skinner, B.F. 20, 140
social model of disability 22, 24
social skill 6, 50, 53, 94, 96, 113, 132
Social Stories 132
sounds 25, 56, 58, 61, 86, 93, 109, 140, 144, 146, 156, 166, 167, 181, 183
space 37, 43, 44, 58, 62, 68, 116, 117, 119, 129, 134, 142, 166, 168, 180, 189, 196
special educational needs and disabilities (SEND) 7, 20, 35, 123, 132, 133, 141, 158, 178, 190
speech 54, 110, 113, 115, 118, 130, 139–142, 144–146, 148, 150–156, 160, 162, 167, 170, 182, 183, 194
speech and language therapy 5–7, 10, 39, 41, 145, 146, 149, 179
speech, language and communication needs (SLCN) 6, 11, 15, 141–143, 147, 153, 166, 168, 170, 171
spelling 94, 155, 156, 173, 174
stammering 145–146
states 24, 37, 39, 41, 43, 44, 50, 66, 77, 97, 101, 105, 110, 115, 118, 121, 123, 133, 141, 191, 192, 195

stigma 22, 71, 123
strategies 12, 13, 15, 24, 27, 32, 34, 40, 47, 48, 56, 58, 67, 71, 75, 76, 78–80, 82, 83, 87, 104, 111, 124, 134, 136, 143, 159, 163–165
strengths 6, 16, 23–30, 39, 72, 84, 90, 93, 108, 112, 149, 155, 163, 176, 181, 188, 197
stress 1, 2, 8, 11, 32, 35–39, 55, 82, 92, 106, 109, 123, 127, 135, 180, 188, 197
student choice 14, 24, 28, 38, 39, 49, 52, 63, 78, 81, 82, 85, 102, 110, 111, 116, 126–128, 132, 136, 172, 173, 180, 187
symbols 61, 62, 157–158, 161, 167, 170–172, 182

touch prompts 112, 182
traits 52, 84, 101, 103, 119, 187
trauma 9, 12, 27, 35–39, 47, 54, 100, 108, 118, 122, 123, 126
trust 33, 36–38, 46, 51, 60, 64, 92, 105, 108, 125, 128, 129, 177, 187, 189, 190
turn-taking 46, 50, 55, 67, 78, 145, 152, 154

understanding of language 26, 27, 38, 41, 48, 58, 80–82, 87, 114, 117, 128, 144, 150–154, 162, 170, 184
Universal Design for Learning 10, 27
upset 14, 24, 36, 46, 55, 69, 88, 117, 131, 148, 174

values 100, 104, 107, 119
visually-impaired 17, 42, 51
visual material 25, 58, 81, 83, 85, 87, 89, 107, 110, 114, 127, 135, 141, 142, 156, 163
visual skills 25, 53, 158, 164
vocabulary 9, 54, 82, 94, 139, 142, 146, 147, 150
Vygotsky, L. 4, 15, 20, 63, 64, 140, 178

warmth 33, 100, 103–105, 107, 119, 122, 189
writing 65, 125, 128, 148, 159, 166, 168, 180

zone of proximal development (ZPD) 4, 15, 63, 64, 106, 178

For Product Safety Concerns and Information please contact our EU
representative GPSR@taylorandfrancis.com
Taylor & Francis Verlag GmbH, Kaufingerstraße 24, 80331 München, Germany

www.ingramcontent.com/pod-product-compliance
Lightning Source LLC
Chambersburg PA
CBHW071819230426
43670CB00013B/2505